BACKROADS & BYWAYS OF
ALASKA

BACKROADS & BYWAYS OF
ALASKA

*Drives, Day Trips &
Weekend Excursions*

TAZ TALLY

THE COUNTRYMAN PRESS

A division of W. W. Norton & Company

Independent Publishers Since 1923

For information about permission to reproduce selections from this book, write to
Permissions, The Countryman Press, 500 Fifth Avenue, New York, NY 10110

For information about special discounts for bulk purchases, please contact
W. W. Norton Special Sales at specialsales@wwnorton.com or 800-233-4830

The Countryman Press
www.countrymanpress.com

A division of W. W. Norton & Company, Inc.
500 Fifth Avenue, New York, NY 10110
www.wwnorton.com

978-1-58157-405-0 (pbk.)

10 9 8 7 6 5 4 3 2 1

To Johnny and Beth, who are both precious family and friends

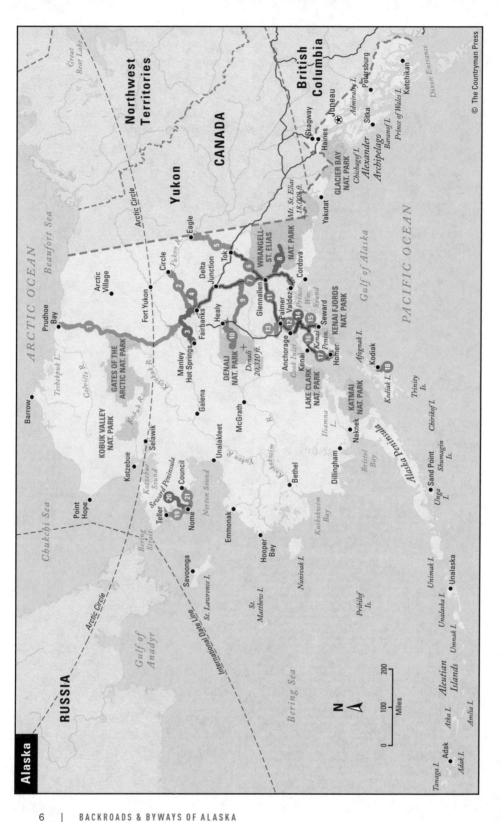

Contents

Introduction

Alaska encompasses a vast topography offering many fascinating wonders. From the midlatitudes of Southeast Alaska to the polar regions of the North Slope, you can sample a wider range of geographic delights than any other state in the United States or province of Canada. The southeast panhandle offers access to the largest midlatitude rain forest in the world. Alaska has more peaks over 14,000 feet, including 20,310-foot Denali, than anywhere in North America. Alaska has more alpine glaciers than anywhere else, and some of the best ocean, stream, and lake fishing on earth. Alaska offers thousands of miles of fjord coastline and hiking trails of all kinds, including uncounted miles and millions of acres of off-trail hiking across glorious alpine tundra. Visitors seeking to explore nature will find more wilderness areas, national parks, preserves, and national monuments than the rest of the U.S. combined. These wilderness areas are home to the two largest bear species (polar and brown bears), plus grizzlies, lynx, moose, caribou, sheep, multiple species of whales (including killer, humpback, gray, fin, and beluga), and sea lions.

Alaska also has a rich human history, both Native and immigrant. Mining, fishing, and logging have provided many historical and current adventures. And throughout Alaska you will find many art, music, history, and food festivals.

STATISTICS AND SUPERLATIVES

The statistics are staggering. By far the largest state, with 663,268 square miles, Alaska is more than twice the size of Texas, the next largest state. Place it over the lower 48 states and it covers a fifth of the landmass. In fact,

LEFT: AUTUMN IN THE BROOKS RANGE IS A TAPESTRY OF COLORS AND TEXTURES

Alaska is larger than all three of the next largest states (Texas, California, and Montana) combined and all but 18 sovereign countries. Alaska is also the state that's the farthest north, farthest west, and believe it or not, the farthest east; a segment of the Aleutian Islands, ironically named the Near Islands, is west of the 180th meridian.

Several of our 620 named glaciers and ice fields, including the Bering Glacier and the Harding Ice Field, are larger than the state of Rhode Island. One of our two-lane gravel roads, the haul road to Prudhoe Bay that leads to the Arctic Ocean, is 414 miles long and terminates 300 miles north of the Arctic Circle. Four of the roads included in this book, one on Kodiak Island and three out from Nome, are not reachable by car; you must fly or boat to them. Alaska is indeed a land of superlatives: In addition to being the largest state, Alaska has the highest peak (Denali), the most dangerous highway (the Seward Highway), the largest fish (300+-pound halibut), the biggest bears (1,300-pound Kodiak bears), and the longest coastline, which at 6,640 miles is longer than the entire Atlantic coast. We also have the most glaciers, the biggest tides, and the world's smallest desert. What we don't have is a large population, and driving experiences here are characterized by long, delightfully empty stretches of road.

Much more of Alaska is roadless than roaded. And even highways mostly have just two lanes, including, for much of its length, the famed 1,390-mile-long Alaska Highway. Turnpikes do not exist. Most of Alaska is rural, and it has the lowest population density of any state, just 1.3 people per square mile compared to Wyoming's six, which has the second lowest population density. Hugh swaths of Alaska are uninhabited wilderness, most of which is inaccessible, but some impressive sections are reachable by road. The Dalton Highway, for example, provides access to the otherwise roadless and untrammeled Gates of the Arctic National Park and Preserve and the Arctic National Wildlife Refuge. Pull-off-the-road camping is common along most roads covered in this book. If you have a self-contained rig, such as camper on the back of a pickup, your lodging opportunities and locations are nearly limitless.

One-way-in, one-way-out roads are common, leading to end-of-the-road communities such as Deadhorse, Valdez, Homer, Seward, Eagle, Circle, Manley, Teller, and Council. It is not unusual to travel great distances and see little or no development. While driving in Alaska, you will come across Native communities that use a variety of travel methods such as snowmobiles (often called snowmachines in Alaska), four-wheelers, bush planes, and dogsleds. Some communities have only twice-yearly delivery services via barge.

GETTING TO ALASKA

Most visitors fly to Alaska. Some take the Alaska Marine Highway System or arrive via cruise ship. Some drive all 1,390 miles of the Alaska Highway from Dawson Creek, British Columbia, which is itself 800 miles north of Seattle. Perhaps the most fun way to venture to Alaska is to combine traveling by the Alaska State Ferry through the Inside Passage to either Hanes Junction or Skagway, and then driving another 600 to 800 miles (depending upon where you disembark) across the Yukon Territory, Canada, and into Alaska. And yes, it's a vehicle ferry, so you can bring your rig; there are no size restrictions. This combination offers plenty of opportunity for travel adventures. The marine highway section takes you along and through Alaska's varied and fascinating coastal communities, for which the ferry often provides the only regular travel access. The overland sections provide extended exposure to the grand expanses of the interiors of the Yukon, the glorious Kluane National Park and Reserve, and Alaska. For more on the Alaska Marine Highway System, see www.dot.state.ak.us/amhs.

GETTING AROUND ALASKA

Unless you bring your own backcountry rig, you'll need to rent a vehicle suitable for exploring all these fun backroads and byways. The two main cities, Anchorage and Fairbanks, offer a variety of vehicle rentals. Most towns, including the fly-in towns of Nome and Kodiak, also offer limited vehicle rental options. Most rental agencies offer car rentals, which can be just fine on many of these roads. However, particularly if you'll be traveling on some of the more remote roads, opt instead for at least a 4x4 SUV or pickup truck. In my opinion the best way to explore Alaska is with a camper unit on the back of a rugged (250/2500–350/3500 series) 4x4 pickup truck. With the 4x4 truck and camper you can confidently drive on any of the gravel or dirt roads covered in this book, as well as many others that beckon you to explore. They provide plenty of ground clearance to safely navigate any water, mud, ice, or snow you may encounter. In addition, this type of rig offers you the kind of independence that allows you to explore without worrying about where you are going to stay. One of the wonderful aspects of traveling the backroads of Alaska is that pull-off camping is the rule, not the exception. You will find an inexhaustible number and variety of hassle-free places to pull off, explore, and camp. What's more, these big pickups all have oversized fuel tanks that should provide you 350 to 400 miles of between-fuel-stops travel. I always carry five 5-gallon cans of diesel fuel on top of my rig to provide me with about 800 miles of carefree perambulation. ABC and GAH RV Rentals both offer stout, well-maintained vehicles and have offices in both Anchorage and Fairbanks. You might also consider renting a rig in the lower 48 (as we refer to mainland U.S.) and driving/ferrying it to Alaska.

Most roads in this book have mileage signs that we call mileposts, or MPs. I use these MPs where they exist. Due to weather or other mishaps, they may be obscured or missing. There are times where I will encourage you to set your trip odometers to help with navigation, and I'll provide other geographic reference points where appropriate. When traveling, and especially in remote communities, it's a good idea to carry some cash. Many small businesses in rural communities don't accept checks or credit cards.

RENTAL VEHICLES

Pickup trucks with a camper on the back are the prime vehicle for traveling Alaska roads, in particular the long gravel roads such as the Dalton, Nabesna, Taylor, McCarthy, and Skilak Lake, along which you are likely to encounter snow, mud, ice, and water. Many companies that rent cars place restrictions on which roads you can travel; many rental cars have GPS tracking systems, so they will know where you've been. Before you leave the rental location, be sure you know how to change your vehicle's tires. Modern pickup trucks commonly use a rod and socket system that may not be immediately obvious.

Recommended Rental Companies

GONORTH: 866-236-7272, www.gonorth-alaska.com. Offers gravel-road-capable auto rentals.

ABC RV: 800-421-7456, www.abcmotorhome.com. Experts on RV travel in Alaska, offering a wide range of Alaska-ready RV rentals, including my recommended pickup trick plus camper rigs.

GREAT ALASKAN HOLIDAYS RV RENTAL: 888-225-2752 (toll-free U.S., except Alaska) or 800-642-6462 (toll-free Alaska), www.greatalaskanholidays.com. Offers a variety of RV vehicles for travel in Alaska.

MAINTAINING YOUR VEHICLE

Driving on gravel roads adds a lot of wear and tear to your vehicle, whether you're driving your own or a rental. All that shaking and jarring tends to

SELF-CONTAINED TRAVEL ALLOWS FOR UNTETHERED EXPLORATION

loosen things up. Set up a daily preventive maintenance schedule that includes at least the following: check and tighten all tie-downs and monitor tire pressure, engine oil, brake fluid, and windshield washer fluid, replacing as needed. And keep an eye on all those gauges that you normally ignore, such as engine temperature and oil pressure. Also, set up at least a twice-daily schedule of washing your windshield and windows, inside and out, your headlights (most important), and your taillight/turn signals. Carry an extra gallon of windshield washer as well as an extra quart of engine oil and can of brake fluid.

PLANNING YOUR TIME

You could spend years driving the backroads of Alaska and still not see it all. If you ferry and drive to Alaska, allow for at least a week for the ferry portion of the trip. Just getting to Alaska is a grand adventure, so give yourself time to enjoy it! If you take the Marine Highway System, you may well want to disembark the ferry for a few days and hang out in one or more of the coastal towns. And along the Alaska Highway, through both Canada and Alaska, there are all sorts of worthy distractions, from the sign forest in Watson Creek to Summit Lake and Pass to Kluane National Park and Reserve.

Some of the routes covered here, such as the Haul Road to Prudhoe Bay, require a week all by themselves. For each trip I have provided minimum travel times you will want to devote; use them when planning your schedule. If your time is very short, plan to fly into Anchorage or Fairbanks and rent your rig there.

DERELICT ROAD SEGMENTS

As you travel the various routes described in this book, keep your eyes open for previous sections of roads that are now derelict but often still passable. These sections are commonly labeled as "Old Highway . . . ." These are often excellent opportunities for semi-off-road explorations and much fun. Throughout this book I recommend some of these derelict sections, such as sections along the Dalton, Richardson, and Steese Highways and the Tok Cutoff, just to name a few. My coverage of these abandoned road sections is by no means comprehensive, so I encourage you to keep your eyes open for your own derelict exploration opportunities. Note: Many of these derelict road sections are in poor repair, so they should always be traveled at low speed and with great care.

ALASKA ROADHOUSES

During the late 18th and early 19th century a system of roadhouses was built to accommodate the travel needs of miners and explorers. Many of these roadhouses have faded into the boreal forest, but a few have been protected as historical sites (Rika's Roadhouse), others have been restored (Sullivan Roadhouse), and still others have taken on new lives as updated versions of their former selves (The Lodge at Black Rapids). I reference many of these roadhouses on various roads throughout the book, and many are worth visiting. If you are interested in investigating the rich history of Alaska roadhouses, start here: www.alaskanroadhouses.wordpress.com

TOURING THE TUNDRA

As you head cross-country on various Alaskan adventures, unless you are hiking exclusively along maintained trails or braided stream channels, you'll be crossing tundra-covered terrain. You'll quickly discover that there are many kinds of tundra. All are beautiful and some are passable. I have my own three-tiered tundra classification based upon hikeability:

- Slogging tundra—marshy tundra that is essentially a wetland, usually found in lower elevations, and characterized by large, unstable, soggy tundra tussocks (flimsy mounds of grass) and tall, intertangled, aggressive willow trees that will challenge the skills, endurance, and ankles of any who attempt to pass through them.

- Brushy tundra—characterized by tall grasses and bushes of willows and alders, more passable than the marshy tundra but still a challenge to traverse.

- Walking tundra—known as dwarf tundra, typically found on higher and drier ridgelines and characterized by very short grasses, small bushes, and a firm, thin veneer of lichens. Pay attention and you will quickly learn to pick your routes across the tundra by sticking to the higher, drier slopes that offer an easy walking tundra, the superhighways of tundra hiking. I often hike the tundra in my XTRATUFs, rubber boots that allow me to navigate various tundra environments with dry feet. I always carry an extra set of socks that I swap out every hour or so. Another approach is to simply hike in sneakers you expect to get wet and muddy.

DEVELOPED CAMPGROUNDS VERSUS DRY/PRIMITIVE CAMPING SITES

Most of the roads covered in this book have access to a variety of developed public campground systems, including Bureau of Land Management (BLM), National Park, National Forest, State of Alaska, and National Wildlife Refuges. Developed campsites typically include toilets (most commomly pit toilets), fire rings, hand-pump water spigots, and picnic tables. I note where campgrounds also provide access to hiking trails, boat ramps, and other recreational amenities. When I refer to a fully developed campground, these usually have running water and nicer restrooms and may have some paved roadways. Partially developed campgrounds are usually designated campgrounds that might have a picnic table, usually have dirt roads, typically lack a ready water source, and may have primitive toilets.

Unlike the lower 48 states, where developed camping is the most common and in fact the norm, dry/primitive camping is a widely accepted part of our outdoor culture in Alaska. This involves pulling off the road and finding a flat area, preferably next to a stream channel, where you can enjoy the landscape by yourself. Many people are used to developed campsites with established toilets, running water, and an overall sense of safety. However, dry/primitive camping offers you freedom, privacy, and a sense of being an

The Alaska Marine Highway System

While it is not a road system you can drive, the Alaska Marine Highway System is one of only 27 federally designated All-American roads. Its ferries serve the coastal communities of the southeast panhandle rain forest, the south central communities of the Kenai Peninsula and Kodiak, and the windblown and storm-tossed southwest archipelago islands of the Aleutian chain, traversing a marine byway that is an important and fascinating part of Alaska's transportation system. The "Blue Canoes," as they are sometimes called, ferry people and vehicles among 33 ports along a 3,500-nautical-mile ferry route that stretches from Bellingham, Washington, to Dutch Harbor in the Aleutians. These ferries, which are the size of small cruise ships, offer passage for everything from hikers to tractor-trailers. You can stake your tent on the deck, sleep in a lounge, or rent a modest berth and enjoy excellent food, all for a very reasonable price.

You can reach Alaska on the Marine Highway by traveling the Inside Passage from Bellingham, Washington, or Prince Rupert, British Columbia. You can also enjoy the Alaska Marine Highway System as a journey all its own, taking in the glacier-carved mountainous landscapes of southeast and south central Alaska or the volcano-formed islands and stormy seas of the Aleutian chain.

integrated, more intimate part of your travel environment. And it's free! If you've never tried dry/primitive camping before, Alaska is a great place to start. I always make a habit of having a couple of gallons of my own drinking water on hand to encourage and facilitate my dry/primitive camping pleasures.

General Useful Alaska Info

THE MILEPOST TRAVEL GUIDE: www.milepost.com

GEOGRAPHY AND WILDLIFE GUIDE FOR ALASKA: www.alaska.guide

TRAIL GUIDES TO MANY TRAILS IN ALASKA: www.alaska.guide/routes

A CAMPGROUND GUIDE TO ALASKA: www.campgroundalaska.com

ROAD LOGS AND GUIDES FOR MUCH OF ALASKA: www.alaska.org/tours/driving-tours

ALASKA TRAVEL PLANNING: www.alaskatrekker.com

CAMPING RESOURCE GUIDE: www.wikicamp.org

ALASKA STATE PARKS INFORMATION: www.dnr.alaska.gov/parks

ALASKA STATE PARK CAMPING: www.dnr.alaska.gov/parks/units

A GOOD GUIDE TO BED & BREAKFASTS: www.bedandbreakfast.com

OUTDOORS DIRECTORY: www.forums.outdoorsdirectory.com

TOURS OF NORTHERN ALASKA: Northern Alaska Tour Company, 800-474-1986 or 907-474-8600, www.northernalaska.com

FOREST CAMPSITES: Chugach National Forest, www.forestcamping.com/dow/alaska/chug.htm

TRANS-ALASKA PIPELINE: www.alaskacenters.gov/the-alyeska-pipeline.cfm

ALASKA TOURS: 866-317-3325, alaskatours.com

BUREAU OF LAND MANAGEMENT RECREATION SITES IN ALASKA: www.blm.gov/alaska

ALASKA CAMPING RESERVATIONS: www.reserveamerica.com, then type "Alaska" in the search field at the top of the home page or search by individual site name.

How This Book Works

This book covers a lot of ground, literally and figuratively! Alaska has more area than the next largest three states combined and covers latitudes ranging from the midlatitudes to above the Arctic Circle. Therefore these backroads and byways cover a lot of distance (the Dalton Highway alone is over 400 miles long) and traverse lands and environments, such as boreal forest and tundra, with which you may not be familiar.

The core of this book is the descriptions of 21 backroads and byways that traverse large portions of Alaska, including two areas (Nome and Kodiak) that are only reachable by plane or boat. I have organized the book from north to south, starting with the Dalton Highway, which travels 300 miles north of the Arctic Circle to the Arctic Ocean, and ending with the most southerly road on the island of Kodiak. I placed the fly-in areas of Nome (in northwest Alaska) and Kodiak (south central Alaska) at the end of the book.

Each road description includes nuts and bolts about where the road begins and ends, some of my favorite highlights, the length and conditions of the roads, estimated travel times, and recommendations of places to fuel both you and your vehicle, keeping in mind that in Alaska the fuel stop you just passed may be the last one for 200 miles.

Throughout the book, I've also added boxes including various side trips and further information. The side trips include brief descriptions of some of the side roads off of the main Backroad & Byway journeys that I think you might like to explore. In addition to the side trip descriptions, I've included some other side road options at specific mile post (MP) descriptions included in the *Attractions and Recreation* segments for each trip. In the other boxes, I cover topics of particular interest such as road conditions, driving tips, and environmental or ecological information.

In the camping sections I list some of the available developed campsites and a few undeveloped ones, keeping in mind that pull-off camping is routine, and desirable, in Alaska. My list of fuel stops, restaurants, camping areas, outfitters, and tour operators is not exhaustive but should provide you with a good foundation. Price codes refer to the price of a night's accommodation for two people.

$ $100 or less
$$ $101–$200
$$$ $201–$300
$$$$ $301 and above
* Call for pricing

Seasonal Note: Many Alaskan businesses earn a lion's share of their annual income during the summer season from Memorial Day to Labor Day. Traveling before Memorial Day or after Labor Day, you may find significantly lower prices than traveling during the summer. This applies to airfares as well.

Visit www.backroadsandbywaysofaslaska.com for information not included in this book, updates, and more, or to provide feedback and suggestions directly to the author.

1

THE DALTON HIGHWAY: HIGH ARCTIC ADVENTURE

Into and Through the Heart of Arctic Alaska

FROM → TO: Livengood to Deadhorse

WHERE IT STARTS: 72 miles north of Fairbanks on the Elliott Highway

WHERE IT ENDS: Deadhorse, 300 miles north of the Arctic Circle

ESTIMATED LENGTH: 414 miles (75 percent gravel)

ESTIMATED TIME: Four days to two weeks

HIGHLIGHTS: South and Middle Forks of the Koyukuk River, Wiseman/Nolan, Chandalar Shelf, Atigun Pass, Galbraith Lake

GETTING THERE: Drive 72 miles northwest of Fairbanks on the Elliott Highway (AK 2), 1 mile west of the tiny town of Livengood to the southern terminus of the Dalton Highway

---

The Dalton Highway, also known as "The Haul Road" because it is the primary transportation corridor for hauling people and materials back and forth between the oil fields of Prudhoe Bay and the town of Fairbanks, is the longest, most isolated, and most northerly road in Alaska. This highway traverses two major mountain ranges, the lovely White Mountains and the spectacular Brooks Range; crosses six major rivers, dozens of valleys, and hundreds of stream channels; cuts through massive sections of boreal forest; and traverses vast stretches of beautiful Arctic and alpine tundra. It skirts the edge of, and provides access to, the Arctic National Wildlife Refuge and the Gates of the Arctic National Park and Preserve. Along the way you will likely encounter a variety of wildlife, including moose, bear, fox, caribou, musk ox, and if you're really lucky, a wolf or two. This is the only road-system-connected-road in Alaska that ventures north of the Arctic Circle, and it does so in a big way: Its northern terminus is 300 miles north of

LEFT: FINGER ROCK JUTTING ABOVE THE HIGH TUNDRA POINTS TO AN ENDLESS SKY

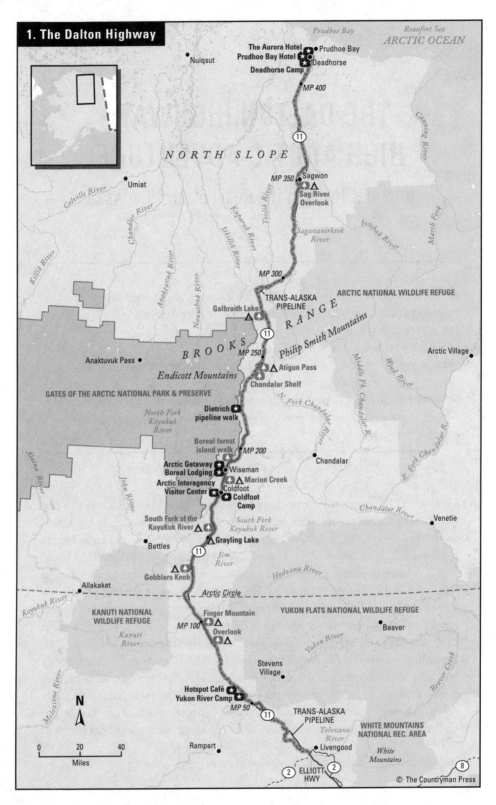

1. The Dalton Highway

Beaufort Sea
ARCTIC OCEAN

Prudhoe Bay

The Aurora Hotel
Prudhoe Bay Hotel
Deadhorse Camp

Prudhoe Bay
Deadhorse

MP 400

Nuiqsut

Canning River

(11)

N O R T H   S L O P E

Colville River

Umiat

Chandler River

MP 350   Sagwon
Sag River
Overlook

Ikakrak River

Marsh Fork

Toolik River

Sagavanirktok River

Ivishak River

MP 300

Killik River

Anaktuvuk River

Nanushuk River

ARCTIC NATIONAL WILDLIFE REFUGE

TRANS-ALASKA
PIPELINE

Galbraith Lake

R A N G E

Philip Smith Mountains

(11)

Arctic Village

B R O O K S

MP 250   Atigun Pass

Middle Fk. Chandalar River

Wind River

Anaktuvuk Pass

Endicott Mountains

Chandalar Shelf

N. Fork Chandalar River

GATES OF THE ARCTIC NATIONAL PARK & PRESERVE

Dietrich
pipeline walk

Chandalar

E. Fork Chandalar R.

North Fork Koyukuk River

Boreal forest
island walk   MP 200

Arctic Getaway
Boreal Lodging   Wiseman

Marion Creek

Alatna River

John River

Arctic Interagency
Visitor Center   Coldfoot
Coldfoot
Camp

Chandalar River

Venetie

South Fork of the
Koyukuk River

South Fork Koyukuk River

Bettles

Grayling Lake

(11)

Jim River

Hodzana River

Gobblers Knob

Allakaket

Arctic Circle

Koyukuk River

KANUTI NATIONAL
WILDLIFE REFUGE

YUKON FLATS NATIONAL WILDLIFE REFUGE

Finger Mountain

Beaver

Kanuti River

MP 100

Overlook

Yukon River

Beaver Creek

Melozitna River

Stevens
Village

Hotspot Café
Yukon River Camp

N

MP 50   (11)

TRANS-ALASKA
PIPELINE

WHITE MOUNTAINS
NATIONAL REC. AREA

0   20   40

Miles

Rampart

Tolovana River

Livengood

White Mountains

(2)   ELLIOTT
HWY

(2)

(8)

© The Countryman Press

THE BEGINNING OF THE 414-MILE JOURNEY INTO THE ARCTIC

the Arctic Circle. If you are a lover of wide-open spaces, wilderness, wildlife, and areas with very few people, and if you're looking for some diverse and awe-inspiring landscapes to enjoy, as well as access to numerous world-class wilderness adventures, then the Dalton Highway is for you!

During your nearly 500-mile-long journey from the interior of Alaska around Fairbanks to the shores of the Arctic Ocean, you will pass through eight different geographic regions. On the first 72-mile-long leg of your journey, from **Fairbanks** along the Elliott Highway (Drive #3) to the actual beginning of the Dalton Highway at MP 0, you will drive up, into, and through the lovely **White Mountains**, which are terrific for multiseason recreation. Your route twists and turns along and through boreal forested ridges and valleys of the 2,000- to 3,000-foot-tall, Arctic tundra–covered mountains. Once through the White Mountains you will pass through the upper reaches of the Tatalina and Tolovana River Valleys on your way to the historic mining community of **Livengood** and the actual milepost start (MP 0) of the Dalton Highway.

Part Two, beginning at the formal start of the Dalton Highway, is about 86 miles of steeply rolling, spruce-dominated boreal forest that traverses the southern and the northern drainage slopes of the Yukon River. Part Three, beginning around the 86-mile overlook and extending through **Gobblers Knob** (MP 132), is characterized by rolling uplands featuring broad expanses of open tundra-covered plains interspersed with sections of boreal forest that cross numerous stream channels. This section includes the granite outcrop **Finger Mountain** area (MP 98), which offers some fabulous cross-tundra hiking and expansive views. Part Four is all about multiple river crossings up to where the highway meets the Middle Fork of the Koyukuk River at around MP 182. The rivers you cross include the Jim River (numerous times) and the South Fork of the Koyukuk River, which offers a fabulous place to camp streamside and hike down its fascinating, gravel bar–strewn channel. Part Five, beginning about MP 185, just south of historic Wiseman, is the section where the Dalton Highway is parallel to, and often immediately next to, the glorious Middle Fork of the Koyukuk River.

BACKPACKERS CROSS THE KOYUKUK RIVER HEADING INTO THE GATES OF THE ARCTIC NATIONAL PARK

MASSIVE LIMESTONE SENTINELS OF THE BROOKS RANGE SOAR INTO THE MIST

The landscape is dominated by the stream channel and floodplain of the river as it cuts and flows through the steep, high-walled canyons in the **Brooks Range**, with massive mountain fronts and spectacular displays of enormous gray walls of 300- to 400-million-year-old limestone and marble. Part Six, which begins around MP 230, is the high alpine Brooks Range section where the Dalton Highway begins its climb in earnest up toward the ridgeline of the Brooks Range and the drainage divide between the Yukon River and the Arctic Ocean. This section includes the lovely, broad, brushy and spongy tundra–covered alpine valley of the **Chandalar Shelf**—which during autumn is like an impressionistic painting of yellows, reds, and golds—and the rocky and rugged Atigun Pass. Part Seven, the Atigun River section, begins at the north end of Atigun Pass, near MP 246, and continues for about 50 miles until you move up and out of the Atigun River drainage. Along this section the highway loosely follows the river's valley, bounded by dramatic peaks and ridgelines. This is the section of the highway where the rugged Brooks Range transitions into the broad, Arctic tundra–covered plane known as the North Slope. Included in this section of the drive is the spectacular **Galbraith Lake** area, which is set at the edge of the valley, nestled alongside the northern front slopes of the Brooks Range. The final section, Part Eight, begins around MP 300, where you enter the "Sag" (short for **Sagavanirktok**) River drainage and travel north for the final 114 miles across the North Slope. This huge, open section of landscape offers some of

the best opportunities for viewing muskox and, in spring and fall, herds of migrating caribou.

One of the other interesting features of the Dalton Highway is that it loosely parallels the northern half of the fascinating and storied **Trans-Alaska Pipeline System (TAPS),** the construction and maintenance of which the Dalton Highway/Haul Road was built to serve. The southern half of TAPS is paralleled by the Richardson Highway (Drive #7). In addition to the primary Dalton Highway road, there is a secondary pipeline access and maintenance road that hugs the pipeline and is used to monitor and maintain it. This pipeline maintenance road is accessible at numerous points and is often hikeable for miles. The pipeline is frequently visible along much of the 414-mile length of the Dalton Highway. Approximately 420 miles of the 800-mile-long pipeline is located aboveground, with 380 miles buried beneath the surface. The pipeline is elevated over sections of permafrost and buried where the ground is not permanently frozen. The entire length of the pipeline is insulated to protect the fragile permafrost tundra and boreal forest ecosystems and habitats. In addition, elevated sections of the pipeline are suspended from refrigerated pilings that further protect the tundra from melting. You can easily view the refrigeration cooling fins that are located on the top of each of the pipeline suspension pilings. The Alyeska Pipeline Service Company, which maintains the pipeline, is happy to have you hike along the maintenance road, they just ask that you obtain a permit to do so (see the "TAPS Permit" sidebar for more information on obtaining a permit).

At each pipeline access point along the highway there are brown signs with white lettering with various designations and numbers such as 67 APL 5, MP 412.3 RGV 67N, OMS 68-1. These provide location information and mileages for various kinds of pipeline access and maintenance activities. However, the designation and number you might find most useful is the milepost designation, starting at MP 0 in Deadhorse near Prudhoe Bay

on the Arctic Ocean and ending at MP 412.3 in Valdez. Notice that the Dalton Highway MP numbers, on green signs, and the pipeline MP numbers, on brown signs, are the inverse of each other, with the pipeline MP numbers beginning in Valdez and the Dalton Highway MP numbers beginning in Deadhorse.

Yes, you can drive this road in four days, but plan to take at least a week to drive up to Deadhorse and another week to drive back. Each day, eschew having any particular destination in mind and drive at a leisurely pace. Having a self-contained camping unit is a big bonus here! Plan to stop early and often, and allow yourself time to explore whatever catches your eye. On your way up, make notes of places to stop on the way back. Traveling the haul road in an unfettered and unstructured manner will be one of the peak driving experiences, if not *the* peak driving experience, of your life. Of all the roads in Alaska that lend themselves to turning off the road and camping wherever you like, this really is the crown jewel. There are only three

TAPS Permits

Contact the Alyeska Pipeline Service Company to obtain Trans-Alaska Pipeline System Right-of-Way (TAPS ROW) permits for hiking/traveling the pipeline maintenance road: 907-787-8170, alyeskamail@alyeska -pipeline.com, P.O. Box 196660, Anchorage, AK 99519. Or call Valdez at 907-834-6480, Fairbanks at 907-450-5707, or Anchorage at 907-787-8971. You can also download a PDF of the TAPS Right-of-Way Users Guidelines (RUG) from www.backroadsandbywaysofalaska.com. Some of these pipeline access points and maintenance road sections are actually wheelchair accessible (see MP 219 below).

towns with dependable accommodations until you reach Deadhorse—**Yukon Crossing/Hot Spot**, **Coldfoot**, and **Wiseman**—and most of these lodgings are only available during the summer months.

IN THE AREA

Accommodations, Fuel, and Food

There are only three dependable areas for lodging along your 414-mile-long Dalton Highway journey, which is why I strongly recommend traveling with a camper. Notice that the Yukon River Camp and Hot Spot lodgings are within 5 miles of each other just north of where the Dalton Highway crosses the Yukon River (MP 56-60), and the communities of Coldfoot and Wiseman are only 14 miles apart (MP 175-189). The Yukon River/Hot Spot and Wiseman facilties are typically open from mid-May to mid- to late September. Only Coldfoot is open year-round.

MP 56: YUKON RIVER CAMP, 907-474-3557, www.yukonrivercamp.com. They offer fuel (gas and diesel), lodging (seasonal), and food. $–$$.

THE HOTSPOT CAFÉ HAS THE BEST BURGERS FOR 500 MILES

MP 60: HOTSPOT CAFÉ, 907-378-9161. Lodging, camping, and food, particularly hamburgers. They don't offer fuel. See their Facebook page for updates. $–$$.

MP 175: COLDFOOT CAMP, 907-474-3500, www.coldfootcamp.com. Fuel (gas and diesel), lodging, and food. The only year-round supply depot available between MP 0 and Deadhorse. $–$$.

MP 189, WISEMAN: 9000 Dalton Highway, Wiseman Village, Wiseman, Alaska, 907-678-4566. Very cozy cabins with food are available at the **Arctic Getaway Lodge** ($$), www.arcticgetaway.com, and **Boreal Lodging**, www .boreallodge.com. $$.

MP 414, DEADHORSE: Year-round accommodations in Deadhorse range from bare-bones dormitory rooms, such as those at **Deadhorse Camp**, 877-474-3565, www.deadhorsecamp.com ($), to more luxurious accommodations such as the **Prudhoe Bay Hotel**, 907-659-2449, www.prudhoebayhotel.com ($$), and **The Aurora Motel**, 907-670-0600, www.theaurorahotel.net, my favorite for great food and nice rooms ($$). General information on Deadhorse is available at www.prudhoebay.com/communities_Deadhorse.htm.

Camping

There are numerous developed campsites (meaning there are restrooms and sometimes water) and undeveloped campsites that accommodate car and RV camping along the Dalton Highway. The following are among my favorites from south to north. Public campgrounds are free or have a minimal fee, are open from May to November, and are clean and well maintained. Because there are so many interesting undesignated camping sites to explore and enjoy, I often drive the entire distance without staying in a single established campground.

MP 28 (ELLIOTT HIGHWAY), WICKERSHAM DOME TRAILHEAD: Located 28 miles north of Fox on the Elliott Highway, this is not actually on the Dalton Highway, but it's a great first night camping stop if you start your Dalton Highway trip later in the day. It also provides access to some spectacular White Mountain hiking if you are so inclined.

MP 86, OVERLOOK: Stop at the high point on the road for expansive views north over the tundra-covered plain of the Finger Mountain region.

MP 98, FINGER MOUNTAIN: This is a basic parking/camping area that's a great place to stop for hiking across a granite boulder–strewn landscape. Be sure to take the time to explore this fascinating landscape of boulders and alpine tundra plants and lichens. Note there is no water here.

MP 132, GOBBLERS KNOB: Pull off the road at the top of this steep hill to enjoy wide views north over the Jim River Basin.

MP 150, GRAYLING LAKE: There is a small car/RV camping area next to a beautiful alpine lake.

MP 156, SOUTH FORK OF THE KOYUKUK RIVER: Although this is not really a developed or even designated camping area, it's a dandy place to stop and camp on the easy-to-access gravel bar on the banks of the Koyukuk River (unless you arrive in early spring and it is in flood stage). Take the dirt road located across the highway from the restrooms that are just south of the Koyukuk River bridge. I always stop here, don my XTRATUF boots or wet sneakers, and wander south along the gravel bars of the South Fork of the Koyukuk River.

MP 180, MARION CREEK: A lovely, well-developed campsite—complete with hand-pump water, tables, and restrooms—carved out of the boreal forest and along Marion Creek, located just 5 miles north of Coldfoot. Take the time to follow the trail north along the creek for a delightful, if wet, journey through the forest. Along the way enjoy the spectacular tundra with its variety of fascinating lichens.

MP 244, ATIGUN PASS: This is another nondesignated campground at which I always camp. Pull off in the flat area on the east side of the road a quarter mile north of the Atigun Pass summit to sleep among soaring Brooks Range peaks. You'll likely experience dynamically changing weather conditions, including scudding clouds and fog, alpine winds, precipitation of various kinds, and sometimes even calm, clear skies. Take a walk along the lovely stream channel that forms the headwaters of the Atigun River.

MP 275, GALBRAITH LAKE: Stop here for one of my "can't miss" campsites. This one is about a mile and a half west of the Dalton Highway, set in an open tundra atmosphere. Hike west up the stream channel and out onto the walking tundra–covered slopes formed at the joining of the northern flanks of the Brooks Range and the vast North Slope.

MP 348, SAG RIVER OVERLOOK: This provides an elevated view of the Sag River and its valley from an information kiosk. Snow and ice remain along this section of the river well into the summer months.

Attractions and Recreation

Established trails in the wilderness are few and far between by design. Both the National Park Service and the Bureau of Land Management purposefully manage this land as wilderness, and they actively encourage hikers to seek their own adventures and make their own way. That said, you should not venture off into this country without the proper equipment and skills, and you should always contact either the Park Service or the BLM to obtain permits and to let them know generally where you'll be.

Here is a very partial list of some things to do along the Dalton Highway:

MP 5 ON ELLIOTT HIGHWAY, TRANS-ALASKA PIPELINE VIEW AND INFORMATION KIOSK: Particularly if this is your first trip north of Fairbanks, just after you begin your journey to the Dalton Highway, be sure to

---

Rules of the Road

The Dalton Highway is likely to be a different and more challenging driving experience than any other highway you've ever driven. Here are some tips to help keep you safe, happy, and on the road:

- **Bring a roadworthy vehicle**, preferably a four-wheel drive with good ground clearance.
- **Bring at least two extra spare tires** (rims included) and check to make sure that both spares are well inflated. If you get a flat tire, be sure to get it fixed as soon as you can, likely at Coldfoot or Deadhorse.
- **Drive slowly!** Yes, these roads are well maintained, and there's even some paved sections. However, driving gravel roads at 60 or 70 miles per hour is a recipe for disaster. If you maintain high velocities with passing vehicles coming in the opposite direction, you will be creating passing velocities of 150 plus miles per hour, which means any rocks thrown from the oncoming vehicle will be moving that fast. Plus, once you start to slide or skid on gravel, it's not like being on pavement. You don't slow down very quickly and you're likely to end up in a ditch at the very least, perhaps worse.
- **Trucks rule the road**. The Dalton Highway was constructed and is maintained primarily as a commercial haul road for moving equipment, supplies, and materials between Deadhorse/Prudhoe Bay and Fairbanks.

Slow down and pull off a bit whenever you meet an oncoming truck, and let trucks by with some cushion room. If a big truck comes roaring up behind you, simply pull over and let it by with a wave and a smile.

- **Plan your gas and stock up on food and provisions (including water) for your entire trip**. Provisions are very expensive along the way, and there is really not much in Deadhorse for tourists to purchase in terms of food and supplies. There is one small grocery store in town, but the choices are sparse and the prices are understandably high.

- **If you need repairs, both Coldfoot and Deadhorse offer vehicle repair facilities**. However, keep in mind that, as a tourist, you are not necessarily a top priority, particularly in Deadhorse. Patience and courtesy will go far, unless of course you'd like to stay the winter.

TRUCKS RULE THE ROAD

stop at the pipeline viewpoint and information kiosk on the east (right) side of the road 5 miles north of Fairbanks. This provides an excellent up-close view of the pipeline, a pipeline "pig" used for cleaning, and lots of fascinating information about the construction and characteristics of the pipeline.

MP 0–414, HIKE THE TRANS-ALASKA PIPELINE SYSTEM: The oil pipeline parallels both the Dalton and Richardson (Drive #7) Highways along its entire 800-mile length from the oil fields at Prudhoe Bay, located along the

Arctic Biomes

The far north Arctic and subarctic environments are dominated by two types of ecosystems/biomes: the boreal forest, also known as taiga, and various types of tundra. The terms *boreal forest* and *taiga* refer to the coniferous forest biome that covers much of the arctic north and is characterized by spruce-dominated forest interspersed with patches and groves of aspen, birch, and larch that are often growing on an understory of various kinds of tundra. The small, scraggly spruce trees are black spruce, which tend to grow very slowly on poorly drained permafrost, permanently frozen ground whose top meter or so may melt during the summer but refreeze in the winter. A 5-foot-tall black spruce may be several hundred years old. The larger and statelier white spruce thrives on better-drained, non-permafrost soils. The term *tundra* refers to a variety of near-ground vegetation—adapted to various cold, wind, and moisture conditions—characterized by short to tall grasses, low to high bushes, and a fascinating diversity of lichens.

Arctic coast just north of Deadhorse, to the Valdez Marine Terminal, located at the north end of Prince William Sound on the Gulf of Alaska, with numerous access points for viewing and even hiking along the pipeline maintenance road. Locate a pipeline access point at a section where the highway turns away from the pipeline (so that you get away from any vehicle noise along the road). Walk over to the pipeline and hike along the dirt and gravel double-track maintenance road for a chance to see wildlife and enjoy an easy hike away from the highway.

MP 98, FINGER MOUNTAIN AND MORE HIKES ACROSS OPEN TUNDRA: You must walk across the tundra at least once. Choose a section of tundra that is high and dry and relatively short, what I call walking tundra, so that your traverse will be easy. You'll be amazed at how beautiful it is and how much there is to see. Finger Mountain is a terrific place to hike cross-country because you're on granite uplands that provide opportunities for hiking across everything from dry to spongy to marshy tundra. Don your boots or wet-sneakers and venture forth!

MP 189–235, HIKE A STREAM CHANNEL: Many of the stream channels along the Dalton Highway still don't have a name. Choose one that heads up into the mountains. This section of the road along the Koyukuk River offers numerous opportunities for hiking upstream channels that climb into the gorgeous, soaring limestone canyons of the Brooks Range.

MP 189–235, THE MIDDLE FORK OF THE KOYUKUK RIVER: Stop at any number of the dozens of access points and enjoy the blending of the river, the Arctic tundra, and the boreal forest.

MP 175, ARCTIC INTERAGENCY VISITOR CENTER: Open 11 AM to 10 PM daily from May 24 to September 9, 907-678-5209 or 907-678-2014. The center, located in the town of Coldfoot, offers all sorts of information about the Arctic north country in general and the Dalton Highway in particular. There is also an excellent display of Dalton Highway rocks and their descriptions.

MP 189, WISEMAN: This historic town keeps on going and is worth a visit. Join Ranger Jack, if he is in town, for his fascinating interpretive presentation and ask for Clutch, a longtime resident, who is a fun character with many stories to tell. Read Bob Marshall's fascinating wilderness adventure story, *Arctic Village: A 1930s Portrait of Wiseman, Alaska,* and drive west 6 miles on the Nolan Road to follow his footsteps into the Gates of the Arctic National Park and Preserve.

MP 192, WALK THROUGH A BOREAL FOREST ISLAND: Pull off the road on the gravel pit access road and walk west through the gravel pit toward the Middle Fork of the Koyukuk River. There's no formal trail here; just make your way through the willows and aspens, across a small, high-water side channel of the river. Earlier in the spring, the side channel may carry enough water to be impassable, so use your common sense. Once you cross the side channel, you're on a forest-stabilized gravel bar island that is covered with tundra-floored boreal forest. The understory tundra is a delight to walk across. Most of it is spongy tundra that is like walking on pillows covered in lichens and mosses and a whole range of mushrooms. After a short distance you'll reach the main-stem channel of the middle fork of the river. Take some time to hang out by the stream channel and enjoy the sur-

THE CHANDALAR SHELF MESMERIZES WITH SWEEPING VIEWS

rounding environs, including great views into the high peaks of the Brooks Range. I found this delightful island by just following my nose. You can find hundreds of similar gems on your own by just exploring.

MP 219, OLD ROAD TO DIETRICH AND WHEELCHAIR-ACCESSIBLE PIPELINE WALK: Pull off here to walk about a quarter mile out to where the Koyukuk River has devoured most of the old road to Dietrich for some wonderful views across the river and into the Brooks Range. Walk the pipeline maintenance road south away from the highway. This is a relatively flat and smooth-bottomed section to attempt with a wheelchair or if you have other mobility challenges.

MP 238, VIEW AND WALK INTO THE CHANDALAR SHELF: Located just south of Atigun Pass and bisected by the Chandalar River, this broad, high-elevation, tundra-covered valley needs to be savored. Pull off the road, set up your camp chairs, and enjoy the view and atmosphere. It's particularly spectacular during late August during the high point of the fall colors.

MP 244, CAMP AND HIKE AROUND ATIGUN PASS: Enjoy the high alpine environments of the Brooks Range, including dwarf tundra, the headwaters of the Atigun River, and rapidly changing weather that often includes swirling clouds and misting rains.

MP 275, CAMP AND HIKE AT GALBRAITH LAKE: Hiking west from the campground, up the stream channel and across the broad walking tundra–covered slopes that lap up against the feet of the mighty Brooks Range is likely to be one of the peak hiking experiences of your life. Give yourself at least one entire day here. Or better yet, hike out, camp on a high tundra-covered ridge, and hike back the next day via another route.

MP 414, TAKE A TOUR OF DEADHORSE: Take a fascinating tour of the oil facility man camp of Deadhorse, including a trip out to the Arctic Ocean on the Arctic Ocean Shuttle (www.deadhorsecamp.com/arctic-ocean-shuttle), which is run out of the camp. If you are interested in seeing more of Deadhorse and the oil complex community, ask your driver for a private tour the next day.

Festivals and Fairs

FAIRBANKS SUMMER ARTS FESTIVAL (THIRD WEEK IN JULY): www .alaska.org/detail/fairbanks-summer-arts-festival

MIDNIGHT SUN FESTIVAL (JUNE 21): www.alaska.org/detail/midnight
-sun-festival

Outfitters and Tour Operators

FRONTIER OUTFITTERS: Fairbanks, 907-452-4774, www.frontieroutfitters
fairbanks.com

ALASKAN ARCTIC TURTLE TOURS: Fairbanks, 907-457-1798, wildalaska
.info/prudhoe-bay-tour

ARCTIC OUTFITTERS: Fairbanks, 907-474-3530, www.arctic-outfitters.com

NORTHERN ALASKA TOUR COMPANY: Fairbanks, 800-474-1986, www
.northernalaska.com

DALTON HIGHWAY EXPRESS: Fairbanks, 907-474-3555, www.daltonhigh
wayexpress.com

ALASKA TOURS: 866-317-3325, alaskatours.com

PEACE OF SELBY WILDERNESS: 907-672-3206, www.alaskawilderness
.net. Ecotourism and guiding services in the southern Brooks Range.

USEFUL INFORMATION

TRANS-ALASKA PIPELINE: www.alaska.org/detail/alyeska-pipeline

THE MILEPOST TRAVEL GUIDE: www.themilepost.com/highway-info/
highways/dalton-highway

ALASKA.ORG ROAD GUIDE: www.alaska.org/guide/dalton-highway

YUKON RIVER CAMP: www.yukonrivercamp.com

COLDFOOT CAMP: www.coldfootcamp.com

DEADHORSE CAMP AND ARCTIC OCEAN SHUTTLE: www.deadhorse
camp.com/arctic-ocean-shuttle

BLM PDF ROAD GUIDE AND MAP: www.blm.gov.

2

THE STEESE-CIRCLE HIGHWAY (AK 6): CIRCLE CITY TO FAIRBANKS GOLD MINING ROUTE

Mining and Much More Along a Road to the Yukon River

FROM → TO: Fox to Circle

WHERE IT STARTS: MP 0 on the Steese Highway, Fairbanks

WHERE IT ENDS: Circle, on the Yukon River

ESTIMATED LENGTH: 161 miles (first half is paved, second half is gravel)

ESTIMATED TIME: Two days to one week

HIGHLIGHTS: Nome Creek Valley (Tabletop Mountain hike), Twelvemile Summit, Eagle Summit, Pinnell Mountain Trail, the Yukon River at Circle

GETTING THERE: Begin on the Steese Expressway (AK 2) in Fairbanks and drive 11 miles north to where AK 2 continues northwest as the Elliott Highway (Drive #3) and the Steese Highway continues northeast as AK 6. Top off your fuel tanks and fill up any extra gas cans where K-6 and AK 2 diverge. Fuel prices in Circle are typically $4.50 plus per gallon.

Like many roads in Alaska, the **Steese Highway**, originally known as the Circle City to Fairbanks Road, was built in pursuit of gold. Much of the history, and most of the remaining structures along the highway, are related to the prospecting, mining, and transportation of gold through and from what was known as the **Circle Mining District**, which was all abustle in the 1890s. There are many gold boom–era artifacts to discover along the Steese Highway. Numerous gold-mining operations are currently active here, including the huge **Fort Knox Gold Mine** at MP 20.

The Steese Highway trends northeast, initially along the southern slopes of the White Mountains, eventually all the way to the banks of the Yukon

LEFT: A GORGEOUS GROVE OF BIRCH TREES NEAR THE TOWN OF CENTRAL

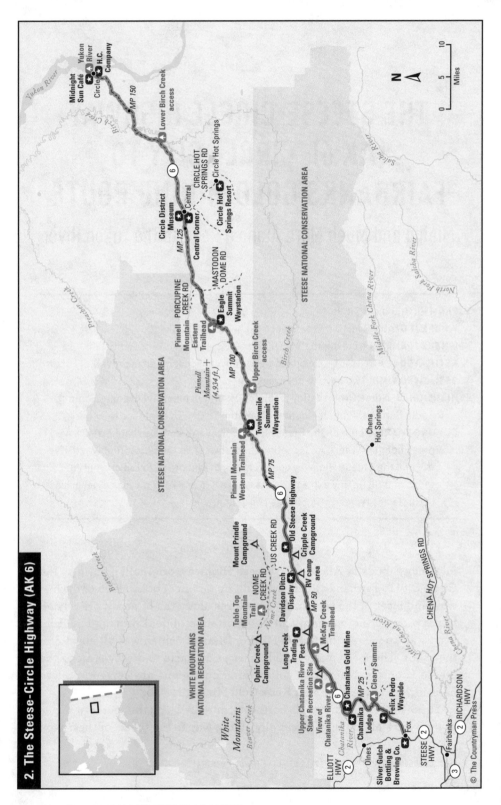

2. The Steese-Circle Highway (AK 6)

N

0 5 10
Miles

Yukon River

Midnight Sun Café
Circle
Yukon River
Circle H.C. Company

MP 150

Lower Birch Creek access

Beaver Creek

Preacher Creek

Birch Creek

6

CIRCLE HOT SPRINGS RD
Circle Hot Springs

Circle District Museum
Central
Central Corner
MP 125
Circle Hot Springs Resort

MASTODON DOME RD

PORCUPINE CREEK RD
Pinnell Mountain Eastern Trailhead

Eagle Summit Waystation

STEESE NATIONAL CONSERVATION AREA

Upper Birch Creek access

Pinnell Mountain (4,934 ft.)

MP 100

Birch Creek

STEESE NATIONAL CONSERVATION AREA

North Fork Chena River

Salcha River

Twelvemile Summit Waystation

Pinnell Mountain Western Trailhead

MP 75

6

Middle Fork Chena River

South Fork Salcha River

WHITE MOUNTAINS NATIONAL RECREATION AREA

White Mountains

Beaver Creek

Table Top Mountain Trail

Mount Prindle Campground

NOME CREEK RD

Nome Creek

US CREEK RD

Old Steese Highway
Cripple Creek Campground
RV camp area

Davidson Ditch Display

MP 50

McKay Creek Trailhead

Ophir Creek Campground

Long Creek Trading Post

Upper Chatanika River State Recreation Site

6

View of Chatanika River

Chatanika River

Chatanika Lodge

MP 25

Chatanika Gold Mine

Cleary Summit

Felix Pedro Wayside

Fox

Chena Hot Springs

CHENA HOT SPRINGS RD

Little Chena River

Chena River

ELLIOTT HWY

2

Olnes

Silver Gulch Bottling & Brewing Co.

STEESE HWY

2

RICHARDSON HWY

2

3

Fairbanks

© The Countryman Press

River at the tiny town of Circle, so named by early settlers who thought this town was on the Arctic Circle. While it is in fact 50 miles south, it's located on a lovely, long bend in the Yukon River and has a fascinating history.

At MP 20 you reach **Cleary Summit** (2,233 feet), which is the first of three road summits along the highway. From there, take a long, slow drive down into the lovely Chatanika River Valley. The Steese Highway follows upstream along the westward-flowing **Chatanika River** through spruce-dominated boreal forest, with many groves of aspens and birches intermingled with large sections of marshy tundra, which are great for viewing but not so great for hiking. You will notice several large, burned-out areas of forest along the Steese Highway in various stages of recovery and rejuvenation from periodic fires. The dimensions and frequencies of these fires have increased in recent years due to higher temperatures and drier seasons.

SERENE AND SCENIC FLOATING ON THE CHATANIKA RIVER

Following your descent from Cleary Summit, you'll find numerous access points to several major stream channels, including, on the western end of the road, the Chatanika River and then Birch and Crooked Creeks on the eastern end. These access points provide multiple put-in and take-out locations if you are interested in some kayak or rafting adventures. During the summer and fall, the relatively low water volumes and low gradients of these stream channels make them prime for safe floating activities. And if fishing is in your future, be sure to look for the numerous small, brown, fish-with-fishhook signs indicating fishing locations stocked by the Alaska Department of Natural Resources.

As you continue eastward, you'll pass the historical Davidson Ditch and side road access to **Nome Valley** at MP 57 (see Side Trips) as the highway continues to gradually climb until you reach **Twelvemile Summit** at MP 85. Along the way you will rise up out of the boreal forest and into the wide-open landscape of the Arctic alpine tundra. As you approach the tree line, notice that the boreal forest becomes thinner and shorter and gradually disappears.

As you drive eastward, observe that, unlike many mountain ranges in Alaska, which tend to be sharp and jagged, these mountains are smooth and rounded. Rather than being made of erosion-resistant granite or sandstone, most of these mountain peaks and ridges are made of mica-rich metamorphic rocks known as schists. These mica minerals are easily weathered and therefore break down and spread out, contributing to the beautifully soft, rounded landscape before you.

Continuing east of Twelvemile Summit, you switch drainage divides and will now be traveling through the eastward-flowing drainages of Birch and Crooked Creeks, with access to the **Birch Creek Wild and Scenic River**. At MP 107 you reach the high point on the Steese Highway at **Eagle Summit** (3,624 feet). As you descend out of the mountains from Eagle Summit, look east to see fresh dredge piles being created along Bonanza and Mammoth Creeks from currently active placer gold-mining activities. In the fall along

this long descent you will be treated to some spectacular sections of gold covered hillsides painted by large groves of aspen and birch trees that form high-contrast patchworks against the dark green spruce trees. The descent from Eagle Summit leads you across the flat-lying wetlands and floodplains of Birch and Cripple Creeks as you approach the lovely community of **Central** (population 94) at MP 127, which is a checkpoint along the Yukon Quest International Sled Dog Race. From Central you continue across a landscape of diminutive black spruce–dominated tundra wetlands. During this stretch you will pass the Lower Birch Creek wayside, and then cross over the Birch Creek bridge as you head toward the small town of **Circle** (population 95), located on the banks of the Yukon River at MP 161. From the Birch Creek bridge to Circle you may notice that the vegetation changes in some sections from small, marshy tundra–supported, scraggly black spruce to the larger, statelier white spruce trees that are growing on the slightly more elevated and well-drained gravel uplands. You also drive along the edge of

SIDE TRIPS

MP 57, Nome Creek Valley

Study the information-packed Wayside kiosk and drive north 7 miles on US Creek Road to reach 16-mile-long Nome Creek Road for year-round access to camping, hiking, fishing, skiing, skijoring, snowshoeing, gold panning, and ATV riding or snowmachining in the White Mountains. This area is often as busy, or busier, in the winter as it is in the summer. Free camp along Nome Creek or at the developed Mount Prindle or Ophire Creek Campgrounds. I particularly recommend hiking the 3-mile-long Table Mountain Trail. For a week-long wilderness paddle with a take-out on the Yukon River, consider the Beaver Creek National Wild and Scenic River.

AN OXBOW LAKE ON THE FLOODPLAIN OF THE YUKON RIVER

some cutoff oxbow lakes that have been isolated from previously active river channels as the Yukon River moves back and forth across its floodplain.

Once you reach Circle and the Yukon River, check out the flood gauge information sign located near the end of the road. And stop by the Midnight Sun Café for a bite to eat and the H. C. Co. Store, whose owners have lived here for 50 years, for fuel and groceries.

IN THE AREA

Accommodations, Fuel, and Food

MP 11, SILVER GULCH BOTTLING AND BREWING COMPANY: 2195 Old Steese Highway, Fox, 907-452-2739, www.silvergulch.com/restaurant.htm. This place has a good selection of locally made brews and a wide variety of comfort foods. $.

MP 29, CHATANIKA LODGE: Mile 28.5 Steese Highway, Chatanika, 907-389-2164, www.chatanikalodgeak.com. Open year-round, this is a good location to stay when exploring the western end of the Steese Highway. $–$$.

MP 45, LONG CREEK TRADING POST, CAMPING & CAFÉ: 8721 Steese Highway, Fairbanks, 907-389-5287, www.facebook.com/steesehighway. Open 8 AM–9 PM. General and liquor store, good food, with cabins, camping, and gold panning. $.

MP 127, CENTRAL CORNER: 128 Steese Highway, Central, 907-520-5800. Lodging, restaurant, fuel, bar, groceries. Also, **Jeff's Cabins** offers lodging and RV parking. It's a good location to stay for exploring the eastern end of the Steese Highway. $–$$.

MP 161, CIRCLE: The **Midnight Sun Café** is your best bet for a bite to eat, and the **H. C. Co.** sells fuel and groceries. No accommodations are available as of this writing. The closest accommodations are in Central.

Camping

MP 40, UPPER CHATANIKA RIVER STATE RECREATION SITE: Lovely tree-shaded camping with direct access to the river. Includes restrooms, tables, and fire rings.

MP 56–57, DRY CAMP AREA FOR RVS NEXT TO STREAM POND: Undeveloped unofficial state gravel and equipment storage site, but also a large, quiet area for good RV camping.

MP 57, MOUNT PRINDLE AND OPHIR CAMPGROUNDS IN NOME VALLEY: These two are developed BLM streamside campgrounds. There are also numerous primitive camping locations along Nome Creek (see Nome Creek Valley in Side Trips).

MP 60, CRIPPLE CREEK BLM CAMPING AREA: Developed campsites nestled into high-canopy, white spruce–dominated boreal forest along the

RELICS OF THE GOLD RUSH AT THE HISTORIC CHATANIKA GOLD CAMP

shores of beautiful Cripple Creek. These sites are OK for car, small RV, and walk-in camping. Don't miss the unheralded, delightful nature trail that follows along Cripple Creek.

Attractions and Recreation

MP 16.5, FELIX PEDRO WAYSIDE: At this information-packed wayside, explore the fascinating Gold Rush photographs and descriptions contained in the numerous kiosk exhibits.

MP 27.5, GOLD OPERATIONS AT CHATANIKA: Here you will find a well-preserved gold mining operation with numerous ore-processing facility buildings. There are also some buildings that have been converted for current hotel and restaurant use that are intermittently open for business. One and a half miles down the road, at MP 29, stop in at the Chatanika Lodge and take a look at the 1927-built gold dredge right across the highway. Ask at the lodge for information about the gold dredge.

MP 35, ROADSIDE TURNOUT: Stop here for a beautiful view of all the various environments along the Chatanika River, including the stream channel, the boreal forests, the tundra, and both north- and south-facing slopes of the surrounding White Mountains.

MP 40, UPPER CHATANIKA RIVER STATE RECREATION SITE: This is a beautiful camping area with large spruce and birch trees with direct access to the Chatanka River and its gravel bars. It's a popular spot to paddle and fish.

MP 42, MCKAY CREEK TRAILHEAD ACCESS TO WHITE MOUNTAINS NATIONAL RECREATION AREA: This trail is appropriate for ORV, dogsled, and skijoring access to the White Mountains. There is a large, flat gravel RV camping and staging area across the road from the McKay Creek trailhead.

GRAVEL-BAR CAMPING ON THE CHATANIKA RIVER

VAST VIEWS OF THE YUKON RIVER AND FLOODPLAIN AT CIRCLE

MP 57, DAVIDSON DITCH DISPLAY: Across the US Creek Highway from the MP 57 wayside is a short access road to an old section of the 83-mile-long Davidson Ditch water pipe that was used for placer gold-mining operations during the heyday of gold mining along the Steese Highway. This huge pipe carried 3 million gallons of water a day when mining activities were at their peak. This is well worth a stop to see the fascinating remnants of this mining water pipe. With a bit of scrambling and some care you can walk across the top of the pipe.

MP 57, ACCESS TO HIKING AND KAYAKING IN NOME VALLEY: Study the information kiosk with a location map and details about access points to White Mountains National Recreation Area and Steese National Conservation Area and Nome Valley (see Side Trips). Take US Creek Road up and over into Nome Valley. There are multiple access points to the White Mountains for hiking, skiing, and kayaking, including access to the wilderness portions of the Birch Creek Wild and Scenic River. There's plenty of camping locations, both developed and undeveloped, and numerous hiking and ORV trails to enjoy.

MP 60, EXPLORE OLD STEESE HIGHWAY SECTION: Around MP 60, just east of the Cripple Creek Campground, you can drive on and explore a previous section of the Steese Highway that has since been abandoned but remains at least partially navigable.

MP 85, PINNELL MOUNTAIN WESTERN TRAILHEAD: Pull over and hike north across the wide-open Arctic walking tundra to the near ridgeline that

is along the first part of the 27-mile-long Pinnell Mountain Trail. You will be treated to some fabulous views of the surrounding countryside. And if you're up for a long, multiday trek through the high alpine tundra, the Pinnell Mountain Trail, whose eastern trailhead is the Eagle Summit wayside at MP 107, should be first on your list of overnight hikes.

MP 85, TWELVEMILE SUMMIT WAYSTATION: Stop here at the second of three road summits along the Steese Highway. Check out the historic Circle City to Fairbanks information kiosk and the side road to an undeveloped and unofficial camping site that serves as a staging area for hunters in the fall. Twelvemile Summit is a wonderful starting point for a variety of terrific cross-tundra hiking opportunities, including the western trailhead for the Pinnell Mountain Trail.

MP 94, UPPER BIRCH CREEK ACCESS: If you are a kayaker or rafter, this is an excellent put-in point for a several-day float down the Birch Creek Wild and Scenic River, with the take-out at the Lower Birch Creek Wayside at MP 140 on the Steese Highway.

MP 107, EAGLE MILE SUMMIT WAYSTATION: Stop here at the third of three road summits along the Steese Highway to walk the short (⅓ mile) nature trail and enjoy the Arctic tundra environment and information plaques. This is also the eastern trailhead for the Pinnell Mountain Trail. For a real treat, invest an hour or two into hiking northwest along the trail to appreciate the many joys of the tundra and vast views. Caribou Peak, about a mile to the west of the trailhead, is a terrific half-day hike. A good plan is

HISTORIC BUILDINGS OF CENTRAL HOT SPRINGS

to camp here overnight at the wayside and get an early start in the morning. In the winter, there are expansive views of the northern lights from here.

MP 114-115, MASTODON DOME AND PORCUPINE CREEK ROADS AND OTHERS: For some off-highway adventure, engage your four-wheel drive and follow these old mining roads, though be aware that there are still current claims that are being mined, so be respectful of people's property.

MP 127, CENTRAL AND CENTRAL HOT SPRINGS: Linger in the lovely community of Central and visit the Central District Museum and the multi-tasking Central Corner community hub. You can also drive 8 miles south from Central to check out the now "officially inactive" Central Hot Springs Resort. Depending upon circumstances and conditions, you may be able to enjoy a nice soak in the huge hot springs pool. Ask the locals for information and permission.

MP 140, LOWER BIRCH CREEK ACCESS: This is another good lunch stop, as well as a natural take-out for kayaking/rafting trips along the Birch

Creek Wild and Scenic River from the put-in at MP 94 at the Upper Birch Creek access point.

MP 161, END OF THE ROAD AT THE YUKON RIVER: Plan to hang out for a while in your lawn chair at the end of the road along this big, beautiful bend in the Yukon River.

Outfitters and Tour Operators

PROSPECTOR OUTFITTERS: Fairbanks, 907-457-7372, www.prospector outfitters.com.

ALASKAN ARCTIC TURTLE TOURS: Fairbanks, 907-457-1798, wildalaska .info/steese-highway-tour.

NORTHERN ALASKA TOUR COMPANY: 800-474-1986 or 907-474-8600, www.northernalaska.com. Tours of Northern Alaska.

USEFUL INFORMATION

THE MILEPOST TRAVEL GUIDE: www.themilepost.com/highway-info/ highways/steese-highway

ALASKA.ORG ROAD GUIDE: www.alaska.org/guide/steese-highway

ALASKAJOURNEY: www.alaskajourney.com/interior/white.html

3

THE ELLIOTT HIGHWAY (AK 2): THE ROAD TO MANLEY HOT SPRINGS

Hot Springs, High Country Tundra, and Wetlands

FROM → TO: Fairbanks to Manley

WHERE IT STARTS: Mile 0 on the Steese Highway in Fairbanks

WHERE IT ENDS: Manley

ESTIMATED LENGTH: 156 miles to the banks of the Tananna River

ESTIMATED TIME: Two to four days

HIGHLIGHTS: Wickersham Dome hikes, viewpoints between MP 86 and MP 95, the walking tundra between MP 95 and MP 100, Tolovana Hot Springs Trail, the town of Minto and Minto Flats, the Manley Roadhouse, and the Manley Hot Springs

GETTING THERE: Begin on the Steese Expressway (AK 2) in Fairbanks and drive 11 miles north to where AK 2 continues northwest as the Elliott Highway and the Steese Highway continues northeast as AK 6 (Drive #2)

If you don't have the time to drive the Dalton Highway but still want to sample and enjoy the far north subarctic and Arctic environments, the **Elliott Highway** past the turnoff to the Dalton Highway is a wonderful alternative that will not disappoint. Plus, the Elliott Highway has some treasures all its own. Here you'll be able to sample all of the major subarctic and Arctic environments, including the spruce-dominated boreal forest with interspersed birch and aspen groves, marshy tundra and walking alpine tundra, stream channels, mountains, wide-open Yukon Flats–type wetlands, and some real seclusion. Toss in a couple of hot springs and you have quite an exciting adventure in store.

Top off the fuel tanks in Fox, just north of Fairbanks, because fuel gets significantly more expensive north of there, and before May and after September the next fuel you find may be 150 miles away in Manley.

LEFT: LICHEN FORMS A TEXTURED CARPET IN THE BIRCH FORESTS ALONG THE TANANA ROAD

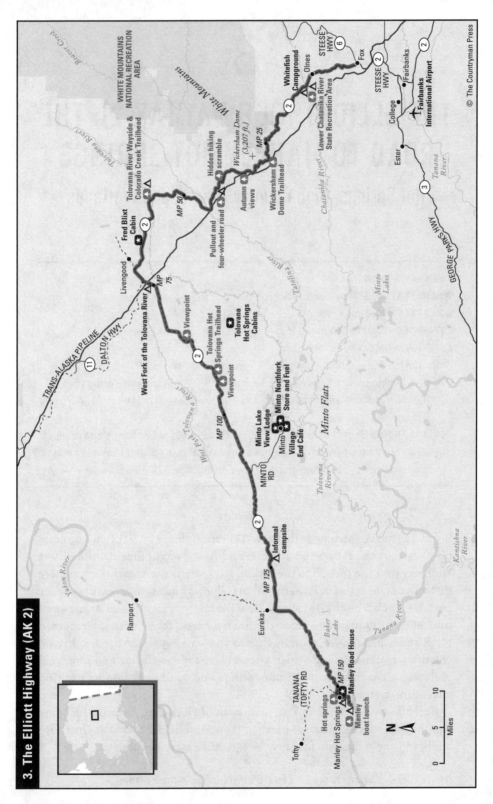

3. The Elliott Highway (AK 2)

Bristol Creek

WHITE MOUNTAINS
NATIONAL RECREATION
AREA

White Mountains

STEESE HWY

Whitefish
Campground

Olnes

Fox

6

2

Fairbanks

2

STEESE
HWY

Fairbanks

Lower Chatanika River
State Recreation Area

College

Fairbanks
International Airport

Ester

Tanana River

3

GEORGE PARKS HWY

Wickersham Dome
(3,207 ft.)

MP 25

Hidden hiking
scramble

Autumn
views

Wickersham
Dome Trailhead

Tatalina River

Chatanika River

Tolovana River

Tolovana River Wayside &
Colorado Creek Trailhead

MP 50

Fred Blixt
Cabin

2

Pullout and
four-wheeler road

Livengood

MP
75

Minto Lakes

Minto Flats

TRANS-ALASKA PIPELINE

DALTON HWY

11

West Fork of the Tolovana River

Viewpoint

Tolovana Hot
Springs Trailhead

2

Tolovana
Hot Springs
Cabins

Viewpoint

West Fork Tolovana River

MP 100

Minto Lake
View Lodge

Minto Northfork
Store and Fuel

Minto

Village
End Café

MINTO
RD

Tolovana River

2

Informal
campsite

MP 125

Yukon River

Rampart

Eureka

TANANA
(TOFTY) RD

MP 150

Manley Road House

Hot springs

Manley Hot Springs

Tofty

Manley
boat launch

Baker
Lake

Tanana River

Kantishna
River

N

0   5   10

Miles

© The Countryman Press

For much of its length the Elliott Highway travels across the southern flanks and core of the **White Mountains**. Almost immediately after leaving Fairbanks you begin to climb into and wind your way through the forested foothills. If you travel this route in the fall, you will be greeted with a beautiful patchwork of golden yellow birch and aspen trees against the dark green backdrop of white and black spruce.

This country is packed with old mining camps and towns, including the town of **Olnes** at around MP 10. Olnes is not much to see today, but it was once a bustling mining community of 300 miners complete with stores, lodges, hotels, and even a post office. At MP 12 you cross the lower Chatanika River (the first of three primary tributaries of the Tanana River that you will cross on this road), where you are downstream from the upper and middle portions that you enjoyed on the Steese-Circle Highway drive (Drive #2).

As you continue your drive north and westward, you cross two more major tributaries to the Tanana River (the large river that flows through Fairbanks and is a major tributary of the Yukon River), the **Tatalina** and **Tolvana Rivers**. Each of these river crossings offers rest areas where you can camp. If you would like a taste of a wilderness cabin experience, consider the beautifully restored Fred Blixt cabin at MP 62.5. As you continue north and westward on your Elliott Highway journey, another point of interest is the town of **Livengood** (MP 71), another bustling mining community in the early 20th century. Today you'll find a road maintenance storage complex here. There's still a dirt track along Livengood Creek that takes you past small-scale gold-mining operations that continue to this day. Feel free to venture forth and explore, but be careful not to trespass on active mining sites.

Just about a mile farther west from Livengood is the start of the Dalton Highway (Drive #1), where you will turn left to continue your journey toward Manley. At the junction with the Dalton Highway, the sign marker indicates the Elliott Highway to the south and Manley Hot Springs to the west, which is the western continuation of the Elliott Highway. Within the first couple miles you'll pass an access road to, and then cross, the Trans-Alaska Pipeline, which you will then leave behind as it continues south and you continue west.

The Elliott Highway climbs steadily toward the tree line through a birch-, aspen-, and spruce-dominated forest as it gradually transitions into the Arctic tundra. The road dips back and forth between the boreal forest and the Arctic tundra as it follows the mountain front high above the Tolovana and then the Tanana. You are treated to frequent spectacular views north into the boreal forest– and Arctic tundra–topped ridges of the White Mountains. To the south you have views of the floodplain of the Tolovana River, including Minto Flats, which is the Tolovana River's version of the Yukon Flats. From MP 94 to MP 100 the highway flirts with the tree line and offers a wonderful cross-tundra hiking opportunity. Stop at the MP 106 turnout for a

MP 109.5, Native village of Minto

Drive 11 miles south into the friendly Native village of Minto, located on the shores of the Minto Flats of the Tolovana River, for access to prime boating, fishing, birding, and moose habitat. Stop by the Village End Café, where the owner, Walt Buchanan, prepares good hamburgers and offers friendly conversation and information.

VAST WETLANDS OF THE MINTO FLATS

beautiful north-facing view into the **Sawtooth Mountains** and an interesting tundra and moose information kiosk. The road continues along the mountain front, passing the road to the Native village of Minto at about MP 109 (see Side Trips) and continuing in the mountains until about MP 123, where you'll find spacious turnouts with expansive views on both sides of the road. The south side turnout is on top of the cut bank, accessible by a short dirt road, and is a good site for a picnic with a view or overnight camping. From MP 123 the road begins a slow descent onto the floodplain of the Tanana River and into the town of Manley.

IN THE AREA

Accommodations, Fuel, and Food

MP 109.5 PLUS 11 MILES TO MINTO: Minto Northforks Store and Fuel, 101 First Street, Minto, 907-798-7181. Offers groceries and fuel (gas and #4 diesel).

VILLAGE END CAFÉ, 13 Main Street, Minto, 907-798-7470. Good food, conversation, and information.

TOLOVANA HOT SPRINGS CABINS, trailhead at MP 93.5 plus 11-mile hike, ski, snowshoe, or 45 mile fly in from Fairbanks, 907-455-6706, www .tolovanahotsprings.com. There are three fully stocked solar powered LED lighted cabins for rent open all year. $–$$.

MINTO LAKE LODGE, Lake View Street, 907-798-7448. A couple of rooms to rent in lakeside lodge. $–$$.

MP 152: MANLEY ROADHOUSE, 100 Front Street, Manley, 907-672-3161, www.manleylodge.com. Established in 1903, this roadhouse offers rooms, cabins, a restaurant, and a bar. Be sure to stop in for a drink and some lively conversation with locals at the beautiful and well-stocked bar and per-

THE HISTORIC MANLEY ROADHOUSE OFFERS FOOD, DRINKS, AND ACCOMMODATIONS

haps some lunch or dinner at this classic and iconic Manley establishment. Closes around October 1 except for the Iditarod or for large groups by reservation. $$.

MP 152.25: MANLEY TRADING POST, 100 Landing Road, Manley, 907-672-3221. Food, groceries, fuel, post office, tire repair, and general information.

Camping

MP 12: LOWER CHATANIKA RIVER STATE RECREATION AREA. Lovely tree-shaded camping with direct access to the Chatanika River and Olnes Pond, including the Olnes Pond rental cabin. For state parks rental cabin Information: www.dnr.alaska.gov/parks/cabins/north. $.

MP 12: WHITEFISH CAMPGROUND. RV and tent camping with access to the Chatanika River and Olnes Pond. $.

MP 60: TOLOVANA CREEK WAYSIDE CAMPING AREA AT THE COLORADO CREEK TRAILHEAD. A good rest/camping area where the Elliott Highway crosses the Tolovana River. Also, plenty of parking if you plan to travel up Colorado Creek to access the northern sections of the White Mountain trail system.

DRAMATIC HIGHLY SATURATED RAINBOWS FREQUENT THE SKIES HERE

MP 62.5: FRED BLIXT CABIN. A beautifully restored wilderness cabin accessible from the Elliott Highway. Available year-round. Contact the BLM for reservation information 907-474-2250. $$.

MP 75: WEST FORK OF THE TOLOVANA RIVER BRIDGE INFORMAL CAMPSITES. A good place to pull off and camp for the evening, especially if you arrive at this point late in the day and want to make an early start for Manley in the morning. Look for dragonflies along the stream channel.

MP 93.5: TOLOVANA HOT SPRINGS, 907-455-6706, www.tolovanahotsprings.com. An 11-mile hike, snowshoe, ski, or 45 mile

STRIKING AUTUMN COLORS LINE THE ELLIOTT HIGHWAY

fly-in from Fairbanks to three fully stocked cabins for rent that are open all year. $$.

MP 123: INFORMAL CAMPSITE ON SOUTH SIDE OF THE ROAD. Drive the short access road to a nice south-facing overlook campsite.

MP 152.5: MANLEY MUNICIPAL CAMPGROUND. In-town campground and RV park. Ask at the Manley Trading Post for information. $.

MP 155: MANLEY BOAT LAUNCH. The road terminates at the Tanana River boat launch 3 miles past the town of Manley. Informal RV camping with a restroom.

Attractions and Recreation

MP 12: LOWER CHATANIKA RIVER STATE RECREATION AREA. Lovely tree-shaded camping with direct access to the Chatanika River and Olnes Pond with lots of activities for the whole family, including fishing, boating, hiking, and berry picking.

THE MINTO FLATS FROM AROUND MP 95 OF THE ELLIOTT HIGHWAY

MP 28: WICKERSHAM DOME TRAILHEAD. Camp overnight and plan to enjoy a half or full day of hiking across the open tundra. There is a large parking area, restrooms, and access to over 200 miles of hiking trails. For a quick trip to the wide-open alpine tundra, take the White Mountains Summit Trail from the west end of the parking lot, and in less than half a mile you will be cruising across gorgeous walking tundra with spectacular views of the surrounding White Mountains. From the trailhead on the east end of the parking lot, you can eventually connect with the Quartz Creek Trail, whose trailhead is down in the Nome Creek valley (see Drive #2 Side Trip).

MP 33–35: FABULOUS AUTUMN VIEWS. During the autumn, slow down as you drive down this section of road to enjoy amazing views of blazing golden groves of birch and aspen trees that light up the hillsides of dark green spruce.

MP 39: TRAILHEAD FOR HIDDEN HIKING SCRAMBLE. Look for a turnoff at the end of the guardrail on the north side of the road (the MP 39 marker is often hidden behind the alder brush on the side of the highway) for a short access road to a steep hike/scramble up into beautiful blue limestone outcrops and some spectacular views of the surrounding mountainsides, particularly in the fall. Be sure to bring and use your hiking poles. Camp at MP 40.

MP 40: PULLOUT REST/CAMPING AND FOUR-WHEELER ROAD. Just a mile up the road from the hike at MP 39 is a pullout on the west/left side of the road. Walk out the four-wheeler path to a granite promontory and spectacular views of the surrounding countryside. This is a good camping spot if you want to enjoy day-hiking from the trailhead at MP 39.

MP 60: TOLOVANA CREEK WAYSIDE CAMPING AREA AND COLO-RADO CREEK TRAILHEAD. A nice place to stop for lunch to enjoy the Tolovana River. If you are an ATV enthusiast, this is a popular trailhead for four-wheelers who want to explore the Tolovana River drainage and the northern portions of the extensive 200-plus-mile White Mountains National

THE ROAD TO TANANA ROLLS ACROSS BOREAL FOREST AND MEADOWS

Recreation Area trail system. Note: From spring through fall this trail is often very wet, and early in the season is mosquito heaven, so dress and prepare properly.

MP 93.5: TRAILHEAD FOR TOLOVANA HOT SPRINGS TRAIL. A moderately difficult 11-mile trail to the south over the 2,316-foot Tolovana Hot Springs Dome leads to the Tolovana Hot Springs. There are three fully stocked cabins for rent. Open all year.

MPS 86, 93, 94 AND 95: OUTSTANDING TURNOUT VIEWPOINTS. Stop at these turnouts for some particularly stunning views of the Tolvana River basin, in particular the broad, lake- and island-dotted Minto Flats. This is a mini, and more accessible, version of the Yukon Flats.

MP 151: TANANA ROAD (FORMALLY THE TOFTY ROAD). Drive this 50-mile-long, often muddy gravel road all the way to the Yukon River through Native-owned land (a high-clearance four-wheel-drive vehicle is recommended). Enjoy a rolling-road journey across and through beautiful boreal forest, with some spectacular sections of lichen-covered understory, and a variety of marshy and spongy tundra and lake environments. The first 15 miles are unremarkable, but the next 35 are a delight. There are no services here, so check in at the Manley Trading Post for current road information, and the Doyon Native Corporation (907-456-6259 or 800-455-6259) to access lands outside the road right-of-way. There may be parking at road's end at the Yukon River.

MP 151.5: MANLEY HOT SPRINGS RESORT SOAK TUBS. A favorite attraction, particularly in the winter, these hot springs soak tubs are enclosed inside a greenhouse. You retrieve a key for access to the hot tubs at a private home that is a quarter mile past the Manley Trading Post in the middle of town. Follow the sign for the BATHHOUSE KEY to the left and ask for Elaine, or call 907-672-3213. Or stop at the Manley Trading Post for information on how the keys are currently being distributed. It costs $5 per person for an hour of hot tub usage. Note: In spring and summer wear a long-sleeve shirt and pants to enter and leave the greenhouse to avoid mosquito bites.

MP 155: MANLEY BOAT LAUNCH. Three miles past the town of Manley, the road terminates at the boat launch on the Tanana River. Contact Manley Boat Charters for boat rentals and guided trips: 907-672-3271.

Outfitters and Tour Operators

MANLEY BOAT CHARTERS, Manley, Fairbanks, 907-672-3271. Offers boat rentals and guided trips.

NORTHERN ALASKA TOUR COMPANY, 800-474-1986 or 907-474-8600, www.northernalaska.com. Tours of Northern Alaska.

PEACE OF SELBY WILDERNESS, 907-672-3206, www.alaskawilderness .net. Ecotourism and guiding services in the Southern Brooks Range.

USEFUL INFORMATION

THE MILEPOST TRAVEL GUIDE: www.themilepost.com/highway-info/ highways/elliott-highway

ALASKA.ORG ROAD GUIDE: www.alaska.org/guide/elliott-highway-fox -to-manley

4

THE CHENA HOT SPRINGS ROAD
River Sports, ATV, and Hiking Paradise

FROM → TO: Fairbanks to Chena Hot Springs
WHERE IT STARTS: 1 mile north of Fairbanks on the Steese Highway (AK 2)
WHERE IT ENDS: Chena Hot Springs Resort
ESTIMATED LENGTH: 56 miles, all paved
ESTIMATED TIME: One to two days
HIGHLIGHTS: Gorgeous birch trees at Rose Hip Campground, the marshy tundra walk on the Granite Tors Trail, floating the Chena River, Lower and Upper Chena of Dome Loop Trail, Chena Hot Springs Resort
GETTING THERE: Begin on the Steese Expressway (AK 2) in Fairbanks and drive 1 mile north to the start of the Chena Hot Springs Road

This road closely follows and crosses back and forth over the Chena River, remaining at river level for most of its length. For about half of its 56 miles, the Chena Hot Springs Road passes through the middle of the **Chena River State Recreation Area.** This proximity provides a plethora of river access opportunities for a variety of river-related activities such as kayaking, rafting, canoeing, fishing, and hiking. This road is an all-season attraction that is kept open to the Chena Hot Springs Resort all year. The winter months are some of the most active for the residents, many of whom are household names in the world of dogsledding. If you drive this road in the fall and winter you're very likely to see dogsled teams out training.

The Chena Hot Springs Road and the Chena River have the closest relationship of any major river-road combination in Alaska, and therein lies much of their appeal. In addition to the many miles of stream channels with over

LEFT: CHENA HOT SPRINGS RESORT, AT THE END OF THE ROAD

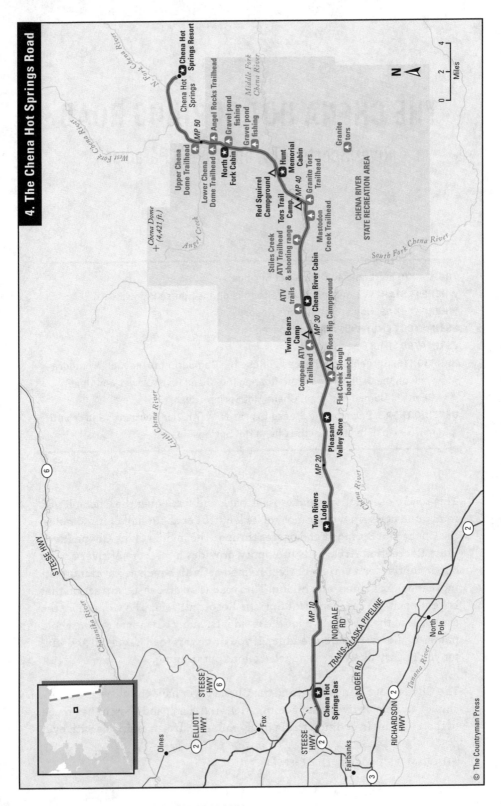

4. The Chena Hot Springs Road

© The Countryman Press

THE CHENA RIVER CHANNEL

20 access points, there are over 100 miles of maintained trails, including ATV, hiking, snowshoeing, skiing, and skijoring trails. The managers of the Chena River State Recreation Area have wisely designated different trails for machine-powered (ATV/snowmachines) and human/animal powered (hiking/skiing/biking/horseback) recreation. The proximity of the road to Fairbanks provides easy access to all sorts of opportunities for floating the river, from half-hour to all-day excursions, including floating all the way back to Fairbanks. In addition, the many access points allow you to leap-frog from one location to another along the road and river. And, of course, there are many opportunities for fishing. Just look for the small brown fish and fishhook signs that indicate Alaska Department of Natural Resources–stocked fishing ponds. In addition to all these activities, there is even a practice shooting range.

One of the more stunning features of the Chena River State Recreation Area is its numerous groves of spectacular old-growth birch trees, many of them streamside. The **Rose Hip Campground** is the crown jewel of the birch grove areas. All the developed camping areas also offer day-use picnicking, often smack dab in the middle of one of these gorgeous groves of birch trees. This drive also offers access to a variety of diverse environments, including backwater sloughs, wetlands, and an array of tundra environments.

BEAVER DAM, LODGE, AND POND ON THE TORS HIKE

IN THE AREA

Accommodations, Fuel, and Food

MP 3: CHENA HOT SPRINGS GAS, 700 Gold Medal Drive, Fairbanks, 907-451-8104. Quick-stop service offering fuel, food, and groceries.

MP 16: TWO RIVERS LODGE, Chena Hot Springs Road, 907-488-6815. For accommodations, restaurant, and groceries away from Fairbanks. Open for dinner 5–10 PM Tuesday–Sunday. $–$$.

MP 23: PLEASANT VALLEY STORE, 907-488-9501. Open 9 AM–8 PM daily for fuel, food, groceries, and a post office.

MP 56.5 (END OF THE ROAD): CHENA HOT SPRING RESORT, 17600 Chena Hot Spring Road, 907-451-8104, www.chenahotsprings.com. A world-class, year-round, destination resort with a full slate of outdoor activities, lodge and cabin accommodations, and of course a very large, indoor hot spring pool. There's a shuttle between all the major hotels in Fairbanks and the resort, as well as a fly-in airstrip. $$–$$$.

Camping

MP 26: CHENA RIVER STATE RECREATION AREA. Fully developed camping facilities as well as eight public use cabins with direct access to the Chena River. $.

MP 27: ROSE HIP CAMPGROUND. Spectacular groves of gorgeous, large, old-growth birch trees are home to fully developed camping facilities and river access. $.

MP 28: SLOUGH LAKE CAMPGROUND. Parking and restrooms for RV camping with access to the Chena River via a side slough. $.

MP 30: TWIN BEARS CAMP, 907-452-5343. Group and individual camping area featuring 12 rustic cabins, each with sleeping platforms to accommodate six to eight people. Summer and winter rentals. Cabins have running water in summertime (May 15–September 15). For rental information: dnr .alaska.gov/parks/cabins/north. $$.

MP 32.2: CHENA RIVER CABIN. This first of three road-accessible rental cabins sleeps nine for some quiet individual accommodations overlooking

THE RESORT OFFERS A FULL RANGE OF FOUR-SEASON SUB-ARCTIC ADVENTURES

the Chena River. Open year-round. For rental information: dnr.alaska.gov/
parks/cabins/north. $.

MP 39: TORS TRAIL CAMPGROUND. Fully developed camping facilities
with direct access to the Chena River. Includes a large paved parking area
and information kiosks. $.

MP 42.3: HUNT MEMORIAL CABIN. The second of three road-accessible
rental cabins. Sleeps six. Open year-round. For rental information: dnr.alaska
.gov/parks/cabins/north. $.

MP 43: RED SQUIRREL CAMPGROUND. Fully developed camping facilities with direct access to the Chena River and some good fishing. $.

MP 47.8: NORTH FORK CABIN. The third of three road-accessible rental
cabins sleeps eight and is near the river. Open year-round. For rental information: dnr.alaska.gov/parks/cabins/north. $.

Attractions and Recreation

MP 26–50: CHENA RIVER STATE RECREATION AREA. A fully developed
camping facility with over 20 direct access points to the Chena River, put-
ins for floating, fishing, and over 100 miles of hiking/snowshoeing/skiing/
skijoring and ATV trails as well as winter dogsled trails. There are numerous day-use picnic sites at most of the camping, fishing, parking, and trail
access sites along the drive.

MP 27: FLAT CREEK SLOUGH BOAT LAUNCH. This is the first access to
the Chena River inside the state recreation area. There is a parking area,
restrooms, and a nifty little nature trail into the boreal forest with some

NUMEROUS LAKES ARE ACCESSIBLE FROM THE CHENA HOT SPRINGS ROAD

spectacular old, large birch trees as well as a sprinkling of balsam poplar trees among the spruces. There is also easy launch access to the Chena River via a short backwater slough.

MP 27: ROSE HIP CAMPGROUND AND PICNIC SITES. In addition to the fully developed camping facilities with direct access to the Chena River, the Rose Hip site offers delightful day-use picnic areas. It's worth the drive here just to enjoy the lovely groves of old-growth birch trees.

MP 30: COMPEAU ATV TRAILHEAD. This provides access to an ATV trail that goes up, over, and along a ridgeline, then down to the Colorado Creek Cabin. It meets up with the Colorado Creek Winter Trail that rejoins the highway at Mile 31.6.

MP 30, 45, AND 47: GRAVEL PONDS FISHING. These are Department of Natural Resources–stocked gravel ponds, full of grayling.

MP 31.4: SOUTH FORK WINTER TRAIL AND RIVER ACCESS TRAILHEAD. Find winter snowmachine and dogsled trails to the Nugget Creek Cabin.

MP 31.6: ATV TRAILS. There is access here to two ATV trails: Colorado Creek Winter Trail and Lower Stiles Creek Trail. The latter provides access to the Stiles Creek Cabin and beyond.

MP 36.4: STILES CREEK ATV TRAILHEAD AND SHOOTING RANGE. Here you'll find access to the Stiles Creek ATV trail and a practice shooting range.

MP 38.5: MASTODON CREEK HIKING TRAILHEAD. The Mastodon Creek Trail takes you south up into ridgelines that lead to the Nugget Creek Cabin, one of six off-road cabins you can rent in the Chena River State Recreation Area. Check out www.dnr.alaska.gov/parks/cabins/north for more information on all nine Chena River State Recreation Area cabins.

MP 39: GRANITE TORS HIKING TRAIL. As advertised in its name, this trail features some notable granite tors. However, I think the real gem here is gorgeous tundra along the first 2 miles of the trail, where the trail is made of free-floating wooden planks placed end-to-end directly on the soggy tundra, providing hikers with the rare opportunity to get up-close-and-personal with the lovely and fascinating marshy tundra, typically too wet and unstable to allow for foot traffic. Here, the often partially submerged and sometimes rotten flat boards provide intimate access to the wonderful variety of plants, mosses, and lichens that populate this spectacularly diverse environment. While walking across the boards can be a bit unstable, the unparalleled access is well worth the modest challenge. Plan to enjoy at least a half a day here. If you enjoy macro photography, hike this trail in the autumn, bring your tripod, and prepare to be totally immersed in the amazing cornucopia of colors, textures, and fabrics that are the hallmarks of this marshy tundra kingdom. Just past the marshy tundra, you will walk along some lovely stream channels flowing through beaver enhanced ponds as you make your way into the high country on your way up to the granite tors.

MP 48: ANGEL ROCKS TRAIL. This is a good introductory trail for young or mobility-challenged walkers. Much of this is wheelchair accessible. If you would like a longer but not necessarily more challenging trail, you can hike about 8.6 miles from the Angel Rocks trailhead to Chena River Hot Springs Resort along a flat trail with only a slight uphill grade.

MP 49.5 AND 50.5: LOWER AND UPPER CHENA DOME LOOP TRAILHEAD ACCESS. Take this trail for a strenuous but delightful (29 miles long and 2,800 feet of elevation change) semiloop trail that takes you on top of and along a ridgeline above tree line, providing spectacular views of the surrounding countryside and the Chena River basin. For a shorter day hike

WOODEN PLANKS PROVIDE A DELIGHTFUL TRAIL ACROSS THE MARSHY TUNDRA

CONTRASTING COLORS AND TEXTURES OF THE AUTUMN MARSHY TUNDRA

to access the great views, start from the Upper Chena Dome Trailhead and hike up onto the ridgeline and back.

MP 56.5: CHENA HOT SPRINGS RESORT, www.chenahotsprings.com. In addition to the namesake indoor hot springs pool, this first-class resort offers access to a variety of sports, including rafting, kayaking, hiking, biking, skiing, skating, and horseback riding. Vintage mining vehicles and equipment dot the property. This resort is known worldwide for using the hot springs to power much of the property, including hothouses where they grow all their vegetables. The resort also hosts an annual renewable energy conference.

USEFUL INFORMATION

ALASKA.ORG ROAD GUIDE: www.alaska.org/detail/chena-hot-springs -road

CHENA RIVER STATE RECREATION AREA: Information and cabin reservations, dnr.alaska.gov/parks/units/chena

PUBLIC USE CABIN INFORMATION: dnr.alaska.gov/parks/cabins/north

5

THE TAYLOR HIGHWAY (AK 5): THE ROAD TO EAGLE ON THE YUKON RIVER

Fortymile River Country and the Chickenstock Music Festival

FROM → TO: Tetlin Junction to Eagle Village

WHERE IT STARTS: Tetlin Junction, MP 1301 on the Alaska Highway

WHERE IT ENDS: Eagle Village on the Yukon River

ESTIMATED LENGTH: 160 miles (the first 60 miles is paved, the remainder gravel; closed in winter)

ESTIMATED TIME: Two to four days

HIGHLIGHTS: The town of Chicken and the Chickenstock Music Festival, Mosquito Fork Dredge hiking, entrenched meanders of the Walker Fork of the Fortymile River, tundra hiking trail between MP 95 and MP 105, walking tour of the town of Eagle

GETTING THERE: Drive 12 miles east of Tok on the Alaska Highway (AK 2) to Tetlin Junction. The Taylor Highway extends north from there. (Note: There is no fuel or accommodations for 78 miles between Tok on the Alaska Highway and the town of Chicken on the Taylor Highway.)

Like many of Alaska's most northerly roads, the **Taylor Highway** is often a lonely route, which of course is one of the recommendations for driving it! This road traverses wide-open country, often hugging high slopes and ridgelines, providing spectacular views not only across the countryside but down into deeply incised valleys of the massive Fortymile Wild and Scenic River system, a major tributary of the Yukon River.

LEFT: ROLLING ALONG THE TAYLOR HIGHWAY

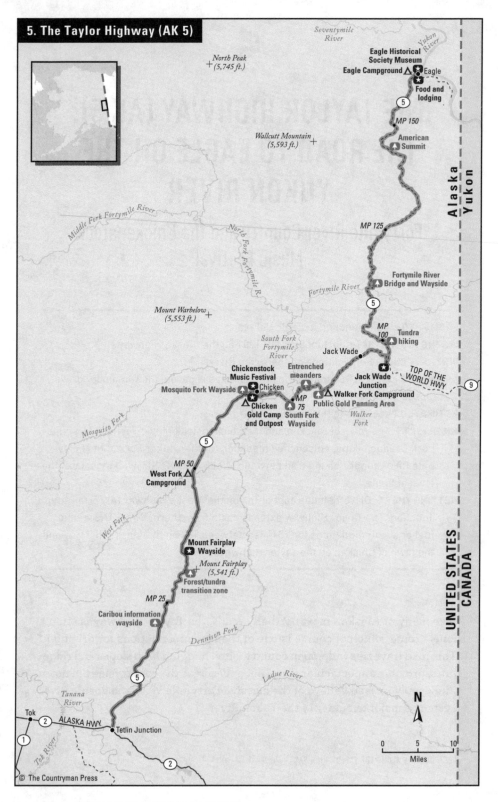

5. The Taylor Highway (AK 5)

Seventymile River

Yukon River

Eagle Historical Society Museum
Eagle Campground — Eagle
Food and lodging

North Peak (5,745 ft.)

MP 150

American Summit

Wallcutt Mountain (5,593 ft.)

Alaska
Yukon

Middle Fork Fortymile River

North Fork Fortymile R.

MP 125

Fortymile River

Fortymile River Bridge and Wayside

Mount Warbelow (5,553 ft.)

MP 100
Tundra hiking

South Fork Fortymile River

Jack Wade

Chickenstock Music Festival
Mosquito Fork Wayside — Chicken
Entrenched meanders
Jack Wade Junction
Walker Fork Campground
Chicken Gold Camp and Outpost
MP 75 — **Public Gold Panning Area**
South Fork Wayside

Mosquito Fork

TOP OF THE WORLD HWY

Walker Fork

9

MP 50
West Fork Campground

West Fork

UNITED STATES
CANADA

Mount Fairplay Wayside

Mount Fairplay (5,541 ft.)

Forest/tundra transition zone

MP 25

Caribou information wayside

Dennison Fork

Ladue River

N

Tanana River

Tok
2 ALASKA HWY
1
Tetlin Junction
2

0 5 10
Miles

© The Countryman Press

The southern portion of the **Taylor Highway** is the southern extension of the Top of the World Highway from Dawson Creek, Yukon Territory, into Alaska, and it's well worth a look if you have a bit of extra time. This is favorite territory for caribou hunters.

Your drive up the Taylor Highway begins with a beautiful open canopy boreal forest. In the autumn, and particularly in mid-September, this broad, open landscape is a brilliant patchwork of bright golds and yellows from the aspen, birch, and willows painted in sharp contrast against the dark green of the spruce-dominated backdrop. The landscape surrounding the Taylor Highway lacks the high rugged peaks of the Wrangell and St. Elias Ranges to the south or the Brooks Range to the north, but instead offers a beautiful rolling and largely rounded montane landscape carpeted with boreal forest at lower elevations and alpine tundra on the higher peaks and ridgelines. The rolling nature of the landscape, absent sharp high peaks and ridgelines, is what provides the spectacular long-distance views. Some of the most interesting places along this highway, and many other Arctic and subarctic highways in Alaska, are the zones where the boreal forest interfingers with the Arctic tundra. These zones are always fascinating, with their changes in vegetation, textures, and colors. Driving through during the fall, you'll notice that the road is often defined in the distance by a ribbon of yellow and gold as it traces its path through the dark green of the spruce forest. This golden ribbon is formed by the autumn-colored willow trees, which thrive in the disturbed zones along the side of the road.

All along your journey you pass over the stream channels and through the drainage basins of the many forks and tributaries of the Fortymile River, including the Dennison River, the Mosquito Fork, the Walker Fork, and others.

The town of **Chicken** (population 23, three in the winter), at MP 67, is the only mining community remaining of the many that flourished in the Fortymile mining district in the 19th century and is well worth visiting. The road north of Chicken is narrower and with tighter turns; therefore, more care needs to be taken with your driving. The road gradually gains in elevation until **Jack Wade Junction** (MP 95), where you continue left and north on the Taylor Highway toward Eagle rather than continuing northeast toward Canada. Here you reach another one of the beautiful transition zones between the boreal forest and the Arctic tundra. For the next 10 miles you ride a high ridgeline through the Arctic tundra, with many places to pull off and dry camp and uncounted cross-tundra hiking opportunities with spectacular views both north and south of the ridgeline. This is probably my favorite section on the Taylor Highway. Take a hike!

At MP 105 the Taylor Highway dips back down into boreal forest as you descend toward the main channel of the **Fortymile River**, which you cross at

A HISTORIC CABIN IN EAGLE

MP 112.5, where you can take a rest and throw your fishing line in the river before you continue on to Eagle. The road beyond Jack Wade Junction, and particularly the road beyond the Fortymile River bridge, is narrower and tighter than anywhere else on the highway. Be particularly mindful, especially during twilight hours, of large trucks that can come barreling down this nearly single lane section of road. If you have a big or long rig, exercise extra caution.

After you cross the Fortymile River you climb up into the transition zone between the boreal forest–covered slopes and Arctic tundra–covered ridges. At around MP 143 you reach what's known as the **American Summit**, where you are treated to more spectacular cross-tundra hiking opportunities and some amazingly expansive views. Much of this area has been burned, and the brilliant summer fireweed is one of the natural pioneer plants in the plant succession series that blankets large areas with its saturated hues. During the mid-to-late summer, the charred forest is carpeted with brilliant magenta fireweed creating a striking visual contrast.

From the American Summit drive about 17 miles downhill through the boreal forest, following American Creek to the town of **Eagle** (population 86), which sits on the banks of the mighty Yukon River. Eagle has a fascinating history as a mining community and as a supply and transportation depot along the Yukon River. Eagle has its most exciting moments during the spring breakup, when the Yukon River, which is frozen all winter, breaks up and roils into a huge ice-filled flood. In 2009 the flooding, ice-choked Yukon destroyed many of the riverside buildings in Eagle, bulldozing them with huge rafts of ice. Such are the wonders and challenges of living on the mighty Yukon. Plan to enjoy a whole day in Eagle, including admiring the Yukon River itself and the views to the north. You can also drive 5 or so miles north of town along the banks of the Yukon for some extra exploring.

IN THE AREA

Accommodations, Fuel, and Food

TOK ON THE ALASKA HIGHWAY, Fuel up in Tok, 12 miles west of the start of the Taylor Highway on the Alaska Highway.

MP 66: CHICKEN GOLD CAMP AND OUTPOST, Chicken, 907-782-4427, 907-399-0005 (November–March), www.chickengold.com/cabins.html. Room and rustic cabin rentals near all the action in Chicken. $–$$.

MP 160: THE RIVERSIDE HOTEL AND CAFÉ AND EAGLE RIVER TRAD-ING COMPANY, 1 Front Street, Eagle, 907-547-7000 or 907-547-2220, www .riversidehoteleaglealaska.com. This store offers rooms, a restaurant, groceries, fuel (gas and diesel), propane, laundry, RV hookups, and information. $$.

THE CHICKENSTOCK MUSIC FESTIVAL IS A UNIQUE LOCAL HIGHLIGHT

FALCON INN BED & BREAKFAST LODGE, 220 Front Street, Eagle, 907-547-2254, www.falconinnlodgelogcabins.com. Beautiful log cabin rooms and individual log cabins are available in this bed & breakfast. $$.

Camping

MP 49: BLM WEST FORK CAMPGROUND. Partially developed, 18 back-in and seven pull-through RV sites at the edge of a boreal forest and spongy tundra. $.

MP 66: CHICKEN GOLD CAMPGROUND AND RV PARK, 907-235-6396, www.chickengold.com. Full-service park for tents and RVs near store, restaurant, and gold-mining exhibits and next to the Chickenstock Music Festival. $–$$.

MP 82: BLM WALKER FORK CAMPGROUND, 907-883-5121. Partially developed, 18 camping sites along the Walker Fork River in a grove of Aspen trees. $.

MP 160: EAGLE BLM CAMPGROUND, 907-474-2200. Partially developed, 18 lovely campsites nestled among tall, stately, old-growth white spruce trees within walking distance of the town of Eagle. $.

Note: All three of the above BLM campgrounds are open late spring to mid-fall and are closed when the Taylor Highway closes for the winter. For more information on all three campsites, visit www.campgroundsalaska.com/tay lorhighwayalaska.php. $.

Attractions and Recreation

MP 21: CARIBOU INFORMATION WAYSIDE AND KIOSK. This stop offers information signs about the Fortymile caribou herd which at one time boasted herds of 500,000.

MP 32: TRANSITION ZONE OF THE BOREAL FOREST INTO ARCTIC TUNDRA. This is a lovely zone of transition between the forest and the tundra as you cross the northern slopes of Mount Fairplay. In the fall the dark greens and golds of the boreal forest give way to the largely red-dominated Arctic tundra. It's quite a lovely visual contrast.

CONFLUENCE OF THE MOSQUITO FORK AND DENNISON RIVERS—A VIEW WORTH THE HIKE

MP 35: MOUNT FAIRPLAY WAYSIDE AND INFORMATION AREA. This wayside rest area contains information about the boreal forest/taiga environments, historical mining activity, Mount Fairplay, and the local caribou population. It also provides a road map showing camping locations.

MP 60: MOSQUITO FORK WAYSIDE. This undeveloped area next to the Mosquito Fork is a favorite base camp and staging area for caribou hunters. It also offers a put-in for canoeing or rafting on the Mosquito Fork.

MP 67: CHICKEN. There's lots of mining history hereabouts to explore, including many mining-related artifacts and displays. As you enter Chicken, take the short road to the left off the Taylor Highway to visit what may well be the most quaint and picturesque post office you've ever seen. Near the post office is a fascinating information kiosk and display about the Forty-mile Mining District and the Gold Rush, including mining equipment artifacts and information about the dredges. Drive into the main area of Chicken across the highway from the post office, and stop in at the **Chicken**

HISTORIC (AND CURRENT) GOLD-MINING FUN IN CHICKEN

Creek Outpost for one of their chicken sandwiches and a cup of the soup of the day. It's also a good stop if you're in need of a coffee fix, a glass of wine, or a bottle of Alaskan-brewed beer. You will find multiple accommodations, restaurants, and cafés, camping, fuel, and a variety of fun mining-oriented activities, including gold panning and tours of old mining equipment. There are also outfitters that offer float trips on the nearby Mosquito Fork and Dennison Rivers.

MP 68: MOSQUITO FORK DREDGE HIKING TRAIL. This one's easy to miss, so watch for it because it's well worth the stop. Park at the pullout on the left side of the road about a mile north of Chicken and hike the 1.5 miles down to an overlook of the Mosquito Fork of the main Dennison Rivers. You have spectacular views of the confluence of these two rivers, the rolling countryside, and a once mighty, now-derelict dredge. This is a beautiful hike through a spongy tundra–floored boreal forest.

MP 75: SOUTH FORK WAYSIDE. Stop at this beautiful wayside along the South Fork of the Fortymile River, which offers spectacular floating opportunities as well as fishing and dry camping. Inquire in the town of Chicken about guiding as well as pickup and drop-off services. You can put in on the

Mosquito Fork in Chicken and take out here at the South Fork wayside or farther below if you prefer.

MP 78–80: ENTRENCHED MEANDERS. Along this high ridgeline between the South Fork wayside and the Walker Fork Campground, look down over 1000 feet below and miles across to see where the Walker Fork carves a beautiful series of S-shaped meanders into the landscape. The road is narrow along this section, so pull off carefully.

MP 82: PUBLIC GOLD PANNING AREA. Directly across from the Walker Fork Campground is a good, safe area designated for public gold panning. Note that local miners continue to engage in active placer gold mining along the stream channels, and it's often hard to know where someone's claim begins and ends. These miners can be plenty crusty about people jumping their claims, even if it's just for a little afternoon tourist fun.

IMPRESSIVE ENTRENCHED MEANDERS OF THE TAYLOR FORK

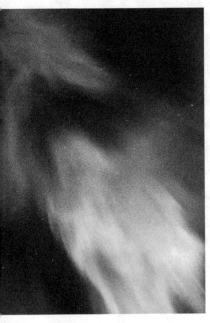

SPECTACULAR LATE SUMMER DISPLAYS
OF NORTHERN LIGHTS

MP 95.5: JACK WADE JUNCTION. Turn left/northwest to continue on the Taylor Highway toward Eagle. Turn right/northeast to drive a section of the Top of the World Highway to the Canadian border and beyond to Dawson City in Yukon Territory.

MP 95–MP 105: TUNDRA HIKING. Pull off along this 10-mile segment of Arctic tundra–covered ridgeline and hike to the top of one of the nearby rounded ridges. There are many great dry camping and excellent aurora-viewing opportunities here too.

MP 112.5: FORTYMILE RIVER BRIDGE AND WAYSIDE. Stop at this wayside and walk across the Fortymile River bridge for some spectacular views up and downstream. This is also a good dry camping location if you favor stream channels.

MP 143: AMERICAN SUMMIT. Magnificent views populate this fireweed-filled landscape in a transition zone between boreal forest and Arctic tun-

HIGH RIDGELINES PROVIDE GREAT CAMPING AND CROSS TUNDRA HIKING

dra. Wonderful macro photo opportunities of the fireweed and burned forest wood, too, and good dry camping locations.

MP 160: EAGLE. There is all sorts of history to explore in Eagle. Plan to walk around the town and visit the Eagle Historical Society Museum, which is housed in an old courthouse where you can sign up for a guided walking tour; Fort Egbert; and the Eagle Visitors Center for the Yukon-Charley Rivers National Preserve. Be sure to stop by the Riverside Hotel and Café, have a meal, and chat with the owner, Dennis, who has a wealth of knowledge about Eagle and its history.

Festivals and Fairs

CHICKENSTOCK MUSIC FESTIVAL (SECOND WEEK IN JUNE): www .facebook.com/ChickenstockMusicFest. Very fun far-north music gathering.

Outfitters and Tour Operators

CHICKEN GOLD CAMP & OUTPOST, 907-782-4427 or 907-399-0005 (winter mobile, November–March), www.chickengold.com/cabins.html. Offers a wide variety of services and trips, including gold panning, kayak rentals, and day floating trips.

USEFUL INFORMATION

THE MILEPOST TRAVEL GUIDE: www.themilepost.com/highway-info/ highways/taylor-highway

ALASKA.ORG ROAD GUIDE: www.alaska.org/guide/top-of-the-world -highway

TOWN OF CHICKEN: www.townofchicken.com

6

THE TOK CUTOFF (AK 1)

Copper River and Wrangell Mountains Adventures

FROM → TO: Gakona Junction MP 128.5 on the Richardson Highway to Tok
WHERE IT STARTS: Richardson Highway, MP 128.5 near Gakona
WHERE IT ENDS: Tok
ESTIMATED LENGTH: 139 miles, all paved
ESTIMATED TIME: One to two days
HIGHLIGHTS: MP 1 overlook, Historic Gakona Lodge and Trading Post, Nabesna Road into Wrangell-St. Elias National Park and Preserve, The Mentasta Mountains, access to south end of Old Tok Cutoff (a.k.a. Mile 91 Loop), Eagle Trail State Recreation Site
GETTING THERE: Drive the Glenn Highway (Drive #11) northeast 189 miles to the town of Glennallen and the intersection with the Richardson Highway (AK 4) MP 114.5, then drive 14 miles north on the Richardson Highway (Drive #7) to MP 128.5 at the Tok Cutoff (AK 1). Fill your fuel tanks and obtain supplies at Glennallen, particularly if you intend to drive the Nebesna Road (see Side Trips).

I always look forward to driving the Tok Cutoff, which is a 140-mile-long connection between the Alaska Highway at Tok and the Richardson Highway (Drive #7) 12 miles north of Glennallen. The Tok Cutoff is officially an extension of the Glenn Highway (Drive #11), but is a road with its own distinctive features and characteristics.

Your drive begins in a classic spruce, birch, and aspen boreal forest, with your first stop only 1 mile down the road at a turnout that overlooks the Copper River and the Wrangell Mountains from a bluff high above the river. I often time my driving so that I stop here for the evening and enjoy spectacular views of the Wrangell Mountains and the Copper River Valley.

LEFT: TRAIL CREEK LEADS FROM THE NABESNA ROAD INTO THE HIGH COUNTRY

A mile and a half east of this first pullout is the historic mining town of **Gakona** and the **Historic Gakona Lodge and Trading Post**, where you can stay overnight and arrange for guided fishing trips on the Copper, Gulkana, and Klutina Rivers. Traveling east from the Historic Gakona Lodge, the Tok Cutoff alternates between streamside and slopeside as the road follows the Copper River gradually upstream. The higher and drier slopes are dominated by spruce trees, while streamside you'll find more birch and aspen. As you drive east, watch south for some beautiful views (east to west) of Mount Wrangell, Mount Sanford, Mount Blackstone, and Mount Drum around MP 5, MP14–15, and MP 21. As you traverse the lower marshy areas, keep your eyes peeled for beaver dams and lodges, and plan to stop at the Chistochina wayside at MP 35.

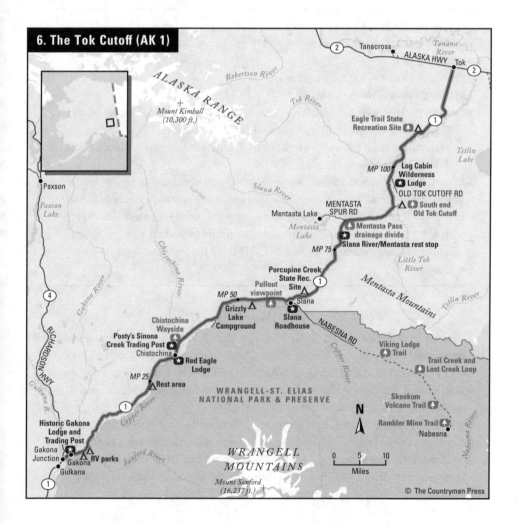

THE HISTORIC GAKONA LODGE AND TRADING POST

Continuing eastward on the Tok Cutoff, you pass numerous marsh and lake environments. Beginning near mile 44 you begin to climb higher onto south-facing slopes that provide increasingly wider views of the surrounding landscape, including the craggy **Mentasta Mountains** to the east and north. The elevated pullout rest area at MP 56 offers some of the most spectacular views. Following the MP 56 viewpoint, the Tok Cutoff turns north and heads downhill to where, at MP 60, the highway intersects with the Nabesna Road (see Side Trips), which will take you past the town of Salana and into the heart of **Wrangell–St. Elias National Park and Preserve**. Near the intersection with the Nabesna Road, the Tok Cutoff turns farther north, following the lovely **Slana River** and its beautiful valley, which supports a lovely and rich riparian environment, complete with plenty of beaver dams and lodges, while it heads into the heart of the **Mentasta Mountains**. At MP 81 you reach the turnoff to the Native village of Mentasta. At Mentasta Pass, near MP 82, you cross the drainage divide between the Salana River, which is a tributary of the Copper River, which in turn flows to Prince William Sound and the Gulf of Alaska, and the Tok River drainage basin, a tributary of the Yukon River, which flows into the Bering Sea. It's interesting to consider that raindrops falling just a few feet from each other on either side of this drainage divide will take very different paths to their respective oceans over a thousand miles apart. For the remainder of your Tok Cutoff adventure you will be following first the **Little Tok River** and then the main channel of the **Tok River** downhill through the boreal forest to the town of **Tok**, located on the Alaska Highway. The last 10 miles is a pretty straight shot through fairly consistent boreal forest directly into Tok. However, about 16 miles before you charge into Tok, at about MP 109, you come to one more hidden gem, the Eagle Trail State Recreation Site, which is well worth a visit before you head into Tok.

VIEW OF THE COPPER RIVER AND MOUNT SANFORD FROM MP 0.5

IN THE AREA

Accommodations, Fuel, and Food

MP 2.5: HISTORIC GAKONA LODGE AND TRADING POST, 907-822-3482, www.gakonalodge.com. Lodge rooms and cabins, dining, tavern, gift shop, and food and supplies store. They offer guided trips on the Copper River May through October. $$.

THE RUGGED MENTASTA MOUNTAINS FROM THE MENTASTA SPUR ROAD

MP 33: RED EAGLE LODGE, Chistochina, 907-822-5299, www.redeagle lodge.net. Fly or drive into this historic roadhouse location, with log cabins, RV, and tent sites. $–$$.

MP 34: POSTY'S SINONA CREEK TRADING POST, Chistochina, 907-822-5454. Gas, diesel, propane, groceries, snacks, and Native arts, crafts, and gifts. Open daily year-round.

MP 78: SLANA RIVER/MENTASTA REST STOP. Rest stop with store and gas station.

MP 98.5: LOG CABIN WILDERNESS LODGE, 907-883-3124, www.log cabinwildernesslodge.com. Drive 2 miles along Old Tok Cutoff Road to the beautiful lodge, hand built by owners John and Jill Rusyniak. Lodging, meals, and tours are available. This intimate, full-service resort is open year-round. $$$–$$$$.

Camping

MP 1: PULLOUT DRY CAMP. Lovely views of the Copper River Valley and the Wrangell Mountains, in particular the volcanoes of Mount Sanford and Mount Drum.

MP 2.5: COPPER RIVER RV PARK AND CABINS. 907-822-3550. Full service, 50 sites, RV hookups, cabins, and tent sites. $.

MP 4.5: GAKONA ALASKA RV PARK, 907-822-3550, www.gakonarvpark .com. Full service park with 20 RV sites, cabins, and 15 tent sites. $.

MP 24: REST AREA. Dry camping with restrooms and a short trail back to the Copper River.

THE SOLANA RIVER AND WETLANDS BACKED BY THE MENTASTA MOUNTAINS

MP 53: GRIZZLY LAKE CAMPGROUND, 907-822-5214, www.rv52.com/rvparks/grizzly-lake-campground. RV sites and a few tent sites with hiking trails and boat rentals. $.

MP 60: PORCUPINE CREEK STATE RECREATION SITE, 907-822-3973, www.dnr.alaska.gov/parks/aspunits/matsu/porcksrs.htm. Small, quiet location with 12 campsites and access to streamside hiking. Includes an interesting road log for the road to Nebesna.

MP 109.5: EAGLE TRAIL STATE RECREATION SITE, 907-833-3686, www.dnr.alaska.gov/parks/aspunits/northern/eagletrailsrs.htm. Thirty-five developed campsites and a picnic shelter with nature and viewpoint trail.

SWEEPING VIEW OF THE TOK RIVER VALLEY LOOKING SOUTH FROM THE EAGLE TRAIL LOOKOUT

The 3 G's

When you are traveling the western end of the Tok Cutoff Highway or the central section of Richardson Highway (Drive #7), you will likely encounter a series of towns and rivers that are spelled and sound similarly and that are all close to each other geographically. These include the towns of Gakona, Gakona Junction, and Gulkana. **Gakona** is the telegraph station town containing the Historic Gakona Lodge and Trading Post located at MP 2.5 on the Tok Cutoff. **Gakona Junction** is located at the intersection of the Richardson Highway and the Tok Cutoff, 2.5 miles east of Gakona. **Gulkana** is a small Native village on the Richardson Highway 2 miles south of Gakona Junction. To add to the confusion, there is also the **Gulkana River**, which flows parallel to the Richardson Highway north of Gakona Junction, and the **Gakona River**, which flows by Gakona on the Tok Cutoff. It's worth taking a few minutes to familiarize yourself with the location and spelling of these various communities and features, and then keep your map handy!

Attractions and Recreation

MP 1: PULLOUT/TURNOUT ABOVE COPPER RIVER. Catch spectacular views from a bluff high above the Copper River of 16,237-foot Mount Sanford and 12,010-foot Mount Drum as well as the beautiful braided stream channel of the Copper River. This a great place to dry camp for the evening. Look for the access trail down to the Copper River on the west end of the pullout. You can hike for a mile along the north bank of the Copper River to the historic town of Gakona located at the confluence of the Gakona and Copper Rivers.

MP 2.5: HISTORIC GAKONA LODGE AND TRADING POST, 907-822-3482, www.gakonalodge.com. Stop by and enjoy this historic lodge and trading post, now a full-service resort. Spend the night, book a fishing trip, and take the time to read about the early telegraph system here.

MP 35: CHISTOCHINA WAYSIDE. This is a rest stop with access to an ATV and hiking easement along the west side of the beautifully braided Chistochina River, a major tributary to the Copper River. I love to stop here and hike along this glacially fed stream channel of the Chistochina. Standing out on the gravel bars and looking north on clear days, you'll have some nice views of the snowcapped peaks of the Alaska Range. To the south

MP 60: Nabesna Road

Drive along this 42-mile-long, mostly gravel, wild road (requires stream crossings) to an old mining camp and into the heart of the northern section of Wrangell–St. Elias National Park. Enjoy photography, hiking, camping, and wildlife viewing opportunities. There is no fuel or other services along this road, so fill up on the Tok Cutoff either in Mentasta, 15 miles north, or in Chistochina, 20 miles west. If you can, first visit the **Wrangell–St. Elias Visitor Center**, located 15 miles south of Glennallen on the Richardson Highway (Drive #7), and/or stop in at the Salana Ranger Station located near the western end of the Nabesna Road. Highlights along this road include: the original Slana Roadhouse, many spectacular views of the Wrangell–St. Elias Mountains and Copper River, Viking Lodge Trail, Trail Creek and Lost Creek Loop, Skookum Volcano Trail, and the Rambler Mine Trail.

rise the high volcanic peaks of the Wrangell Range. The Chistochina River, like many Alaskan rivers, serves as a wintertime ice highway that locals use for snowmobile and dogsled travel.

MP 56: PULLOUT VIEWPOINT. Stop here for some of the most spectacular views of the Wrangell–St. Elias Mountains and a wide swath of the Copper River drainage. There is also an information kiosk on the exploration history of the Copper River Valley.

MP 60: See Nabesna Road side trip.

MP 81: MENTASTA SPUR ROAD. This road runs through the heart of the scenic Mentasta Mountains to the Native Village of Mentasta and Mentasta Lake. Stop in at the Tribal Office in town to ask permission to visit the lake.

MP 82: The drainage divide between the Copper River that flows to Prince William Sound and the Gulf of Alaska, and the Yukon River that flows into the Bering Sea.

MP 91: ACCESS TO SOUTH END OF OLD TOK CUTOFF (A.K.A. MILE 91 LOOP). Drive 1.5 miles along this derelict section of the Old Tok Cutoff. Park or camp in the gravel pad near the bulldozed barricade, and walk or bike for up to 6 miles along this lovely path. You will be delighted by all the flowers, trees, light, and shadows along this quiet, abandoned section of the highway that is slowly being reclaimed by the boreal forest. The abandoned roadbed is totally bikeable as well as hikeable. Early morning or late afternoon/evening walks along this lonely roadbed are particularly enjoyable.

MP 98.5: ACCESS TO NORTH END OF OLD TOK CUTOFF AND LOG CABIN WILDERNESS LODGE. Drive 2 miles along this picturesque road to its end, where you will find the beautiful, hand-built Log Cabin Wilderness Lodge. This is worth the drive down just to see this gorgeous property, and then make plans to return for a stay and to enjoy the numerous outdoor adventures they offer.

MP 109.5: EAGLE TRAIL STATE RECREATION SITE. This recreation site is an unexpected beauty, with with some information kiosks about the history of the Valdez-Eagle Trail, a mile-long nature trail, and another 1.5-mile trail through the spruce, aspen, and cottonwood trees to an overlook with expansive views of the Tok River Valley.

THE CHISTOCHINA RIVER DURING SPRING RUNOFF, LOOKING TOWARDS MOUNT SANFORD AND MOUNT DRUM

MP 139: END OF THE ROAD AT THE TOWN OF TOK ON THE ALASKA HIGHWAY. Full services and accommodations available.

Festivals and Fairs

UPPER TANANA MIGRATORY BIRD FESTIVAL (THIRD WEEK IN MAY): www.facebook.com/tetlinnationalwildliferefuge.

Outfitters and Tour Operators

TOK AIR SERVICE, South Ramp, Tok Airport, 907-322-2903, www.tokair service.com. Offering a variety of guiding services, including hiking, rafting, skiing, climbing, and hunting.

THE LOG CABIN WILDERNESS LODGE AT THE END OF THE OLD TOK CUTOFF

LOG CABIN WILDERNESS LODGE, MP 98.5 off Tok Hwy, 907-833-3124, www.logcabinwildernesslodge.com. Beautiful accommodations and meals along with numerous outdoor activites such as hiking, skiing, fishing, birding, and other wildlife viewing, and skeet shooting.

USEFUL INFORMATION

THE MILEPOST TRAVEL GUIDE: www.themilepost.com/highway-info/highways/glenn-highway-tok-cutoff

ALASKA.ORG ROAD GUIDE: www.alaska.org/guide/tok-cut-off

CHISTOCHINA RIVER INFORMATION: www.alaska.guide/River/1400335/Chistochina-River

7

THE RICHARDSON HIGHWAY (AK 4): THE HISTORIC VALDEZ TO FAIRBANKS ROAD

Pipeline to Adventures

FROM → TO: Valdez to Fairbanks

WHERE IT STARTS: Valdez

WHERE IT ENDS: Fairbanks

ESTIMATED LENGTH: 368 miles, all paved

ESTIMATED TIME: Three to four days

HIGHLIGHTS: Thompson Pass, Worthington Glacier, side road to Gulkana Glacier, Old Richardson Highway, Rika's Roadhouse

GETTING THERE: Drive the Glenn Highway (Drive #11) northeast 189 miles to the town of Glennallen and the intersection with Highway MP 114.5, then drive 114.5 miles south to the town of Valdez to begin this trip. Alternatively, fly into or take the Alaska Marine Highway System to Valdez, or drive the Richardson Highway (Drive #7) from north to south starting in Fairbanks at MP 368.

The start of the Richardson Highway at MP 0 is located at the Prince William Sound coastal town of Valdez. The end of the Richardson Highway is 368 miles north at Fairbanks. This route traverses two major drainage basins, the Copper River, which flows south into Prince William Sound and the Gulf of Alaska, and the Delta River, which flows north into the Tanana, a tributary of the Yukon River, which in turn empties into the Bering Sea. Along this route you also pass through two major mountain ranges: the Coast Range and the Alaska Range. Because this is such a long trip with so much to see and do, and since you can access this road from six different entrance points (Valdez, Glennallen, Gakona Junction, Paxson, and the Alaska Highway at

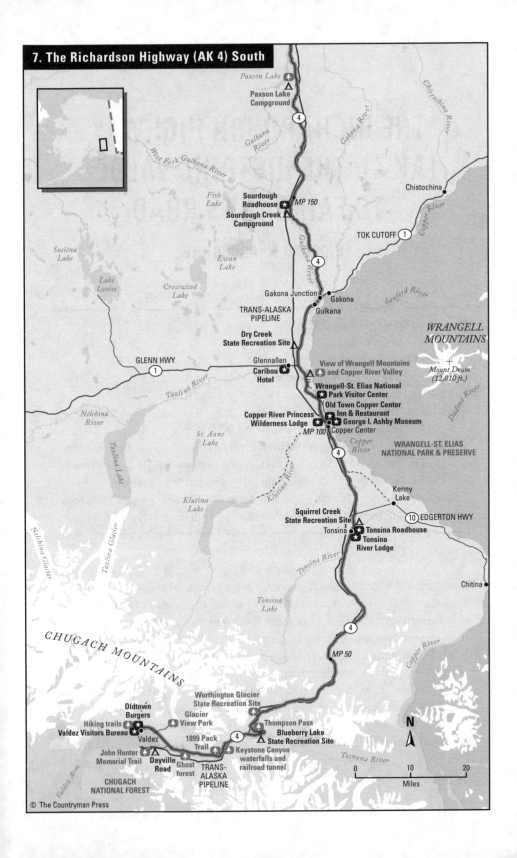

7. The Richardson Highway (AK 4) South

Paxson Lake

Paxson Lake
Campground

4

Chistochina River

Gulkana River

West Fork Gulkana River

Gakona River

Chistochina

Copper River

Fish
Lake

Sourdough
Roadhouse — MP 150
Sourdough Creek
Campground

TOK CUTOFF 1

Susitna
Lake

Ewan
Lake

Gulkana River

Sanford River

Lake
Louise

Crosswind
Lake

Gakona Junction — Gakona
TRANS-ALASKA
PIPELINE   Gulkana

WRANGELL
MOUNTAINS

Dry Creek
State Recreation Site

Mount Drum
(12,010 ft.)

GLENN HWY

1

Tazlina River

Nelchina
River

St. Anne
Lake

Glennallen
Caribou
Hotel

View of Wrangell Mountains
and Copper River Valley
Wrangell-St. Elias National
Park Visitor Center
Old Town Copper Center
Copper River Princess
Wilderness Lodge
Inn & Restaurant
George I. Ashby Museum
MP 100 Copper Center

Dadina River

Copper
River

WRANGELL-ST. ELIAS
NATIONAL PARK & PRESERVE

Tazlina Lake

Klutina
Lake

Klutina River

4

Kenny
Lake

10 EDGERTON HWY

Squirrel Creek
State Recreation Site
Tonsina — Tonsina Roadhouse
Tonsina
River Lodge

Nelchina Glacier

Tazlina Glacier

Tonsina River

Chitina

Tonsina
Lake

4

Copper River

CHUGACH   MOUNTAINS

MP 50

Worthington Glacier
State Recreation Site

Oldtown
Burgers
Glacier
View Park

Hiking trails
Valdez Visitors Bureau
Valdez

Thompson Pass

4   Blueberry Lake
State Recreation Site

N

John Hunter
Memorial Trail   Dayville
Road   Ghost
forest
1899 Pack
Trail
Keystone Canyon
waterfalls and
railroad tunnel

Tasnuna River

CHUGACH
NATIONAL FOREST
TRANS-
ALASKA
PIPELINE

0   10   20

Miles

© The Countryman Press

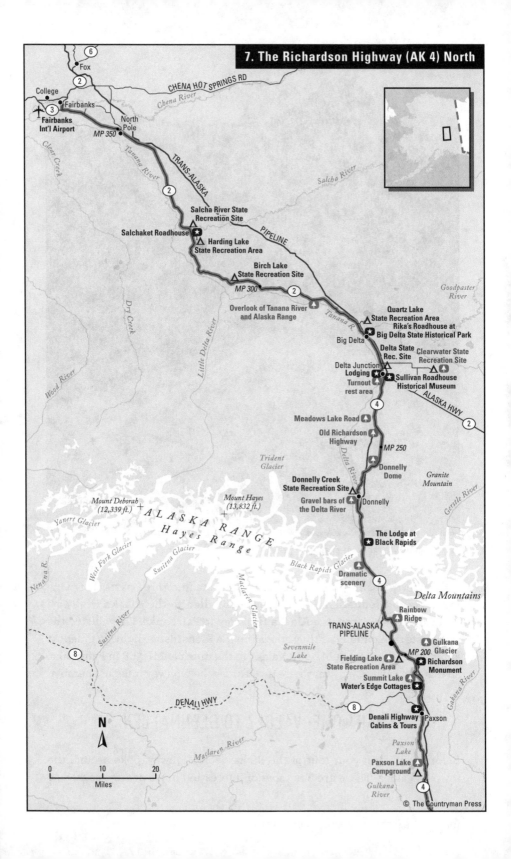

DRIVING SOUTH INTO THE HEART OF THE COAST RANGE

Delta and Fairbanks), I have divided this drive into three parts. Part One is **Valdez to Glennallen,** Part Two is **Glennallen to the Alaska Highway,** and Part Three is from the **Alaska Highway to Fairbanks.** I have listed the mileposts sequentially as they appear on the Richardson Highway milepost signs, from the start at MP 0 in Valdez to the finish at MP 368 in Fairbanks, so that you can jump in anywhere if you know the highway milepost number.

PART ONE: VALDEZ TO GLENNALLEN

Before you begin your tour of the Richardson Highway, poke around the town of Valdez. There are a number of interesting hikes nearby, as well as kayaking, fishing, and winter helicopter skiing. A good place to start is the visitors center, where the staff is routinely well informed and friendly.

Valdez is the southern terminus of the Trans-Alaska Pipeline System (TAPS), and the Richardson Highway parallels the southern half of TAPS, the northern half of which is along the Dalton Highway (Drive #1). The pipeline is alternately raised above the ground on refrigerated towers over the permafrost and buried beneath the surface in areas where there is no permafrost. The highway and oil pipeline crisscross each other along the Richardson Highway. There are numerous pipeline access points through which you can reach the pipeline for viewing and even hiking along the pipeline

THE ACCESSIBLE WORTHINGTON GLACIER IS WELL WORTH THE STOP

PAXSON LAKE OFFERS GREAT FISHING AND BOATING

maintenance road. See Drive #1 for more information on hiking the TAPS maintenance road.

Heading west out of Valdez, for the first 12 miles you will follow (and can access at several points) the braided stream channel of the **Lowe River**. Also look for the entrance to **Robe Lake** for fishing and kayaking fun and, at MP 12, the trailhead for the historic 1889 Pack Trail. At MP 13 the highway turns abruptly north through **Keystone Canyon** with views of lovely waterfalls and interesting railroad tunnels. The highway then begins its climb toward **Thompson Pass**, which at 2,678 feet is the highest road elevation along the Coast Range. Stop in any one of several pull-offs in the area of Thompson Pass to hike across the wonderful alpine tundra and take in the glorious alpine springs, stream channels, and lakes while enjoying a full variety of tundra vegetation from lichens to wildflowers.

Just a few miles north of Thompson Pass you reach the entrance to the **Worthington Glacier State Park**. Here you have a chance to visit and learn about the glaciation of the Thompson Pass area and hike around the glacier. If glacier hiking is of interest, you could also consider the McCarthy Road (see Drive #8) and a hike to and on the Root Glacier.

The current Richardson Highway follows essentially the same path of what was known in the late 19th and early 20th centuries as the **Valdez to Fairbanks Road**, which many miners and explorers took to reach the interior of Alaska, many looking for the riches that they were sure the Alaskan gold fields held in store for them. To help provide accommodations, food, and supplies for these intrepid travelers, a series of roadhouses, spaced at a day's walk (~10 miles) apart, was built in the late 1800s and early 1900s. Many of these roadhouses, such as the Summit Roadhouse once located at the top of Thompson Pass, have long since disappeared, but several, including the Tonsina Roadhouse (MP 79), Yost's Roadhouse (MP 202), Sourdough Roadhouse (MP 150.6), Black Rapids Roadhouse (MP 227.4), Sullivan Road-

house (MP 266), and Rika's Roadhouse (MP 275) are still visible. Rika's, near Delta Junction, is well restored and maintained as a state historic site (definitely worth the stop) and others, such as the Black Rapids, are in the process of being restored. For more, check out www.alaskanroadhouses .wordpress.com.

Five miles south of the town of Glennallen, take a short side trip to the town of Copper Center, which offers the whole range of visitor services, including accommodations, historic buildings, and a museum.

PART TWO: GLENNALLEN TO THE ALASKA HIGHWAY

From Glennallen, drive 14 miles north past the Native Village of Gulkana to the turnoff for the Tok Cutoff at MP 128.5 (Drive #6) at Gakona Junction. North of Gakona Junction, the Richardson Highway follows the path of the Gulkana River, the southern extension of the Gulkana National Wild and Scenic River, which offers multiple access points for floating and fishing. Near the Sourdough Roadhouse at MP 150.6 the highway turns west away from the Gulkana River and begins gaining elevation as you drive toward the turnoff to the **Denali Highway** (Drive #9). Along the way you pass the beautiful **Paxson** and **Summit Lakes**, which are both north-south oriented, glacially carved, boreal forest–surrounded lakes providing plenty of boating, paddling, and fishing opportunities. And Paxson Lake provides access to the Gulkana National Scenic and Wild River System.

Isabel Pass, just a few miles north of Summit Lake, is near the drainage divide between the south-flowing Copper River and the north-flowing Delta River. Take the gravel road northeast from the pass into the heart of the Alaska Range and hike up to the **Gulkana Glacier**. Starting around MP 200, follow the Phelan River as it flows north toward its confluence with the main channel of the Delta River. Look for numerous beaver dams and ponds in the marshy wetlands along the side channels. The open landscape alternates between boreal forest, marshy tundra, and lakes, including the charming and scenic Fielding Lake. Just prior to the confluence of the Delta River you pass some high cliffs made of multicolored rocks (known as Rainbow Ridge), which are the remnants of 200-million-year-old basaltic ocean crust that was formed near the equator and transported several thousand miles by plate tectonics to what is now Alaska.

North of Fielding Lake you will begin a dramatic drive through the middle of the soaring **Alaska Range** along and above the Delta River. This is one of Alaska's great mountain ranges, seen from a wonderful section of road. In the fall you'll be treated to some spectacular contrast of 11,000- to 13,000-foot snowcapped peaks against dark spruce trees interspersed with patchworks of bright golden autumn colors. It seems that the view at each turn in the road and every bend in the river is more spectacular and dramatic than the one before. At around MP 227, weather permitting, there's a decent view up the lower section of the **Black Rapids Glacier.**

As you head toward Delta Junction you have wonderful views back toward the south of the steep, fault-bounded front of the Alaska Range with the braided channels of the Delta River in the foreground. The second part of the Richardson Highway terminates at the historic town of **Delta Junction**, which offers a full range of visitor services. You might want to stop in and peruse all the local information the **Delta Visitor Center** has to offer, as well as the nearby historic **Sullivan Roadhouse.** There are several camping options, but my favorite is the **Clearwater Creek State Recreation Site**, located along the banks of the slow-flowing Clearwater River. It is renowned for its flat-water canoeing and kayaking.

PART THREE: DELTA JUNCTION TO FAIRBANKS

From the town of **Delta Junction**, which is at the end of the Alaska Highway, the Richardson Highway turns northwest and heads toward Fairbanks. The highway follows the northern banks of the Delta and then the Tanana Rivers all the way to Fairbanks. The greatest assets of this section of the Richardson Highway are the many views south across the braided stream channels of the Delta and Tanana Rivers over to the north flank of the massive Alaska Range that forms the backdrop for the entire southern sky. There are many overlooks from which you can enjoy the scenery, but you won't want to miss the overlook at MP 288.5. If you take your time on the way to Fairbanks you can enjoy a variety of state recreation areas, including those at **Quartz, Birch**, and **Harding Lakes** and the **Salcha River State Recreation Site.** From the Salcha River you are about 45 minutes from the city of Fairbanks, which offers a full range of visitor services.

IN THE AREA

Accommodations, Fuel, and Food

MP 0 (VALDEZ): MAGPIES ON THE FLY, 907-255-2267, www.magpies bakery.com, or find them on Facebook. Look around Valdez for Maggie's mobile bakery trailer, which serves tasty breakfast sandwiches, pastries, and lunch to go. $.

MP 0 (VALDEZ): OLDTOWN BURGERS, 139 E. Pioneer Drive, 907-461-8335. Serves breakfast, brunch, burgers, and seafood. Open 5 AM–10 PM. $.

MP 79: THE TONSINA RIVER LODGE, 907-822-3000, www.tonsinariver lodge.com. Wood-paneled lodging and restaurant with tasty Russian and American food in an updated building next to the original Tonsina Roadhouse. Open noon–9 PM, closed Tuesdays. $–$$.

LOOK FOR THE MAGPIES ON THE FLY TRAILER FOR TASTY TREATS

MP 101.2 PLUS 1: OLD TOWN COPPER CENTER INN & RESTAURANT, Old Richardson Highway Loop, 907-822-3245, www.oldtowncoppercenter .com. Rooms and a restaurant are housed in a historic, old-style, low-roof cabin. They also offer information on a wide variety of outdoor activities and adventures. Open all year. $$.

MP 101.6: COPPER RIVER PRINCESS WILDERNESS LODGE, 1 Brenwick Craig Road, Copper Center, 907-822-4000, www.princesslodges.com. Beautiful accommodations on 200 acres near the Copper River. $$$.

MP 115 PLUS 1: CARIBOU HOTEL, 187 Glenn Highway, Glennallen, 907-822-3302, www.caribouhotel.com/rooms.htm. Spacious accommodations at a reasonable price. $$.

MP 147.5: SOURDOUGH ROADHOUSE, 907-822-3636, www.telephone.bouw man.com/Alaska/Valdez/Sourdough.html. Food and spirits at a rebuilt roadhouse near launching for Gulkana River. $$.

MP 188: DENALI HIGHWAY CABINS AND TOURS, 907-987-0977, www .denalihwy.com. Picturesque log cabins, tent cabins, and a cottage near Paxson and the Denali Highway. $$.

MP 191: WATER'S EDGE COTTAGES, 907-822-4443 or 907-388-8299, www .deltanewsweb.com/sponsor/watersedge. Cottages on the edge of Summit Lake. $$.

MP 227.4: THE LODGE AT BLACK RAPIDS, 877-825-9413, www.lodgeat blackrapids.com. Gorgeous, modern, wood beam lodge with integrated restaurant in the heart of the glorious Alaska Range, well described as rugged luxury. They are restoring the original Black Rapids Roadhouse located at the same mile marker. Open in all seasons. $$–$$$.

MP 266 (DELTA JUNCTION): KELLY'S ALASKA COUNTRY INN, 907-895-4667, www.kellysalaskacountryinn.com. Nice, affordable, family-run motel in Delta Junction. $–$$.

MP 266 (DELTA JUNCTION): DIAMOND WILLOW INN, 907-895-7400, www.diamondwillowinn-alaska.com. Beautiful, modern, full-service, log cabin–style village and lodge. $$–$$$.

MP 266 (DELTA JUNCTION): THE GARDEN BED & BREAKFAST, 907-895-4633, www.alaskagardenbandb.com. Private, quiet, modern cabins surrounded by glorious flowers. $$.

MP 276 (DELTA JUNCTION): ALASKA 7 MOTEL, 907-895-4848. Clean, quiet, and affordable motel. $.

MP 322: SHALCHAKET ROADHOUSE, 907-488-4339, www.facebook.com/salchaketroadhouse. Good drinks plus a motel and groceries for sale at a fun, modern roadhouse. $$.

Camping

MP 24: BLUEBERRY LAKE STATE RECREATION SITE, 907-269-8400. Twenty-five lovely developed lakeside campsites nestled into the alpine tundra near Thompson Pass. $.

MP 79–80: SQUIRREL CREEK STATE RECREATION SITE, 907-822-5932. Pleasant, developed streamside camping (25 sites) with access to both a lake and Squirrel Creek for fishing. $.

MP 117.5: DRY CREEK STATE RECREATION SITE, 907-205-0766. Fifty campsites on 360 acres in a white spruce forest near Gulkana with trails and fishing. $.

MP 175: PAXSON LAKE CAMPGROUND, 907-822-3217, www.campgrounds alaska.com/richardsonhighway/paxsonlakecampground.php. Large, forested, lakeside BLM campsite with 40 RV and 50 tent sites and a large boat ramp on the shores of beautiful Paxson Lake. The south end of Paxson Lake is the outflow to the Gulkana River.

MP 201: FIELDING LAKE STATE RECREATION AREA. Camping, fishing, a boat launch into a tundra-surrounded lake, and a state park rental cabin (visit www.dnr.alaska.gov/parks/cabins/north for State Parks rental cabin information). $.

MP 238: DONNELLY CREEK STATE RECREATION SITE. These 12 boreal forest–shaded developed campsites are nestled in among some towering white spruce trees near the east bank of the Delta River. There is access to a levee from which you can access great views of the river and the Alaska Range. However, if you don't mind camping a bit more informally and would like a bit more privacy and full-time access to views, pull off onto the gravel access road at around MP 237.5, about a half mile south of the entrance to the Donnelly Creek State Recreation Site, and drive out onto the gravel bars of the floodplain of the Delta River. Early in the spring, the Delta River may be full; however, by midsummer and into the fall these gravel bars along the Delta River are wide open for exploration and camping. $.

MP 267 PLUS 11: CLEARWATER CREEK STATE RECREATION SITE. Seventeen quiet, lovely campsites next to the languid Clearwater Creek, 11 miles east of Delta Junction on Jack Warren and Remington Roads. Best camping in the Delta Junction area! $

MP 267: DELTA STATE RECREATION SITE. Twenty-five easy-to-access state campsites in a forest just north of the town of Delta Junction. $.

MP 277.7: QUARTZ LAKE STATE RECREATION AREA. About 600 acres of quiet fishing, removed from the highway picnic and campsites, with a boat launch, hiking trails, and two public use cabins (visit www.dnr.alaska .gov/parks/cabins/north for State Parks rental cabin information). $.

MP 305.2: BIRCH LAKE STATE RECREATION SITE. This is a nice picnic stop and camping area, with 22 sites and a motorboat launch next to a military recreation area. It includes a state park rental cabin (visit www.dnr .alaska.gov/parks/cabins/north for State Parks rental cabin information). $.

MP 321: HARDING LAKE STATE RECREATION AREA. This beautiful lakeside area has 78 vehicle and five walk-in campsites and a boat launch nestled among towering white spruce trees, birches, and aspens. The road around the south side of the lake is interesting to explore and has nice homes along it. $.

MP 323.5: SALCHA RIVER STATE RECREATION SITE. Developed campsites nestled in a spruce forest with lots of big birch trees and a boat launch providing access to the Salcha River. There's also access to dry camping on a large gravel bar in a bend of the Salcha River, a nearby marina, and a state park rental cabin (visit www.dnr.alaska.gov/parks/cabins/north for State Parks rental cabin information). $.

Attractions and Recreation

Part One: Valdez to Glennallen

MP 0: VALDEZ VISITOR CENTER. This is a good place to begin your Richardson Highway adventure, with lots of maps, good information, and a fascinating and informative display on the system of roadhouses that was concentrated along the Richardson Highway, previously known as the Valdez-Fairbanks Trail.

MP 0: HIKING TRAILS AROUND VALDEZ. Check out the coastal Shoup Bay, Homestead, and Mineral Creek Trails along an old mining road that heads up into the coastal mountains. There is access to numerous spectacular waterfalls and plenty of opportunities for camping. All three of these hikes are accessible on the west side of town, with maps available at the visitor center.

MP 2–368: HIKE THE TRANS-ALASKA PIPELINE. The oil pipeline parallels the Richardson Highway along its entire length, with numerous access points for viewing and hiking along the pipeline maintenance road. To obtain TAPS ROW permits for hiking/traveling the pipeline maintenance road, contact the Alyeska Pipeline Service Company at P.O. Box 196660, Anchorage, AK 99519; 907-787-8170; or alyeskamail@alyeska-pipeline.com. Or call one of the following numbers: Valdez at 907-834-6480, Fairbanks at 907-450-5707, or Anchorage at 907-787-8971. You can also download a PDF of the TAPS Right-of-Way Use Guideline (RUG) from the website for this book, www.backroadsandbywaysofalaska.com.

MP 2.9: DAYVILLE ROAD. Check out this 5-mile-long road out to the oil pipeline storage terminal, with several pullouts with restrooms for dry camping (I often camp here) and nice views across Valdez Bay. There is access to the 3.8-mile-long John Hunter Memorial Trail, which follows a buried portion of the oil pipeline on its way to the Solomon Gulch Hydroelectric Project, providing some good elevated viewpoints of Valdez Bay along the way.

MP 3: GLACIERVIEW PARK PICNIC SITE. Take Airport Road about 4 miles to reach a picnic site on a glacial meltwater lake.

MP 6–7: GHOST FOREST. Look for sections of standing dead trees in wetlands where the roots have been flooded, the result of this entire region being dropped down more than 10 feet during a 1968 earthquake.

MP 12: OLD RICHARDSON HIGHWAY ROUTE AND ACCESS TO 1899 PACK TRAIL. Look for the north side access to an old section of the Richardson Highway that rejoins the highway after a half mile. Dry camping pullouts and a streamside camp location are here as well as the trailhead for a hiking path that follows the old gold miners' pack trail from 1899.

MP 13–15: KEYSTONE CANYON WATERFALLS AND RAILROAD TUNNEL. At MP 13 the highway turns north into the narrow, steep-walled Keystone Canyon, home to two large, lovely waterfalls, Horsetail and Bridal Veil Falls, and a historic railway kiosk, all of which are worth a stop. Note: You can hike to Bridal Veil Falls on the 1899 pack trail from the trailhead located near MP 12 on the old section of the Richardson Highway mentioned above.

MP 26: THOMPSON PASS (2,678 FEET). Stop at the south side pullout next to the gate on a double track at the top of Thompson Pass and enjoy a couple hours, or more, of lovely alpine tundra hiking with good views to the west of the aptly but not so creatively named 27 Mile Glacier.

MP 29: WORTHINGTON GLACIER STATE RECREATION SITE. Stop here for some hiking to get up close and personal with the two-pronged Worthington Glacier. Information kiosks and restrooms are available. The kiosk area and lower trails are all paved and wheelchair accessible. Enjoy wonderful early-morning hikes across the lower glacial outwash plain trail or to the glacier itself along the higher and more rugged primitive Ridge Trail. It's amazing to ponder that not long ago, geologically speaking, the spot where you are standing was under several thousand feet of ice and the landscape over which you now walk has just recently been released from the grip of thousands of feet and millennia of glacial ice.

MP 79: THE ORIGINAL TONSINA ROADHOUSE. One of the original roadhouse locations on the Valdez to Fairbanks Road, the original Tonsina Roadhouse, built in 1900, sits next to the current version, which is the Tonsina Lodge. It's worth the stop here to take a stroll around the original roadhouse and imagine what a welcome sight it must have been for travelers making their way along this wilderness pathway in the early days of the 20th century.

MP 104.6: COPPER CENTER MUSEUM GOLD RUSH ANNEX, 907-822-3245. Drive 1 mile off the Richardson Highway to see the historic building that now houses the Old Town Copper Center Inn & Restaurant, as well as the Trail of '98 Museum and Gold Rush Annex featuring artifacts from the Gold Rush era and before.

MP 112.5: WRANGELL MOUNTAIN AND COPPER RIVER VALLEY VIEWPOINT. Slow down as you pass MP 112 and look for a dirt road that turns off to the east onto an old section of the Richardson Highway. Don't drive down the old section of the highway, but continue heading east through the opening in the roadside trees and bushes to a high overlook with spectacular views of the Copper River far below and Mount Wrangell beyond. This

PAXSON LAKE PROVIDES ACCESS TO THE GULKANA NATIONAL SCENIC AND WILD RIVER SYSTEM

is an unofficial viewpoint at which I often stop and dry camp if I'm in the Glennallen area near camp time.

Part Two: Glennallen to Delta Junction

MP 175: PAXSON LAKE. Camping, boating, and fishing are available on this beautiful lake. Access the Gulkana National Wild and Scenic River here.

MP 190: SUMMIT LAKE. A gorgeous alpine lake with great paddling and fishing, home to the wild, springtime Arctic Man snowmobile and skiing competition. Summit Lake is also the headwaters of the Gulkana National Wild and Scenic River.

MP 198: ISABEL PASS (3,280 FEET) RICHARDSON MONUMENT AND SIDE ROAD TO GULKANA GLACIER. Stop at the pass for the Richardson Monument and the fascinating Gold Rush Women information kiosk. For some off-road adventure, take the gravel road north to and along the Gulkana River, and then cross over into the College River drainage as you head toward the headwaters at the front of the Gulkana Glacier. Drive as far as you dare, then take off on foot up the College River and across a suspension bridge. Follow the cairns up and over a ridgeline that is directly in front of the Gulkana Glacier. You can continue your hike all the way up to the front of the glacier.

MP 201: FIELDING LAKE STATE RECREATION AREA. Drive 2 miles down to this lovely, scenic, fish-stocked lake with a boat ramp and picnic and camping area surrounded by tundra and boreal forests.

MP 220–230: DRAMATIC DRIVE THROUGH THE TOWERING ALASKA RANGE. Stop at turnouts to enjoy the jaw-dropping scenery, including the Black Rapids Glacier.

MP 237.5: GRAVEL BARS OF THE DELTA RIVER. Explore, and even camp on, the vast gravel bars of the braided stream channels of the Delta River and enjoy amazing views of the towering Alaska Range. If you are a rock hound you have just entered heaven!

MP 256: OLD RICHARDSON HIGHWAY. This 1½-lane-wide gravel road climbs to the top of Windy Ridge, providing wonderful views of the Delta River and the north slope of the snow- and ice-covered Alaska Range. You can also climb Donnelly Dome, walk the oil pipeline, and hike walking tundra–covered ridgelines. Lots of noodling around and dry camping opportunities here—go explore this little-used section of side roads along the Old Richardson Highway!

MP 258: MEADOWS LAKE ROAD/FORT GREELY – Drive 15 miles through Fort Greely amid an open canopy boreal forest which provides access to several side roads leading to lakes offering good fishing and lakeside camping sites and ultimately to the braided stream channels of the Delta River. Contact the Fort Greely Public Affairs office at 907-873-4604 to obtain a

permit to camp on Fort Greely. Few folks use these recreational areas, so you're likely to have your fishing spot to yourself.

MP 263: TURNOUT REST AREA. Stop here for some spectacular views south across the braided channel of the Delta River to the Alaska Range. Study the informative geology kiosk that explains the plate tectonic and geographic significance of the Denali Fault Zone, along which the Alaska Range has been and continues to be uplifted, and the human historical placards as well.

Part Three: Delta Junction to Fairbanks

MP 266: SULLIVAN ROADHOUSE HISTORICAL MUSEUM. Located directly across the highway from the Delta Visitor Center, this beautifully restored roadhouse has fascinating interpretive exhibits.

MP 267 PLUS 11: CLEARWATER CREEK STATE RECREATION SITE. Drive 11 miles east of Delta Junction on Jack Warren and Remington Roads to this quiet campground nestled into a white spruce forest along the calm waters of Clearwater Creek. This gem of a spot offers wonderful flat-water canoeing. Food and drink are available at the Clearwater Lodge next door.

MP 275: RIKA'S ROADHOUSE AT BIG DELTA STATE HISTORICAL PARK. Plan to enjoy at least half a day at this well-restored and well-maintained roadhouse on the Delta River. Lots of history has been recorded and preserved here.

MP 288.5: OVERLOOK OF THE DELTA RIVER AND ALASKA RANGE.
Enjoy splendid views of the braided stream channels of the Delta River several hundred feet below you and the high, jagged peaks of the Alaska Range on the southern skyline. If you drive by this, turn around and go back to it!

Festivals and Fairs

FIREWEED FESTIVAL (LAST WEEK IN JUNE): Copper Center.

DELTANA FAIR & FESTIVAL (LAST WEEK IN JULY): www.deltanafair.com

Outfitters and Tour Operators

RIVER WRANGELLERS (COPPER CENTER), 888-822-3967, www.river wrangellers.com/index.php. Float trips and guided fishing adventures.

GOLDEN EAGLE OUTFITTERS (DELTA JUNCTION), www.alaskawilder nessexpeditions.com. Offers eco-friendly tours, including glacier adventures, air taxi services, and float and fishing trips at many locations in Alaska.

WRANGELL OUTFITTERS (DELTA JUNCTION), 907-388-5968, www .guidefitter.com/wrangelloutfitters. Offers base camp trips for hiking, photography, flora, wildlife, hunting, and fishing,

FIELDING LAKE OFFERS CAMPING, BOATING, AND FLOATPLANE ACCESS

NUMEROUS PULLOUTS WITH PICNIC TABLES PROVIDE SWEEPING VIEWS OF MOUNTAINS AND TUNDRA

DENALI HIGHWAY CABINS & PAXSON ALPINE TOURS, 907-987-0977, www.denalihwy.com. Picturesque log cabins, tent cabins, and a cottage near Paxson and the Denali Highway.

USEFUL INFORMATION

TRANS-ALASKA PIPELINE: www.alaska.org/detail/alyeska-pipeline

TRANS-ALASKA PIPELINE CONTACT INFORMATION: www.alyeska -pipeline.com/NewsCenter/ContactInformation

THE MILEPOST TRAVEL GUIDE: www.themilepost.com/highway-info/ highways/richardson-highway

ALASKA.ORG ROAD GUIDE—VALDEZ TO FAIRBANKS: www.alaska.org/ guide/valdez-to-fairbanks

ALASKA.ORG ROAD GUIDE—VALDEZ TO WORTHINGTON GLACIER: www.alaska.org/guide/valdez-to-worthington-glacier

STATE PARKS RENTAL CABIN INFORMATION: www.dnr.alaska.gov/ parks/cabins/north

8

THE ROAD TO MCCARTHY AND KENNECOTT (AK 10)

Into the Heart of Wrangell–St. Elias National Park and Preserve

---

FROM → TO: Richardson Highway to McCarthy

WHERE IT STARTS: MP 82.5 (north of Valdez) on the Richardson Highway

WHERE IT ENDS: McCarthy

ESTIMATED LENGTH: 93 miles (about 17 miles is paved, the rest is gravel)

ESTIMATED TIME: Two to four days

HIGHLIGHTS: Copper River floodplain with fish wheels, Kuskulana and Gilhina River railroad bridges, Main Street McCarthy, Kennecott Mines National Historic Landmark, stream channels that flow across the Route Glacier and disappear down into moulins

GETTING THERE: Drive 31.5 miles south along the Richardson Highway (Drive #7, AK 4) from its intersection with the Glennallen Highway (Drive #11, AK 1) to MP 82.5 and turn east on the Edgerton Highway, which becomes the road to McCarthy at the confluence of the Chitina and Copper Rivers at the town of Chitina

---

This road to McCarthy is the southern companion to the northern Nabesna side trip road (in Drive #6) because both roads provide access to the superlative-laden Wrangell–St. Elias National Park and Preserve.

I am starting this description of the southern road into the spectacular **Wrangell–St. Elias National Park and Preserve** on the Edgerton Highway, 30 miles east of where the actual 60-mile road to McCarthy that begins in the town of Chitina, because there are a few commendable locations to see along this lead-in section of Edgerton Highway. (Note: the MP numbers I use on this drive begin with MP 0 at the turnoff onto the Edgerton High-

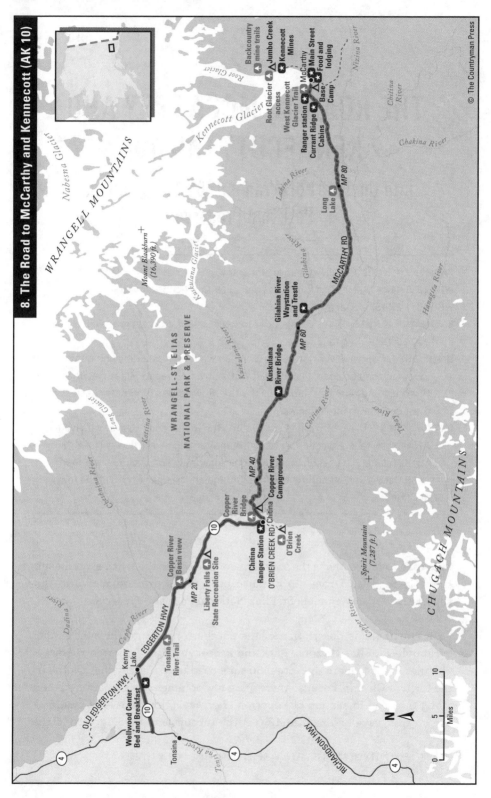

8. The Road to McCarthy and Kennecott (AK 10)

© The Countryman Press

WRANGELL MOUNTAINS

Nabesna Glacier

Mount Blackburn
(16,390 ft.)

Kuskulana Glacier

Root Glacier

Kennecott Glacier

WRANGELL–ST. ELIAS
NATIONAL PARK & PRESERVE

Long Glacier

Katrina River

Kuskulana River

Chetaslina River

Backcountry
mine trails

Jumbo Creek

Kennecott
Mines

McCarthy

Main Street

Food and
lodging

Root Glacier
access

West Kennecott
Glacier Trail

Ranger station

Currant Ridge
Cabins

Base
Camp

Nizina River

Chitina
River

Chakina River

Lakina River

Long
Lake

MP 80

MCCARTHY RD

Gilahina River
Waystation
and Trestle

Gilahina River

MP 60

Kuskulana
River Bridge

Chitina River

Tebay River

Hanagita River

MP 40

Copper River
Bridge

Copper River
Campgrounds

Chitina

Chitina
Ranger Station

O'BRIEN CREEK RD

O'Brien
Creek

Spirit Mountain
(7,287 ft.)

CHUGACH MOUNTAINS

10

Copper River
Basin view

MP 20

Liberty Falls
State Recreation Site

EDGERTON HWY

Copper River

Dadina River

OLD EDGERTON HWY

Kenny
Lake

Tonsina
River Trail

Wellwood Center
Bed and Breakfast

10

4

Tonsina

Tonsina River

RICHARDSON HWY

4

4

Copper River

N

0   5   10
Miles

way; therefore, you might want to set your trip odometer to 0 here.) Even before you reach the Edgerton Highway, I encourage you to stop at the main **Wrangell–St. Elias Visitor Center**, located just north of Copper Center (around MP 107) on the Richardson Highway (Drive #7). Here you will find a wealth of information, including maps, guides, books, and up-to-date details on road conditions and river crossings.

Heading east onto the Edgerton Highway, you drive through prime open farm and ranch country as you make your way toward the **Copper River**. Around MPs 12, 18, and 23 you are treated to some great elevated views of the river and its valley as the road parallels it on its way to Chitina (population about 100) and the Copper River bridge. Along the way you pass **Liberty Falls State Recreation Site** and pass by the glacially carved One, Two, and Three Mile Lakes, named for their distances west of Chitina. The quaint little town of **Chitina** offers a range of visitor services and is a good base camp for taking a side trip along the Copper River. Chitina is also the actual beginning of the road to McCarthy.

As you cross the Copper River Bridge, about a mile east of town, look south to see the confluence of the Chitina and Copper Rivers less than a half mile downstream. On the east side of the bridge are access roads to the gravel bars that line the Copper and the Kotsina Rivers, whose confluence is immediately north of the Copper River bridge. These gravel bars provide many dry camping opportunities and the ability to see how the

Wrangell–St. Elias National Park and Preserve

At 13.2 million acres, Wrangell–St. Elias National Park and Preserve is the largest national park in the United States, equal in size to six Yellowstones. It contains the largest wilderness area in the National Wilderness Preservation System. Its designation, along with the adjoining Canadian Kluane National Park and Reserve and Tatshenshini-Alsek Provincial Park, is a World Heritage Site and the world's largest internationally protected wilderness. This area contains four major mountain ranges, including the Wrangell, St. Elias, Chugach, and the eastern part of the Alaska Range. These ranges encompass 18,000-foot Mount St. Elias, the second highest peak in the United States, second only to Denali, and nine of the 16 highest peaks in the U.S. The park contains the Nabesna Glacier, which at approximately 80 miles long is the longest nonpolar valley glacier in the world, and the largest collection of glaciers in North America, including the Malaspina and Hubbard Glaciers, which are the largest piedmont and tidewater glaciers in North America, respectively. The Malaspina Glacier is so large that you can only view its entirety from the air. A land of superlatives indeed!

MOUNT ST. ELIAS IN THE SUPERLATIVE WRANGELL-ST. ELIAS NATIONAL PARK AND PRESERVE

native fish wheels, which are always present during the summer and fall, operate. Leaving the Copper River, you drive a rough section of the road as it cuts through a rocky, steep-sided ridgeline for a couple miles as you cross over into the Chitina River drainage basin. The river's confluence with the Copper River, which you saw from the bridge, is clearly visible if you look southwest from turnouts along from the western end of the McCarthy Road.

As you continue eastward along the McCarthy Road, you pass through alternating environments of spruce-, aspen-, and birch-dominated boreal forests and spongy and marshy tundra dotted with many lakes. Look for beaver dam–augmented ponds and their lodges.

Like so many roads in Alaska, the McCarthy Road was built for mining. A

If You Only Have One Day in McCarthy and the Kennecott Mine Area

- Rent a pair of ice grips that you can slide over your boots from one of the local gear outfitters in McCarthy.
- Pack a lunch and some water, and take an early morning bus to the mine site.
- Enjoy the mine site in the morning.
- Hike north to the Root Glacier access point, hike down to the glacier, don your ice grippers, and take a stroll across the glacier. It's magnificent, it's safe (with your grippers), and it's fun! One of the highlights of walking across Root Glacier is seeing the surface channels of water that flow across the top and then disappear where they swirl down into vertical shafts, called moulins, which are carved out of the ice by these streams. However, use caution and don't venture too close to these moulins.

railroad once occupied this same route, carrying men and supplies into and out of the Kennecott Mines. You'll find several of the old sections of the rail system still intact, including the big trestles that cross the Kuskulana and Gilahina Rivers, both of which are fascinating stops. As you drive through the alternating forest and tundra environments, slow down and look at some of the details. Many who pass through the boreal forest at high speed believe it to be monotonous and uninteresting, when in fact it is filled with fascinating treasures. In particular, take time to investigate transition environments where the forest blends into the marshy tundra and lakes. These are rich habitats supporting a variety of plant species, including many flowers, grasses, sedges, and mosses. They also provide habitat for many types of wildlife, including moose and beavers. As you approach the end of the road at the Kennecott River, the **Wrangell and St. Elias Mountains** begin to dominate the landscape out your front windshield. There are several camping and accommodation opportunities near the end of the road. The quaint town of **McCarthy**, with numerous attractive lodging and dining options, is fun to wander around. The town was a booming mining hub 150 years ago. Vehicle access to McCarthy and the historic Kennecott Mines area, 4 miles beyond, is limited to local traffic (locals cross the Kennecott River on a private bridge located about a mile south.) Your access is across the narrow bridge either by bicycle or on foot. Plan to park and/or camp at the end

PLAN YOUR STAY TO INCLUDE A HIKE ACROSS THE ROOT GLACIER

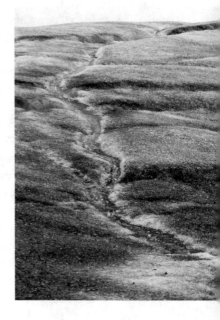

FASCINATING ARTIFACTS AWAIT AROUND THE HISTORIC KENNECOTT MINE NATIONAL PARK

of the road and walk across the Kennecott River footbridge into town. There you can arrange all sorts of hiking, biking, rafting, and fishing adventures, although it's better to make them in advance.

Note: The last few times I drove the McCarthy Road from Chitina, the road was in very good shape, with the exception of the first section just east of the Copper River bridge. Historically, we used to brag about how we, and our vehicles, survived driving this road. In recent years, road maintenance has improved significantly. That being said, the McCarthy Road can still be a challenge. Check in with the rangers at the Wrangell–St. Elias Visitor Center, just south of Glennallen on the Richardson Highway, to ask about road conditions. Four-wheel-drive is not always necessary, but it can be a big benefit. Near the beginning and end of the road to McCarthy, and over numerous bridges, there are sections where the road is single lane, so pay particular attention. As with all gravel roads, I recommend slowing down and pulling off a bit when you pass vehicles coming from the other direction to minimize the likelihood of gravel being slung into and cracking your windshield or radiator. And anyway, what's the rush?

IN THE AREA

Accommodations, Fuel, and Food

MP 6: WELLWOOD CENTER BED AND BREAKFAST, 907-822-3418, wellwoodcenter.com. Bed & breakfast near the beginning of the Edgerton Highway. $–$$.

MP 90.5 (NEAR MCCARTHY): CURRANT RIDGE CABINS, 907-554-4424, www.currantridge.com. Lovely, eco-friendly, private, log-style cabins and a restaurant near the end of the road at McCarthy. $–$$.

MP 93 (NEAR MCCARTHY): KENNICOTT RIVER LODGE, PRIVATE CABINS AND HOSTEL, 907-554-4441 (lodge), 907-554-2329 (summer cell), 907-447-4252 (winter cell), www.kennicottriverlodge.com/lodging. Log-

---

If You Only Have Five Days in McCarthy and the Kennecott Mine Area

To make sure you can capture and enjoy the full flavor of the road to McCarthy and the Kennecott Mines area, I recommend you plan a minimum of a five-day journey, including making arrangements with a local McCarthy outfitter for some river rafting, fishing, biking, or other guided activity.

Day 1: Noodle around Chitina and explore the gravel bars of the Copper River. Drive to the end of the road at the Kennecott River, stopping along the way to enjoy the many natural environments and railway trestles. Then make camp and walk over the footbridge into the town of McCarthy and confirm your outdoor adventure plans with your outfitter.

Day 2: Enjoy your guided (or unguided) outdoor adventure activities around McCarthy and plan to have a late lunch or dinner at one of McCarthy's eateries.

Day 3: This is your day to take an early bus (or bike) to the Kennecott Mines for a morning exploration of the old mine site. The guided tours are really fascinating! Then take an afternoon hike to the Root Glacier to enjoy your gripper-aided cross-glacier walking adventure. I like to have a picnic lunch on the glacier. (It pays to bring a collapsible camp chair or towel to sit on.)

Day 4: Hang out around McCarthy and perhaps take an extended hike up the east side of the Root Glacier and into the country beyond.

Day 5: Drive back to Chitina and down the O'Brien Creek Road to see all the fun that's happening there. Stay overnight in one of Chitina's sweet bed & breakfasts or hotels.

THE HISTORIC MA JOHNSON HOTEL IN MCCARTHY

style buildings and a restaurant within walking distance of the footbridge near the end of the road at McCarthy. $.

MP 93 (NEAR MCCARTHY): MCCARTHY BED AND BREAKFAST, 907-554-4433 (office), 907-554-1133 (cell), www.mccarthybedandbreakfast.com. Affordable bed & breakfast near the end of the road. $–$$.

MP 94 (MCCARTHY): MA JOHNSON HOTEL/THE MCCARTHY LODGE, 907-554-4402, www.mccarthylodge.com. A living museum, hotel, saloon, and bistro. $$–$$$.

MP 94 (MCCARTHY): LANCASTER'S BACKPACKER HOTEL, 907-554-4402, www.mccarthylodge.com. Affordable hotel oriented toward backpackers and other outdoor travelers. $–$$.

MP 94 (MCCARTHY): THE ROADSIDE POTATOHEAD RESTAURANT, 907-554-4504. Tasty American food and drinks plus community gatherings and events in a delightful, homey building. $.

MP 95 (BETWEEN MCCARTHY AND KENNECOTT): BLACKBURN CABINS, 907-231-6227, www.blackburncabins.com. Delightful eco-friendly cabins near Kennecott. $–$$.

MP 95 (KENNECOTT): KENNICOTT GLACIER LODGE, 800-582-5128, www.kennicottlodge.com. First-class hotel and restaurant in the middle of the Kennecott Mines National Historic Landmark offers a full range of outdoor activities with local outfitters May–September. $$$–$$$$.

MP 95 (KENNECOTT): KENNICOTT COTTAGE, www.alaska.net/~oviattws/kennicott/final.htm. Affordable historic cottage in Kennecott. $–$$.

Camping

MP 23.5: LIBERTY FALL STATE RECREATION SITE, 907-823-2265. Lovely picnic and camping site with a beautiful waterfall. $.

MP 35: COPPER RIVER CAMPGROUNDS AND DRY CAMPING SITES, located on the east side of the Copper River bridge. Camp at either of two developed campgrounds with 12 sites, or dry camp on the gravel bars of the Copper and Kotsina Rivers. $.

MP 93: BASE CAMP, 907-277-4321, www.rvparkreviews.com/regions/alaska/chitina. Partially developed campsite and RV parking at the end of the road for tenting and RVs. Often works on the honor system for payment. $.

Attractions and Recreation

MP 12: TONSINA RIVER TRAIL. This is a nice and easy 2-mile trail along the high bluffs above the Tonsina River.

MP 18 AND 23: COPPER RIVER BASIN VIEWS. Enjoy awesome elevated views from north-side pullouts high above the Copper River Valley.

MP 23.5: LIBERTY FALLS STATE RECREATION SITE. Stop at this lovely picnic and camping site, home to its gorgeous namesake waterfall.

MP 33: TOWN OF CHITINA. Small town just west of the Copper River bridge at the beginning of the road to McCarthy with many travelers' amenities, including some nice hotels, sweet bed & breakfasts, restaurants, and a museum.

THE END-OF-THE-ROAD BASE CAMP IS A JUMPING OFF POINT FOR MANY MCCARTHY ADVENTURES

MP 33: O'BRIEN CREEK ROAD. Drive 5 miles along the banks of the Copper River for fishing, boating, and camping at the confluence with O'Brien Creek. This drive crosses Chitna Native Corporation lands: please sign in at the end of the road and pay a modest recreational use fee for the use of their lands.

MP 34.5: COPPER RIVER BRIDGE. Drive slowly as you cross this bridge for good views upstream of Native fish wheels and the braided stream channel of the Copper River, and downstream of the confluence of the Chitina and Copper Rivers.

MP 35: COPPER AND KOTSINA RIVERS GRAVEL BARS AND TWO CAMP-ING AREAS. Have fun exploring the gravel bars of the Copper and Kotsina Rivers, or camp here for the evening to enjoy the river, gravel bars, and fish wheels.

MP 51: KUSKULANA RIVER BRIDGE. One of the original railroad bridges, built in 1910 for the Copper River and Northwestern Railway link between Cordova and the Kennecott Mines at McCarthy, has been reconfigured as a vehicle bridge. It's well worth the stop. On the east side of the bridge is a large and very nice wayside with restrooms and information kiosks. Stop on either side and walk across the bridge for some great views up and down the Kuskulana River (watching for infrequent traffic, of course). You can drive down on the west side and walk down on the east side to scramble around the bridge abutments, You can even walk out on a catwalk that extends under the bridge and high over the river, once you boost yourself up onto the abutments.

RAFTING ON THE MCCARTHY RIVER

THE BRAIDED STREAM CHANNEL OF THE GLACIER-FED AND SALMON-FILLED CHITNA RIVER

MP 67.5: GILAHINA RIVER WAYSTATION AND RAILROAD TRESTLE.
The current bridge is no big deal, but after you cross over it, turn and look to the left into a dirt pullout, to see the remnants of one of the great, old railroad trestles that still stands today. This is also a nice undeveloped camping spot next to the Gilahina River. There's a waystation with restrooms and fascinating information kiosks on the west side of the current bridge. If you are a painter, sketcher, or photographer, you will not be able to resist the geometric lines and shapes presented by the brace work of the old trestle.

MP 78: LONG LAKE. View thousands of sockeye salmon that have arrived here after their long, arduous journey up the Copper and Chitina Rivers to spawn.

MP 93: RANGER STATION AND WEST KENNECOTT GLACIER TRAIL.
Check into the ranger station for local information and hike the West Kennecott Glacier Trail to the Kennecott Glacier, which is only easily accessible from this west side trail along the Kennecott River.

MP 94: MAIN STREET MCCARTHY. Walk across the footbridge over the Kennecott River and about a half mile into the small town of McCarthy. Main Street, about a quarter mile long, offers a variety of accommodations, several outdoor adventure outfitters, and restaurants.

MP 99: KENNECOTT MINES NATIONAL HISTORIC LANDMARK AND ACCESS TO THE ROOT GLACIER. Take a bus (they run about every half hour), bike, or hike about 4 miles northwest from McCarthy to this fascinating historic mine processing facility that also includes the Kennecott Glacier Lodge, where you can stay smack in the middle of the action. You can arrange for guided tours of the old mine site, or wander and enjoy the numerous informative placards that detail the history of the mine. If you are a photographer and you love old buildings, textures, and fabrics, you'll love the old Kennecott mine site, as it's packed with all of them. The gravel

THE FRAMEWORK OF THE HISTORIC GILAHINA RAILROAD TRESTLE

road becomes a trail past the site, providing access to the hiking trail up to the Root Glacier and beyond.

MP 99: THE ROOT GLACIER AND THE BACKCOUNTRY. Hike about a mile and a half to the Jumbo Creek Camping Area and take a side hike down to and onto the Root Glacier. Strap on your ice grippers to hike across the glacier or continue this trail along the east side of the glacier 4 miles to the Erie Trail and the backcountry beyond. There is access to other nearby trails, such as the Jumbo Mine and Bonanza Mine Trails, as well as cross-country routes to Erie Lake and "The Knoll."

Festivals and Fairs

MCCARTHY WHITEWATER FESTIVAL AND PACKRAFT RACE (JULY): www.facebook.com/mccarthywhitewaterfest

Outfitters and Tour Operators

KENNICOTT SHUTTLE, 907-822-5292, www.kennicottshuttle.com. Provides transportation and a variety of tours between and around Glennallen, Kenny Lake, Chitina, McCarthy, and Kennecott. Reliable and affordable transportation if you don't want to drive the road to McCarthy.

WRANGELL MOUNTAIN AIR, 800-478-1160, www.wrangellmountainair.com. Backcountry trips, flight-seeing, charter service.

MCCARTHY AIR, 907-554-4440, www.mccarthyair.com. Backcountry trips, flight-seeing, charter service.

KENNICOTT WILDERNESS GUIDES (KENNECOTT), www.kennicottguides.com. Wide variety of backcountry guiding services.

ST. ELIAS ALPINE GUIDES (MCCARTHY), 800-664-4537, 907-554-4444 (summer), www.kennicottguides.com or www.steliasguides.com. Wide variety of backcountry guiding services.

MCCARTHY RIVER TOURS & OUTFITTERS (MCCARTHY), 907-554-1077, www.raftthewrangells.com. Guided outdoor adventures and gear rental.

ALASKA WILD ALPINE GUIDES, 888-682-2368, www.alaskawildalpine.com. Ice climbing and skiing adventures.

USEFUL INFORMATION

THE MILEPOST TRAVEL GUIDE: www.themilepost.com/highway-info/highways/edgerton-highway-mccarthy-road

ALASKA.ORG ROAD GUIDE—GLENNALLEN TO MCCARTHY: www.alaska.org/guide/edgerton-highway-kenny-lake-to-mccarthy

MCCARTHY ROAD GUIDE AND MAP: www.alaska.org/assets/content/maps/mccarthy-road-guide-map.pdf

WRANGELL–ST. ELIAS DAY HIKING GUIDE: www.nps.gov/wrst/planyourvisit/hiking-trails-routes.htm

9

THE DENALI HIGHWAY (AK 8)
Nonstop Views of the Alaska Range

FROM → TO: Paxson to Cantwell
WHERE IT STARTS: Paxson, MP 188.5 on the Richardson Highway (AK 4)
WHERE IT ENDS: Cantwell, MP 210 on the Parks Highway (AK 3)
ESTIMATED LENGTH: 135 miles, all gravel (open May through October)
ESTIMATED TIME: Two to four days
HIGHLIGHTS: Maclaren River and glacier views, Susitna River and glacier views, Rusty Lake walking trail, Tangle Lakes floating, views of and through Amphitheater Mountains
GETTING THERE: Drive the Glenn Highway (Drive #11) northeast 189 miles to the town of Glennallen, and then drive 71 miles north on the Richardson Highway (AK 4) (Drive #7) to MP 188.5 at the Denali Highway (AK 1)

The **Denali Highway** is considered by many to be one of the most spectacular drives in the world due to the views you have across vast, open, beautiful tundra landscapes; the amazing Alaska Range, with its continuous ridgeline of 10,000- to 14,000-foot peaks; and the wonderful Amphitheater and Clearwater Mountains. In addition to the physical splendor, these wide-open tundra plains are also prime habitat for migrating caribou herds and grazing moose. The dramatic landscape before you continues to be uplifted by massive plate tectonic forces, while glaciers and stream channels carve out spectacular U-shaped valleys and V-shaped canyons, respectively. You are literally watching the tug-of-war between mountain building and erosion. If you only have time for one road trip in this massive state, the Denali Highway should be it, because it truly captures the essence of interior Alaska. Be sure to bring your binoculars and your long camera lens, as you're likely

LEFT: THE BUSHKANA RIVER BUBBLES PAST A CAMPGROUND NESTLED IN THE LUSH BOREAL FOREST

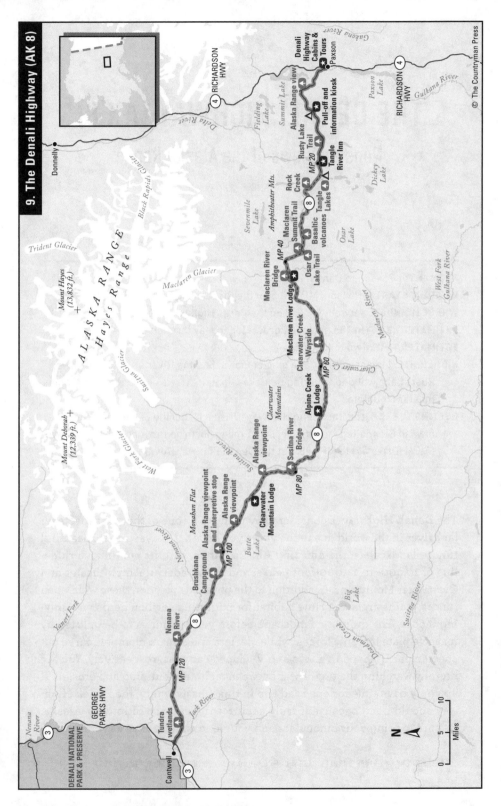

© The Countryman Press

RICHARDSON HWY (4)

RICHARDSON HWY (4)

Gakona River

Paxson

Denali Highway Cabins & Tours

Alaska Range view

Pull-off and information kiosk

Rusty Lake

MP 20 Trail

Tangle River Inn

Paxson Lake

Dickey Lake

Fielding Lake

Summit Lake

Delta River

Donnelly

Black Rapids Glacier

Trident Glacier

Mount Hayes (13,832 ft.)

ALASKA RANGE

Hayes Range

Maclaren Glacier

Amphitheater Mts.

Rock Creek

Maclaren Summit Trail

Basaltic volcanoes

Tangle Lakes

Osar Lake Trail

(8)

Sevenmile Lake

Osar Lake

West Fork Gulkana River

Maclaren River

MP 40

Maclaren River Bridge

Maclaren River Lodge

Clearwater Creek Wayside

Clearwater Cr.

MP 60

Alpine Creek Lodge

(8)

Clearwater Mountains

Clearwater River

Suzitna River

Glacier

West Fork Glacier

Mount Deborah (12,339 ft.)

Suzitna River

Alaska Range viewpoint

Susitna River Bridge

MP 80

Clearwater Mountain Lodge

Alaska Range viewpoint

Monahan Flat

Alaska Range viewpoint and interpretive stop

Butte Lake

Big Lake

Deadman Creek

Susitna River

Brushkana Campground

MP 100

Nenana River

Yanert Fork

Nenana River

(8)

MP 120

Jack River

GEORGE PARKS HWY

(3)

DENALI NATIONAL PARK & PRESERVE

Tundra wetlands

Cantwell

(3)

N

0 5 10 Miles

to spot moose. You may even spot the migrating Nelchina caribou herd if you're driving this road in the fall.

Fuel Note: Be sure to fuel up in Glennallen or Gulkana Junction if you're driving from the south, or in Delta if you're driving from the north along the Richardson Highway, to make sure you have enough fuel to make it along the Richardson Highway plus the 135 miles of the Denali Highway. Make sure you have a range of at least 250 miles. Motorcyclists will be wise to carry an extra couple of gallons of fuel strapped to the back of their cycles. There is often fuel at Triangle Lakes; however, early and late in the season this fuel-up location may not be available. There is no diesel at Triangle.

Mile Marker Note: Unlike most of the backroads and byways in this book, there are not dependable mile markers along the Denali Highway; some are present, some are not. Therefore, you might want to set your trip odometer to zero to help you locate and keep track of the various mileage locations used below.

Driving Note: The Denali Highway is gravel, sometimes muddy, and difficult to maintain. During dry weather, which is very common in the summer, this

THE ALASKA RANGE EXTENDS FOR OVER 100 MILES

road tends to be very dusty. The dust is typically very fine-grained, which means you can create huge clouds when traveling, even at moderate speeds. This dust can be hazardous to oncoming traffic. Here's a good rule of the road for any gravel road, but particularly for the Denali Highway and its super-fine dust: Slow down and pull off to the side of the road for oncoming traffic. Other dust-conscious drivers will do the same. Slowing down will dramatically reduce the dimensions and longevity of the dust clouds, making for safer driving, a lot less dust on and in your vehicle, and an overall more pleasant driving experience.

Traveling Off-Road Note: If you travel off-road, particularly in an ATV, with which you can get many miles away from the highway, be sure to carry some basic survival supplies: a few bottles of water, some food, some matches and a fire starter, a reflective surface for signaling, and a whistle. Dress in layers and bring extra clothes, particularly raingear and a hat and gloves. If your vehicle breaks down you'll likely have to walk back to the highway, and you need to be prepared to do so safely. And if you are injured, you need to be able to have some basic supplies of food, water, fire, clothing, and a way to signal potential rescuers. It doesn't take much time to prepare a simple survival kit that can make the difference between life and death.

Prior to the building of the Parks Highway in the 1970s, this was the only road to Denali National Park, and hence the name. For the most glorious version of your journey along the Denali Highway, plan to drive this road in the autumn, when the over 2,000 square miles of foreground Arctic tundra will be carpeted in the beautiful reds, oranges, and yellows of their fall clothing and juxtaposed against the snow- and ice-topped peaks of the massive Alaska Range. Along much of your Denali Highway tour, your view will be of this gorgeous Arctic tundra in the foreground and the awesome Alaska Range or Amphitheater or Clearwater Mountains in the background. This dramatic two-part landscape of soaring Alaska Range peaks fronted by vast tundra plains is the product of the northerly latitude of this area plus the high altitudes created by the plate tectonic forces that built, and continue to build, the Alaska and associated mountain ranges.

The Denali Highway is mostly gravel, remote, and is often in fair to poor condition. You will frequently encounter washboards, ruts, and potholes, depending upon how the weather has been and how recently the road grader has been along any particular section of road. Drive slowly, enjoy the landscape, and try dry/primitive camping at least one evening.

IN THE AREA

Accommodations, Fuel, and Food

MP 0 (PAXSON): DENALI HIGHWAY CABINS AND TOURS, 907-987-0977, www.denalihwy.com. Offers picturesque log cabins, tent cabins, and a cottage near Paxson and the Denali Highway. $$.

MP 19: TANGLE RIVER INN, 907-892-4022 (winter), 907-822-3970 (summer), www.tangleriverinn.com. Provides lodging (cabins and rooms), food, fuel (unleaded but no diesel), groceries, a liquor store, and canoe rentals. These are the only services along the Denali Highway. Open May–September. $–$$.

MP 80: SUSITNA LODGE, 907-452-2739, www.silvergulch.com/restaurant. htm. Offers a good selection of locally made brews and a wide variety of comfort foods. $–$$.

MP 42: DENALI HIGHWAY TOURS AND CABINS, www.denalihighway tours.com. Accommodations and tour guide services with a green focus, located where the highway crosses the Maclaren River. $$.

MP 42: DELTA OUTDOORS ADVENTURES, 907-388-6039, deltaoutdoor adventures.com. Cabin rentals and tour guiding where the highway crosses the Maclaren River. Guided ATV, dogsled, horseback riding, and hiking tours. $$.

MP 42: MACLAREN RIVER LODGE, 907-331-3518, www.maclarenlodge .com. Rooms, restaurant, store, tire repair, jet boat rides, canoe rentals, and snowmobile tours. $$.

MP 68: ALPINE CREEK LODGE, 907-743-0565, alpinecreeklodge.com. Lodging, restaurant, hunting, fishing, ATV tours, and snowmobiling. $$.

MP 82: CLEARWATER MOUNTAIN LODGE, 907-203-1057, www.clear watermountainlodge.com. Accommodations, restaurant/bar, air taxi service, fuel (no diesel). $$.

Camping

MP 21.5: TANGLE LAKES CAMPGROUND. www.campgroundsalaska.com /tangle-lakes-campground.php. Twenty-five fully developed campsites with

HIKING OPPORTUNITIES ABOUND
ALONG THE DENALI HIGHWAY

a designated put-in on the Delta National Wild and Scenic River. Look for moose and caribou ranging through here and particularly in the fall. $.

MP 104: BRUSHKANA CAMPGROUND. A developed campground with well-separated campsites in the middle of an old-growth white spruce forest next to the north-flowing Brushkana River. Includes a 2.5-mile-long Brushkana Creek trail and streamside walking path and a day-use picnic area. Wonderful family camping location with room for kids to safely ride bikes. $.

DRY CAMPING: There are many dry camping opportunities all along the Denali Highway.

Attractions and Recreation

Section One: Early Views of the Alaska Ridge

MP 6.5: FIRST ALASKA RANGE VIEWPOINT AND GEOLOGY KIOSK. This is a must-stop location to soak in your first awesome views and learn a bit about the local geology. The largest glacier that you see in your view to

VIEW OF THE ALASKA RANGE FROM MP 6.5

the northwest is the Gakona Glacier, flowing down from an ice field at the crest of the Alaska Range.

Section Two: Great Walking Tundra, Camping, Floating, and Views of the Amphitheater Mountains

MP 11.5: SOUTH SIDE PULL-OFF AND INFORMATION KIOSK. Here the highway is wrapping around some foreground tundra-covered hills. Enjoy the information kiosk and the great berry picking along the roadside. However, the real gem at this location is a double-track ORV path on the north side of the road, back about 50 yards, that takes you up to a flat camping spot, and then continues on up to the top of the rounded tundra-covered hills. If you're ready to camp and can negotiate this double track (it's passable with a high-ground-clearance four-wheel-drive vehicle), drive up there and establish a base camp. From your base camp, hike the rest of the way north to the rounded ridgeline across the delightful walking tundra for some jaw-dropping views of the Alaska Range and the vast foreground tundra at your feet. If you can't drive up this double-track ORV track, simply park and camp at the turnout and hike up the mud track.

MP 15–22: TANGLE LAKES (ARCHAEOLOGICAL REGION). There is great canoeing and rafting along this 16-mile-long sequence of stream channels and lakes, formed by retreating glaciers, that makes up the Tangle Lakes area at the headwaters of the National Wild and Scenic River section of the Delta River drainage. There's a designated put-in at the Tangle Lakes

A CLASSIC GLACIAL U-SHAPED VALLEY IN THE AMPHITHEATER MOUNTAINS

Campground for a multiday rafting trip down to the Gulkana River, paralleling the Richardson Highway.

MP 16: RUSTY LAKE WALKING TRAIL. This is less than a mile long but a real treat! Follow the path across a wide variety of tundra environments, including blueberry and currant bush bogs; very short-cropped, lichen-covered walking tundra; and soggy, moss-rich muskeg and tussock tundra characterized by large tussocks of grass. While on the shores of Rusty Lake, notice that this is a beaver dam–enhanced lake, complete with a beaver lodge. Simply follow the rock cairns to the lake.

MP 17–18: TERRIFIC VIEWS OF GLACIAL VALLEY. Look through this classic glacially carved valley, known as Landmark Gap, cut through the middle of the Amphitheater Mountains, framing spectacular views of the high peaks of the Alaska Range beyond.

MP 25: ROCK CREEK. This is a favored fishing spot with streamside primitive camping. Views north offer more great Alaska Range views through the U-shaped Landmark Gap valley. There is also a 3-mile-long ATV, hiking, and biking road that leads north to Landmark Lake, which sits in the middle of Landmark Gap.

MP 30.5: ORV, BIKING, OR HIKING TRACK. Ride or hike 3 miles north to Glacier Gap Lake, laid out along the front of the Amphitheater Mountains,

and then continue another 5 miles through the Amphitheater Mountains to Sevenmile Lake, which lies parallel to the north face of the range.

MP 33–36: BASALTIC VOLCANOES. Hike freely up onto the volcanoes that parallel the south side of the highway for great views of the surrounding landscape—look for moose and caribou.

Section Three: The Maclaren River Valley and Spectacular Views of Alaska Range

MP 37: MACLAREN SUMMIT TRAIL. This is a 2.6-mile trail north to Maclaren Summit with a terrific view of the Alaska Range and the Maclaren Glacier at the head of the Maclaren River Valley.

MP 37: OSCAR LAKE TRAIL. A 7-mile trail south over and through tundra to Oscar Lake. Bring your berry bucket!

MP 42: MACLAREN RIVER BRIDGE AND MACLAREN GLACIER VIEW-POINT. As you drive west across the Maclaren River valley, your view of Maclaren Glacier becomes increasingly complete. It's worth a stop at the bridge to take it all in.

THE SINUOUS SUSITNA RIVER DRAINS THE SOUTHERN SLOPES OF THE ALASKA RANGE

Section Four: The Clearwater Mountains

MP 55: CLEARWATER AND LITTLE CREEK CONFLUENCE BRIDGE CROSSING WAYSIDE. This site offers informal camping on both sides of the road east of the bridge. These are two lovely stream channels whose confluence is just upstream from the bridge crossing. Notice that the water in both channels is clear, hence the name Clearwater, indicating that these streams are not glacially fed. Both drain the Clearwater Mountains, which are directly in front of you to the north. This is a wonderful place to camp for the night.

Section Five: The Susitna River Valley and More Awesome Views of the Alaska Range

MP 80: BRIDGE ACROSS THE SUSITNA RIVER. Stop on the west side of the river and walk back across the bridge (watching for traffic, of course) for some wonderful views up and down the beautifully braided stream channel of the Susitna River. There are also additional dramatic views of the high peaks of the Alaska Range, in whose glaciers rise the waters of the Susitna River. Note the milky look of the Susitna, as contrasted with the clarity of the Clearwater Creek. The milkiness results from all the fine, glacially ground sediment that is released along with the waters of the melting glaciers.

MP 85.5: ALASKA RANGE VIEWPOINT. Pull off on a semicircular gravel area and scramble upslope along a dirt path for a couple hundred yards to enjoy amazing views of the Susitna River Valley, with its gorgeous braided stream channels and lowlands carpeted with white spruce–dominated, lake-dotted taiga forest. The tundra and forest front the massive, jagged, glacier-carved peaks and slopes of the Alaska Range, including Mount Deborah (12,339 feet) and Mount Hess (about 12,000 feet). Take an off-path walk across the alpine walking tundra filled with currants and blueberries. This doesn't look like much from the road, but believe me, this is a must!

THE NORTH-FLOWING NENANA RIVER ULTIMATELY JOINS THE YUKON RIVER

MP 90 PLUS: Gradually descend from tundra-dominated open slopes above the tree line to white spruce–dominated taiga/boreal forest.

MP 95: ALASKA RANGE VIEWPOINT. Drive down a short side road to an Alaska Range viewpoint and peak identification plaque as well as an interesting interpretive earthquake exhibit.

MP 100: ALASKA RANGE VIEWPOINT AND INTERPRETIVE STOP. Take in the view across the drainage divide between the south-flowing Susitna River drainage, which flows into Cook Inlet in the Gulf of Alaska, and the north-flowing Nenana drainage, which flows into the Yukon River and ultimately the Bering Sea.

Section Six: The Nenana River

MP 117: There are numerous places along this section of the highway where the roadbed is close and parallel to the north-flowing Nenana River, surrounded by taiga/boreal forest. Take some time to stop at one of several pullouts to enjoy the stream channel and surrounding forest.

MP 120–135: FINAL ROAD SECTION. Don't ignore the numerous tundra wetlands with beaver-enhanced ponds.

Festivals and Fairs

CANTWELL MUSIC FESTIVAL (SECOND WEEK IN JULY): Contact Gary Markley, garybanjo@gmail.com for details.

Outfitters and Tour Operators

DENALI FLY FISHING GUIDES: 907-768-1127, www.denaliflyfishing.com. Custom fly-fishing trips in the Alaska Range.

DENALI WILDERNESS OUTFITTERS: 907-768-2620. Kayaking and paddleboard adventures and rentals.

DENALI HIGHWAY CABINS AND TOURS: 907-987-0977, www.denalihwy .com. Picturesque log cabins, tent cabins, and a cottage near Paxson and the Denali Highway.

USEFUL INFORMATION

THE MILEPOST TRAVEL GUIDE: www.themilepost.com/highway-info/highways/denali-highway

ALASKA.ORG ROAD GUIDE: www.alaska.org/guide/denali-highway

EXPLORE NORTH ROAD GUIDE: www.explorenorth.com/library/roads/denali_highway_guide.html

TANGLE LAKES INFORMATION: www.en.wikipedia.org/wiki/Tangle_Lakes

10

THE DENALI PARK ROAD
Road to the Great One

FROM → TO: McKinley Park on the Parks Highway to the Kantishna Roadhouse
WHERE IT STARTS: Mile 237 on the Parks Highway (AK 3, Drive #11)
WHERE IT ENDS: Kantishna Roadhouse, MP 92
ESTIMATED LENGTH: 92 miles (first 15 miles is paved, the remainder is gravel); private vehicle access is limited to the first 15 miles unless you obtain a permit either through lottery or by applying for a professional permit
ESTIMATED TIME: One to seven days (13-hour one-day bus tour; single-day private drive with permit; or multiple-day bus and camping tour)
HIGHLIGHTS: Seeing Denali, Polychrome Overlook and Pass, Eielson Visitor Center, Wonder Lake, finding the tundra-covered Muldrow Glacier
GETTING THERE: Drive 237 miles north of Anchorage on Glenn Highway (AK 1) and Parks Highway (AK 3), or 120 miles south of Fairbanks on the Parks Highway (AK 3)

This 92-mile-long road into **Denali National Park and Preserve** is glorious indeed. From the entrance into the park you travel through the rugged foothills of the Alaska Range and over five major glacier-fed braided stream channels, including the Savage, Sanctuary, Teklanika, and two forks of the Toklat Rivers. You also cross the vast tundra plains that front the mighty, high, and saw-tooth-shaped peaks of the western end of the Alaska Range, whose denouement is the 20,310-foot summit of Denali (previously known as Mount McKinley). This is a huge landscape filled with wild glacier-fed rivers, towering glacier-covered peaks, vast stretches of Arctic tundra, and wild freely roaming megafauna. The landscapes and environments of Denali National Park and Preserve are much like they were 1,000 years ago, before

LEFT: MOUNT DENALI LOOMS OVER THE BEAUTIFUL TUNDRA PLAIN IN DENALI NATIONAL PARK

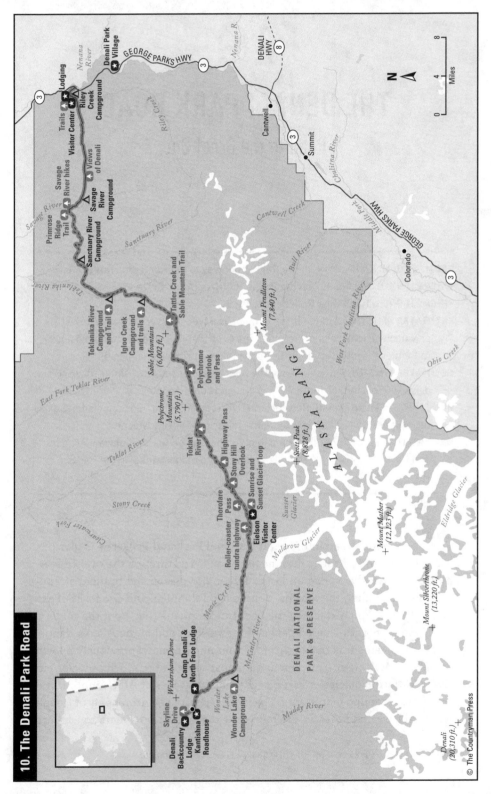

10. The Denali Park Road

Denali Park Village

GEORGE PARKS HWY

DENALI HWY

Nenana R.

Nenana River

Lodging

Trails

Visitor Center

Riley Creek Campground

Riley Creek

Cantwell

Summit

Chulitna River

Primrose Ridge Trail

Savage River hikes

Views of Denali

Savage River

Savage River Campground

Savage River Campground

George Parks Hwy

Colorado

Sanctuary River Campground

Sanctuary River

Teklanika River

Cantwell Creek

Bull River

West Fork Chulitna River

Middle Fork

Obio Creek

Teklanika River Campground and Trail

Igloo Creek Campground and trails

Tattler Creek and Sable Mountain Trail

East Fork Toklat River

Sable Mountain (6,002 ft.)

Mount Pendleton (7,840 ft.)

ALASKA RANGE

Polychrome Overlook and Pass

Polychrome Mountain (5,790 ft.)

Toklat River

Highway Pass

Stony Hill Overlook

Scott Peak (8,828 ft.)

Sunset Glacier

Mount Mather (12,123 ft.)

Eldridge Glacier

Stony Creek

Thorofare Pass

Sunrise and Sunset Glacier loop

Muldrow Glacier

Clearwater Fork

Roller-coaster tundra highway

Eielson Visitor Center

Mount Silverthrone (13,220 ft.)

Moose Creek

McKinley River

DENALI NATIONAL PARK & PRESERVE

Muddy River

Camp Denali & North Face Lodge

Wickersham Dome

Skyline Drive

Wonder Lake

Wonder Lake Campground

Denali (20,310 ft.)

Denali Backcountry Lodge

Kantishna Roadhouse

© The Countryman Press

even the hint of the arrival of Europeans. Many consider Denali National Park and Preserve to be the crown jewel of the national park system because of its wild and pristine nature and the intimate, yet protected, access provided by the Denali Park Road and bus system.

Perhaps the single core value and goal of the National Park Service in its management of the Denali National Park and Reserve is to preserve the wild, unspoiled nature of this vast iconic landscape, and rightly so. Unlike all the other roads in this book, the Denali Park Road is not one that you can simply choose to take a drive on any time you want. Past the first 15 miles, which you can freely drive in your own car without permit, the Denali Park Road is highly regulated. Most people who venture along this road do so on school bus–style transportation operated by the National Park Service. You can drive into campgrounds past the Savage River Campground at mile 13, but you'll need to obtain vehicle and camping permits well in advance to do so. If you prefer to enjoy Denali National Park in the winter, you can access the park via skiing or dogsled.

There are several bus options that all begin at the **Wilderness Access Center** near the visitors center. All the buses offer frequent planned and unplanned (for wildlife viewing) stops. The informal green bus tours vary from 5½ to 13 hours. More formal guided tours (beige buses) are also available. There are also camper buses that you can take out to various campsites along the highway. If you have one day to enjoy Denali National Park and Preserve, I recommend investing an entire day enjoying what is known as the Kantishna Experience, a 12- to 13-hour tour that leaves early in the morning and takes you all the way to the end of the road at Kantishna and back. If you'd like to experience being out in the middle of Denali but aren't really interested in a backpacking adventure, you might take advantage of the get-off-one-bus-and-get-on-another option, whereby you can take one of the informal bus tours, get off along a section of the highway that looks interesting to you, and walk along the road. When you are done walking, you can get on another one of the informal buses heading in either direction. The National Park Service website has good resources to help you plan your Denali road adventure and reserve a bus.

You can also participate in a yearly lottery to be one of 1,600 lucky people who have the opportunity to travel the Denali Park Road on their own for one day. Professional photographers and researchers can also apply for longer multiday permits (see page 157 on Denali Park Road lottery and permits).

Because of the restricted access, traveling this road is something of a logistical challenge. It's so spectacular and offers access to so many visual wonders—not the least of which is the potential for some close encounters with some very wild residents, such as fox, grizzly bear, caribou, moose, and even the stealthy wolves—that it is well worth the planning. Multiple pro-

THE BRAIDED STREAM CHANNEL OF THE TOKLAT RIVER

posals have been made to carve additional roads out into this landscape. To date they have all failed, and rightly so. The Denali Park Road is one that we should continue to both cherish and protect for us and for all who come after us, including the current wild residents and their descendants.

I've traveled the Denali Park Road many times and in various ways, including the 13-hour school bus–style drive, multiple times. I'm not one who is inclined to join large groups of people on outings, but I thoroughly enjoy the journey every time. My most memorable travel along this road is a bicycle trip on which a buddy and I pedaled all the way to Kantishna. And what a glorious trip it was. We were lit up by early morning and late afternoon sun, rained on by some late afternoon thunderstorms, were literally blown sideways and nearly off the road by 50-plus-knot winds when pedaling over Polychrome Pass, and yes, ate some dust from those passing school buses, but I wouldn't have changed a minute of it! We obtained

DENALI NATIONAL PARK IS A WONDERLAND FOR WILDLIFE, INCLUDING MOOSE

Parks Highway Side Trips

Here are three side trips to enjoy on your way up the Parks Highway from Anchorage to Denali National Park and Preserve.

Parks Highway MP 99: Talkeetna Junction and Visitor Information Cabin. Turn off for a 14-mile-long paved road to the town of Talkeetna, which offers numerous galleries and eateries, including the daily-in-summer Artisan Open Air Market.

THE HIGH PEAKS OF THE ALASKA RANGE AS SEEN FROM THE PARKS HIGHWAY

Parks Highway MP 115: Community of Trapper Creek and Petersville Road. This is the location of the pre-bridge Susitna River crossing. Check out the Trapper Creek Historic Post Office too. This is also the turnoff for the Petersville mining road, which provides access to historic and active mining sites as well as hiking and scenic ridgelines in Denali State Park.

Parks Highway MP 137, 156, and 136: Kesugi Ridge Hiking Trail. Hike through an old-growth boreal forest up to a beautiful alpine tundra–covered ridgeline offering spectacular views of Denali and companion peaks as well as other ridgelines and valleys of the Alaska Range and the Talkeetna Mountains. You can access this trail from multiple trailheads, including MP 137.6 (Upper Troublesome Creek Trailhead), MP 147 (Byers Lake Campground Trailhead), MP 156.5 (Ermine Hill Trailhead), and MP163.9 (Little Coal Creek Trailhead).

Denali Versus Mount McKinley

The native Koyukon Athabaskan people lived in the vicinity of the mountain we know as Denali for centuries before white men appeared. These natives called this massive and glorious mountain Denali, which means the high, tall, or great one, depending on how you interpret their language. In 1896 a gold prospector referred to the mountain as McKinley as a nod of political support for presidential candidate William McKinley from Ohio. For some reason that name stuck until 2015, when it was changed back to Denali, which is what Alaskans have always called it anyway.

camping permits to camp at the Riley Creek, Savage River, Teklanika Creek, and Wonder Lake campgrounds. We then stayed at Camp Denali, directly in front of Denali, for a glorious week of Denali adventures, which included hiking across alpine tundra–covered ridgelines behind the camp; navigating the spongy and marshy lowland tundra landscapes; hiking up to, along, and across portions of the braided stream channels of the wild McKinley River; and paddling across Wonder Lake, where we had an opportunity to watch a mother loon teach her single young how to dive and fish for food.

There are indeed many ways to access and enjoy the Denali Park Road. It will require planning, but whichever access method you choose—car, bus, bike, walk, ski, or dogsled—you can expect a grand adventure.

Denali Road Lottery and Professional Permits Note: The Denali Road Lottery typically opens May 1 and closes May 31. See www.nps.gov/dena/plan youryourvisit/road-lottery.htm.

Denali Professional Photography Special Road Travel Permits: The National Park Service also offers a special road permit program for professional photographers. It is a fairly extensive application form that includes documentation proving that you are a professional photographer and a substantial fee ($150 as of this writing). If you secure one of these special road travel permits, you will be able to travel the road in your own vehicle for the purposes of photographing Denali. Visit www.nps.gov and search for "Denali photography permits."

IN THE AREA

Accommodations, Fuel, and Food

PARKS HIGHWAY MP 231: DENALI PARK VILLAGE, 800-276-7734, www
.denaliparkvillage.com. Affordable, kid-friendly lodge 8 miles from Denali
National Park. $$.

MP 238 (NEAR NATIONAL PARK ENTRANCE): GRAND DENALI LODGE,
855-683-8600, www.denalialaska.com. Beautiful full-service hotel overlook-
ing entrance to Denali National Park. $$$.

**MP 238 (NEAR NATIONAL PARK ENTRANCE): MOUNT MCKINLEY
PRINCESS WILDERNESS LODGE,** 800-426-0500, www.princesslodges.com.
Full-service lodging accommodations offering a variety of tours. $$–$$$.

**MP 238.4 (NEAR NATIONAL PARK ENTRANCE): DENALI BLUFFS
HOTEL,** 855-683-8600, www.denalialaska.com. Affordable guest rooms and
a beautiful lodge with restaurant. It also offers tours. $–$$.

**MP 238.5 (NEAR NATIONAL PARK ENTRANCE): MCKINLEY CHALET
RESORT,** 800-544-0970, www.westmarkhotels.com. Large, full-service
resort. $$.

MP 239: 49TH STATE BREWING COMPANY (near National Park entrance),
907-683-2739, www.49statebrewing.com. Great steak and beer. Offers shut-
tle to and from Denali. $.

MP 90: CAMP DENALI AND NORTH FACE LODGE, 907-683-2290, www
.campdenali.com. Cabins and a lodge located 90 miles in, situated high on a
ridgeline above the surrounding landscape. Guests are treated to spectac-
ular views of a vast stretch of the Western Alaska Range directly in front
of the cabins, including Denali itself, Wonder Lake, the McKinley River,
the Muldrow Glacier, and vast tundra-covered plains. This is my favorite
lodging-based place to stay when I am in Denali. It offers many outdoor,
often educational activities, both guided and independent. Reserve your
stay early in the year. $$$.

MP 91: DENALI BACKCOUNTRY LODGE, 844-399-1784, www.alaskacol
lection.com/lodging/denali-backcountry-lodge. Beautiful backcountry lodge
on Moose Creek in the heart of Denali National Park. $$$.

MP 92: KANTISHNA ROADHOUSE, 800-942-7420, www.kantishnaroad house.com. Modern, backcountry, log-style lodge and cabins at the end of the road with all the fixings, including a saloon, a sled dog kennel, and access to many outdoor adventures. $$–$$$.

Camping

MP 5: RILEY CAMPGROUND, 800-622-7275, www.reservedenali.com. Large full-featured campground near the park entrance. A good staging area for launching your Denali National Park adventure.

MP 13: SAVAGE RIVER CAMPGROUND, 800-622-7275, www.reserve denali.com. At the edge of the boreal forest with views of Denali on clear days, this campground is about a mile before the Savage River crossing and within the 15-mile free access area.

MP 23: SANCTUARY RIVER CAMPGROUND, 800-622-7275, www.reserve denali.com. This is a small, quiet, seven-site, tent-only area.

MP 29: TEKLANIKA RIVER CAMPGROUND, 800-622-7275, www.reserve denali.com. You can ride a bus to this larger campground or drive your own vehicle, but you have to obtain both camping and vehicle permits well in advance. There are 53 sites for RVs and tents and there is a three-night stay minimum.

MP 34: IGLOO CREEK CAMPGROUND, 800-622-7275, www.reservedenali .com. Similar to the Sanctuary River Campground, this is a small tent-only area. You have more peace and quiet than in some of the larger camp-grounds such as Riley or Tek.

MP 90: WONDER LAKE CAMPGROUND, 800-622-7275, www.reserve denali.com. This lovely campground is located near the end of the Denali Park Road. Enjoy camping at the edge of the iconic, moraine-formed lake (over 200 feet deep) with access to hiking and canoeing.

Attractions and Recreation

MP 0–15: OPEN DENALI PARK ROAD. The first 15 miles is paved and open to private vehicles without having to obtain any permits or hop on a bus. If you only have half a day to enjoy Denali National Park, driving in these first

15 miles is well worth the journey, and you'll have access to several good hikes. On clear days you may even be able to see Denali around MP 10.

MP 0.75: MOUNT HEALY OVERLOOK TRAIL. Located between the park entrance and the visitors center, this easy-to-access 3- to 5-mile round-trip hike through boreal forest and then up onto tundra-covered slopes provides good views of the Nenana River valley and nearby ridges. You can continue this trail for an all-day hike to the summit of Mount Healy.

MP 1: HORSESHOE LAKE TRAIL. Close to the visitors center, this 3-mile trail is a lovely and easy hike through boreal forest along the Nenana River, providing lots of overviews of oxbow lakes, beaver dams, and beaver lodges along the floodplains of the river.

MP 1.5: DENALI NATIONAL PARK VISITOR CENTER. Plan to spend some time in this beautiful and sprawling log building, packed with information. Apply for bus reservations and hiking permits here, although both are easily and preferably obtained in advance of your arrival at Denali National Park.

MP 9–11: FIRST VIEWS OF DENALI. Around MP 10, the vista opens up as the boreal forest disappears. Look west along the mountain ridge to see the top 8,000 feet of Denali on the skyline, over 70 miles away.

MP 15: SAVAGE RIVER TRAILHEAD. You may drive the first 15 miles to this trailhead near the Savage River without a permit. Enjoy a 2-mile loop trail across tundra along both sides of the Savage River, looking out for Dall sheep, caribou, and gulls that frequent this stream channel. This is a good family hike. For more of a hiking challenge and some expansive views, you can climb to the nearby ridgeline on a steep informal trail, or take the 4-mile-long Savage Alpine Trail.

MP 15.5: SAVAGE RIVER STREAM CHANNEL TREK. The highway crosses the first of the five major glacially fed, braided stream channels on the Denali Park Road here. Scramble down to the stream channel from either end of the bridge and make your way along the gravel streambed.

MP 16: PRIMROSE RIDGE TRAIL. Hike across the Arctic tundra and view pink primrose flowers and red birch trees while keeping your eyes peeled for Dall sheep. This area is also known for its good birding.

MP 30.2: TEKLANIKA RIVER TRAIL. Another great opportunity to hike one of the wonderful braided stream channels that drain the north slopes of the Alaska Range. You can hike either way on the stream channel.

MP 34: IGLOO CREEK CAMPGROUND AND HIKING TRAILS. If you are riding one of the buses, this is a good place to exit for a half day of exploration. Take one of the numerous day-hike trails that lead from the campground around the slopes of Igloo Mountain. Sightings of Dall sheep, moose, and bear are common, and you can visit some honest-to-goodness dinosaur tracks. Catch another one of the buses moving in either direction when you finish with your Igloo area adventures.

MP 37.5: TATTLER CREEK AND SABLE MOUNTAIN TRAIL. Follow Tattler Creek up a steep ravine to a ridgeline overlooking the Sable Pass area. This is a good day hike, but the ridgeline can be a bit hot and dry, so bring extra water.

MP 46–47: POLYCHROME OVERLOOK AND PASS. One of the more stunning viewing areas along the Denali Park Road, this is a wonderful section of road along which to walk. Leave the confines of your bus and walk to your heart's delight, then snag another bus moving in either direction.

MP 53: TOKLAT RIVER. This is another wonderful braided stream channel hiking opportunity. Keep your eyes open for moose, bear, and even wolves using the Toklat gravel streambed as a wild highway.

MP 58: HIGHWAY PASS. At almost 4,000 feet above sea level, this pass is the highest pass on the Denali Park Road. As you drive up onto higher and drier ridges during your 5-mile rise from the Toklat River to the high point on Highway Pass, notice how the healthy, white spruce–dominated forest

THE MULTIPLE BRAIDED STREAMS OF THE TOKLAT RIVER IN FALL

that thrives around the Toklat River thins as you gain elevation and move out of the prime reproduction and growing conditions for the white spruce.

MP 58: STONY HILL OVERLOOK. Stop here for a great view of Denali and some vast views across the wide-open Arctic tundra. Scan your binoculars slowly across the tundra and you just might see a wolf loping across the landscape. Late afternoons and early evenings are the best viewing times.

MP 64.5: THOROFARE PASS. This is a well-known nesting area for migrating birds. Look for, be careful of, and do not touch or disturb nests of migrating birds such as the yellow-legged and golden plover.

MP 66: SUNRISE AND SUNSET GLACIER LOOP. For a spectacular off-trail, cross-country classic Denali journey, consider this two- to four-day backpacking adventure to the twin Sunrise and Sunset Glaciers. Begin from the Eielson Visitor Center, then hike up either Gorge or Sunrise Creeks to the Sunrise Glacier. Return on the Thoroughfare River. This is a wonderful opportunity to see both wolves and grizzly bears on their own terms. Just keep your distance!

MP 66: EIELSON VISITOR CENTER. Enjoy fabulous views of Denali, now only 33 miles away to the west, along with numerous guided and nonguided learning and hiking opportunities. I've seen caribou here on several visits.

MP 66–85: ROLLER-COASTER TUNDRA HIGHWAY AND HIDDEN GLA-CIER. From the Eielson Visitor Center to Wonder Lake, the Denali Park Road rolls across the landscape like a roller coaster and offers wide-open views of the western end of the Alaska Range, including the magnificent Denali. You travel across broad, open stretches of marshy and brushy tundra dotted with literally thousands of kettle lakes, formed when massive glaciers that covered this entire landscape retreated and left behind huge ice chunks, which depressed the ground, melted, and filled in these depressions. These marshy tundra landscapes are prime habitat for moose, and look for caribou that prefer to travel the higher and drier ridges. There's another gem here, a large glacier that is hidden in plain sight. Because the Alaska Range is so high and continuous, it forms a barrier that forces most of the moisture arriving from the Gulf of Alaska to be precipitated, largely as snow, along the southern slopes of the range. Because of this, most of the glaciers, and nearly all of the large ones, flow down the south-facing slopes of the Alaska Range (visible from Drive # 9). Here, on the north slope of the Alaska Range, there are fewer and typically smaller glaciers. One exception to this

A WELL ANTLERED CARIBOU USES THE FACILITIES AT EIELSON VISITOR CENTER

BERRIES ABOUND THROUGHOUT THE
BRUSHY TUNDRA

is the Muldrow Glacier, formed from several smaller glaciers flowing off the northeastern flank of the Denali massif. As you look south toward the southeast flank of Denali, you may wonder where the heck is the glacier? Well, it's right in front of you, but because it is so slow moving there is an entire tundra ecosystem growing on top of it. Most people who drive this road never see this huge glacier, but if you look carefully along the bottom of the south flanks of Mount Silverthrone, Mount Deception, and Mount Mather, the three prominent peaks to the east of Denali, you will indeed see a long, glacier-shaped ridge that is covered with boreal forest and tundra. If you have binoculars, look carefully and you'll see patches of white here and there where the slowly moving glacier has broken open the overlying boreal forest blanket, revealing the glacial ice beneath. Another way to find the Muldrow Glacier is to follow the McKinley River east upstream to its source, which is at the mouth of this hidden glacier.

MP 85: WONDER LAKE CAMPGROUND. Made famous by Ansel Adams's classic photograph of Denali with Wonder Lake in the foreground, this campsite offers some great opportunities for hiking and canoeing. Look for loons rearing their young as they ply the lake. From the south side campground, head off across the tundra to explore, or walk or take one of the passing buses to the north side of the lake for some excellent nob and ridge hiking and berry picking. Large caribou are frequently visible here in August and early September. There is also a hiking trail access through the boreal forest to the braided stream channel of the McKinley River, known as the McKinley Bar, which forms at the mouth of the Muldrow Glacier only a few miles upstream. Be sure to bring your bug spray and watch for grizzly bears, moose, caribou, and wolves.

MP 91.5: SKYLINE DRIVE. Walk this gravel road up into the Kantishna Hills and take advantage of its access to Quigley Ridge and Wickersham Dome. Then hike cross-country on your own path over beautiful, short-cropped walking tundra. The higher you go, the better the views. There are private inholdings sprinkled throughout the lower slopes, so it's best to remain on the gravel road until you reach the ridgeline. Then you're free to roam.

Festivals and Fairs

Denali Area

DENALI MUSIC FESTIVAL (THIRD WEEK IN JULY): www.nps.gov/dena/getinvolved/denalimusicfestival.htm

DENALI WINTERFEST (THIRD WEEK IN FEBRUARY): www.nps.gov/dena/planyourvisit/winterfest.htm

DENALI WILDWATER FESTIVAL (THIRD WEEK IN AUGUST): Search online for Denali Wildwater Festival.

Talkeetna Area

TALKEETNA ARTISAN OPEN AIR MARKET (SATURDAY–MONDAY THROUGHOUT SUMMER): www.talkeetnachamber.org. Local artists show their wares in an outdoor marketplace. Features concerts at 5 PM Fridays and multiple tasty eateries from which to choose.

TRAPPER CREEK BLUEGRASS FESTIVAL (MEMORIAL DAY WEEKEND): www.nps.gov/dena/planyourvisit/calendar.htm.

TALKEETNA WINTERFEST (LAST WEEK IN NOVEMBER THROUGH FIRST WEEK IN DECEMBER): www.talkeetnachamber.org. Features annual Wilderness Woman Contest and the Bachelor Auction and Ball.

Outfitters and Tour Operators

DENALI OUTDOOR CENTER: 888-303-1925, www.denalioutdoorcenter.com. Offers paddle and float trips on the Nenana River.

DENALI RAFT ADVENTURES: 888-683-2234, www.denaliraft.com. Offering whitewater and scenic river adventures in Denali National Park.

DENALI FLY FISHING GUIDES: 907-768-1127, www.denaliflyfishing.com. Custom fly-fishing trips in the Alaska Range.

DENALI SOUTHSIDE RIVER GUIDES (TALKEETNA): 907-733-7238, www.denaliriverguides.com. Kayak and rafting float trips around Talkeetna and the south side of Denali.

DENALI WILDERNESS OUTFITTERS: 907-768-2620. Kayaking and paddleboard adventures and rentals.

K2 AVIATION: 800-764-2291, www.flyk2.com. Flight-seeing tours of Denali and the Alaska Range.

DENALI AIR: 907-683-2261, www.denaliair.com. Flight-seeing tours of Denali and the Alaska Range.

KANTISHNA AIR: 907-644-8222, www.katair.com. Flight-seeing tours of Denali.

FLY DENALI: 907-683-2359, www.flydenali.com. Flight-seeing tours of Denali and the Alaska Range.

USEFUL INFORMATION

THE MILEPOST TRAVEL GUIDE—DENALI NATIONAL PARK AND PRESERVE: www.themilepost.com/major-attractions/denali-national-park-and-preserve

THE MILEPOST TRAVEL GUIDE—PARKS HIGHWAY: www.themilepost.com/highway-info/highways/parks-highway

ALASKA.ORG ROAD GUIDE—DENALI PARK ROAD: www.alaska.org/guide/denali-park-road

ALASKA.ORG ROAD GUIDE—PARKS HIGHWAY: www.alaska.org/guide/anchorage-to-denali-national-park

DENALI NATIONAL PARK PLANNING GUIDE: www.nps.gov/dena/planyourvisit/visiting-denali.htm. Plan your Denali Park Road adventure and reserve a bus.

DENALI PARK ROAD MAP: www.denali101.com/denalinationalpark/Denali_Park_road_map.html

DENALI NATIONAL PARK SHUTTLE BUS AND CAMPGROUND RESERVATIONS: 800-622-7275, www.reservedenali.com

MAPS OF DENALI NATIONAL PARK: www.nps.gov/dena/planyourvisit/maps.htm

TALKEETNA FAIRS AND FESTIVALS: www.alaska.org/destination/talkeetna/festivals

DENALI STATE PARK INFORMATION: www.dnr.alaska.gov/parks/units/denali1.htm

PETERSVILLE ROAD INFORMATION: www.alaskavisit.com/things-to-do/scenic-drives/petersville-road

11

THE GLENN HIGHWAY (AK 1)
Up Close and Personal with Glacier Landscapes

FROM → TO: Palmer to Glennallen

WHERE IT STARTS: MP 49.5 at turnoff to Hatcher Pass

WHERE IT ENDS: Glennallen

ESTIMATED LENGTH: 136 miles, all paved

ESTIMATED TIME: One to two days

HIGHLIGHTS: Matanuska Glacier; Sheep Mountain, Trail and Camp Creeks area; Alascom Dome Road; Lake Louise

GETTING THERE: Drive from the beginning of the Glenn Highway in downtown Anchorage 51 miles north to the turnoff for Hatcher Pass (Drive #13) on the north side of the town of Palmer. Then continue on the Glenn Highway (AK 1)

I begin 50 miles from the start of the Glenn (formally titled the Glennallen Highway, AK 1, and named after Captain Edwin F. Glenn, who explored this route in 1898 while searching for a passageway from Cook Inlet into the interior of Alaska) because this is where the backroad nature of the highway begins. Note: In Drive #12 I cover an older section of the Glenn Highway (the Old Glenn) and several side road adventures. So, we begin our current Glenn Highway adventure at MP 50 near the turnoff to another Alaska drive, #13, the road to Hatcher Pass. I use the physical Glenn Highway milepost signs to reference locations.

The first 50 miles of our **Glenn Highway** journey follow along and provide spectacular views of the Matanuska Glacier–fed, braided stream channel of the Matanuska River and its valley. Much of the first 25 miles is at or near river level, with the Glenn jogging occasionally away from the stream channel, through the boreal forest, and along marshes and lakes. There are

LEFT: ROLLING TOWARD LAKE LOUISE

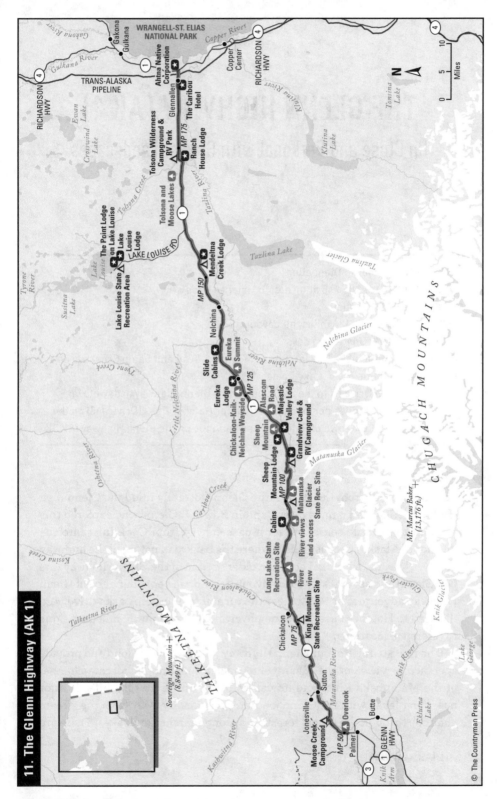

11. The Glenn Highway (AK 1)

WRANGELL-ST. ELIAS
NATIONAL PARK

TRANS-ALASKA
PIPELINE

RICHARDSON
HWY

RICHARDSON
HWY

Gakona

Gulkana

Copper
Center

Ahtna Native
Corporation

Glennallen

The Caribou
Hotel

Tolsona Wilderness
Campground &
RV Park

MP 175

Ranch
House Lodge

Tolsona and
Moose Lakes

The Point Lodge
on Lake Louise

Lake
Louise
Lodge

LAKE LOUISE RD

Lake Louise State
Recreation Area

Mendeltna
Creek Lodge

MP 150

Nelchina

Slide
Cabins

Eureka
Summit

Eureka
Lodge

MP 125

Chickaloon-Knik-
Nelchina Wayside

Alascom
Road

Majestic
Valley Lodge

Sheep
Mountain Lodge

Grandview Café &
RV Campground

Matanuska
Glacier
State Rec. Site

Sheep
Mountain

MP 100

Cabins

River views
and access

Long Lake State
Recreation Site

River
view

Chickaloon

MP 75

King Mountain
State Recreation Site

Sutton

Jonesville

Overlook

Moose Creek
Campground

MP 50

Palmer

Butte

GLENN
HWY

TALKEETNA MOUNTAINS

Sovereign Mountain
(8,849 ft.)

CHUGACH MOUNTAINS

Mt. Marcus Baker
(13,176 ft.)

N

Miles

0   5   10

© The Countryman Press

sections along this first segment where the highway is immediately next to the stream channel. Near one of these, you may witness active erosion of the banks that threatens the road and other surrounding structures during periods of flooding, particularly during the spring runoff. The Glenn Highway in these areas is on the previous floodplain that is now being re-eroded by the natural meandering processes of the **Matanuska River**. You'll also notice that the waters are milky and opaque. This is due to its being fed primarily by the melting of the sediment-filled Matanuska glacier that you drive by between MP 95 and MP 100.

Around MP 75, the Glenn begins its climb up onto the south-facing slopes above the Matanuska River, providing numerous spectacular views up and across this glacially carved valley that is now being modified by stream channel processes. As you drive along the valley, keep in mind that just a few thousand years ago, the **Matanuska Glacier**, as impressive as it is cur-

THE MAIN CHANNEL OF THE MATANUSKA RIVER WEAVES THROUGH FALL COLORS NORTH OF THE CHUGACH MOUNTAINS

THE GLACIER-FED MATANUSKA RIVER

rently, was far more massive. In fact, it occupied the entire length, breadth, and nearly all the height of this valley all the way down to the head of what is now Cook Inlet, where it contributed to an even larger glacier that carved out Cook Inlet. On your journey up to the Matanuska Glacier you have multiple opportunities to view it from a distance. Once you reach the glacier, you can take a side trip down and over to the glacier and actually scramble onto it for a very cool (pun intended) picnic. Traveling this long, deep, and narrow drainage in the fall is spectacular indeed.

Once you pass the Matanuska Glacier, you will move up into the headwaters of the **Nelchina River** and the Copper River drainage basin. Here you drive through and explore wide-open a tundra-covered and lake-dotted landscape. Along the entire length of the Glenn you are treated to spectacular views to the south of the high, rugged ridgeline of the Chugach Mountains. If you look carefully, you'll be able to see a few of the north-flowing glaciers that are grinding slowly down from the high Chugach peaks. Most of the Chugach glaciers flow south into Cook Inlet because the high Chugach Mountains form a precipitation barrier that encourages most of the snow to fall on the south-facing slopes, thereby feeding south-flowing glaciers. One major exception to this is the Tazlina Glacier, which is visible from the Lake Louise side road near MP 160.

From the marshy and lake-filled headwaters of the Nelchina River, which you can investigate on a fascinating side road to Alascom Dome, you will continue on to higher and drier boreal forest–dominated environments, with plenty of interspersed marshy tundra, meadows, and lakes, as you make your way toward Glennallen at the end of the road. Along the way you have

many opportunities to access the backcountry via hiking, biking, skiing, or ORVs and by taking a side road to the lovely Lake Louise. You also pass many state of Alaska–stocked fishing lakes, including Tolsona and Moose Lakes. For the last 10 miles as you approach Glennallen, on clear days you will have some good views of volcanic peaks of 16,237-foot Mount Sanford and 12,010-foot Mount Drum on the eastern skyline.

IN THE AREA

Accommodations, Fuel, and Food

MP 95: BEAR DEN CABINS, 907-745-2395, www.facebook.com/bearden cabins. Two small, sweet cabins near the west end of the road. $–$$.

MP 95: HOMESTEAD GUEST CABINS, 907-745-4514, www.homestead cabinsak.com. Beautiful log cabins nestled at the edge of the forest. $–$$.

MP 102: LONG RIFLE LODGE AND RESTAURANT, 907-745-5151, www .longriflelodge.co. Great views of the Matanuska Glacier. $–$$.

MP 109.5: TUNDRA ROSE GUEST COTTAGES. 907-745-5865, www.alaska .net/~tundrose. Affordable, quiet, comfortable cabins with good views of the Matanuska Glacier. $–$$.

VIEW FROM THE TOP OF THE LAKE LOUISE ROAD LOOKING SOUTH TOWARDS THE TAZLINA GLACIER AND LAKE

MP 109.7: GRANDVIEW CAFÉ & RV CAMPGROUND, 907-745-4480, www.grandviewrv.com. Good food and camping near the Matanuska Glacier. $–$$.

MP 113.5: SHEEP MOUNTAIN LODGE, 907-745-5121, www.sheepmountain .com. Cute, affordable cabins and a lodge restaurant in a historic location with stunning views of the surrounding Sheep Mountain area. $–$$.

MP 115: MAJESTIC VALLEY LODGE, 907-746-2930, www.majesticvalley lodge.com. Weddings, retreats, accommodations, and a restaurant surrounded by the glorious Chugach Mountains. $$.

MP 128: EUREKA LODGE, 907-822-3808, www.eurekalodge.com/Eureka_ Site/Home.html. Fuel, groceries, restaurant, lounge, RV parking, and lodging. $–$$.

MP 135: SLIDE CABINS, 907-822-3883, www.slidemountaincabins.net. Fully equipped cabins and an RV park in Nelchina. $–$$.

MP 153: MENDELTNA CREEK LODGE, 907-822-3346, www.mendeltna creeklodge.com. Eco-friendly cabins, hostel, and tent sites along lovely Mendeltna Creek with a beautiful hand-built log lodge offering a variety of activities, including fly-fishing, biking, and skiing along 50 miles of dog-friendly trails. $–$$.

MP 160: THE POINT LODGE ON LAKE LOUISE, 800-808-2018 or 907-822-5566, www.thepointlodge.com. Lovely lodge on a point that juts out into Lake Louise, located 17 miles north on Lake Louise Road. $$.

MP 160: LAKE LOUISE LODGE, 877-878-3311 or 907-822-3311, www.lakelouiselodge.com. Well-known full-service lodge and restaurant which offers boat rentals on the lakeshore. $$.

MP 173: RANCH HOUSE LODGE, 907-822-5634, www.facebook.com/pg/ranchhouselodge/about. Motel accommodations close to Glennallen. $–$$.

MP 187: THE CARIBOU HOTEL, 907-822-3302, www.caribouhotel.com. Hotel-style lodging in Glennallen. $–$$.

Camping

MP 54: MOOSE CREEK CAMPGROUND. Small but well-developed campsite for both RV and tent campers with access to Moose Creek. Good stopping point for a late-starting day. $.

MP 76: KING MOUNTAIN STATE CAMPGROUND. A 24-space developed campground next to the Matanuska River, located just west of the town of Chickaloon. $.

THE HISTORIC LAKE LOUISE LODGE

MP 101: MATANUSKA GLACIER STATE RECREATION SITE, 907-745-5151. Developed state park campsite next to a formal parking area and viewing platform of the Matanuska Glacier. This is a good family campsite with lots of room to move around, and it's next to a nice slopeside hike through boreal forest offering multiple viewpoints of the glacier. $.

MP 153: MENDELTNA CREEK LODGE, 907-822-3346, www.mendeltna creeklodge.com. Eco-friendly cabins, hostel, and tent sites along lovely Mendeltna Creek with a beautiful hand-built log lodge offering a variety of activities, including fly-fishing, biking, and skiing along 50 miles of dog-friendly trails. $–$$.

MP 160: LAKE LOUISE STATE RECREATION AREA, 907-441-7575. Drive 17 miles north on the Lake Louise Road to twin campgrounds (Lake Louise and Army Point), both with boat launches on lovely Lake Louise. $.

MP 173: TOLSONA WILDERNESS CAMPGROUND AND RV PARK, 907-822-3900, www.tolsonacampground.com. Family-oriented tent and RV camping near Glennallen. $–$$.

Attractions and Recreation

MP 50: KNIK AND MATANUSKA RIVERS OVERLOOK. At the very beginning of the drive, turn into the paved pull-off on the east side of the road and scramble up the bank to some awesome views of the Knik River Valley on the right (southeast) and the Matanuska River Valley on the left (northeast). There are also spectacular views to the south of the Chugach Mountains, including the dominant Pioneer Peak. You can't see these views until you climb the embankment.

MP 84.5: RIVER VIEW. Slow down when you reach mile 84 for small turnout at mile 84.5. This is my favorite view of the Matanuska River Valley. It's a small turnout on the sharp corner, but it's worth the challenge of getting in there!

LAKE LOUISE OFFERS ISLAND-DOTTED SERENITY

MP 85.5: LONG LAKE STATE RECREATION SITE. Day-use picnicking, fishing, and easy-access floating on Long Lake.

MP 95–98: SEVERAL LARGE TURNOUTS WITH GREAT VIEWS. Take the time to pull off at any of several long and broad turnouts for good places to stretch your legs and enjoy some terrific views of the Matanuska River Valley and the high Chugach Mountains. These are excellent turnouts for larger rigs.

MP 96.5: HICKS CREEK LAUNCH SITE. The Nova River Guides launch their rafts from this site for float trips down the Matanuska River. There is also a company store where you can inquire about flow trips.

MP 101: MATANUSKA GLACIER STATE RECREATION SITE. This has a formal viewing area with excellent views up the Matanuska River toward the Matanuska Glacier. There is also a nice trail through a slope-side boreal forest with beautiful birch trees as well as views up toward the glacier. This is adjacent to a State Recreation Site camping area.

MP 102: ACCESS ROAD TO THE MATANUSKA GLACIER. This is a private road (Glacier Park Road), with a fee, that leads down to and then across the outwash plain to the terminus of the Matanuska Glacier. If you've never been up close and personal with a glacier, this is well worth the modest

THE MATANUSKA GLACIER AND CHUGACH MOUNTAINS

VIEW FROM THE ALASCOM HILL

fee. Local outfitters offer glacier adventure trips. This is a great picnic site within an easy day drive from Anchorage. Keep in mind as you drive over the channels of the Matanuska River that all that milky, opaque sediment-filled water is coming off the Matanuska Glacier, and that channel is flowing nonstop. There are massive quantities of water and sediment locked up in these glaciers!

MP 107–120: SHEEP MOUNTAIN, TRAIL CREEK, AND CAMP CREEK AREA. This recreation area includes the Chickaloon-Knik-Nelchina Trail System, a web of multiuse (hiking, skiing, biking, and ORV) trails that crisscross the higher and drier upland side slopes as well as the marshy tundra–covered lowlands. Even a short walk across one of the upland trails is rewarding.

MP 126.5: ALASCOM ROAD. Take this 3.5-mile-long gravel side road south across the lake-dotted drainage divide of the westward-flowing Matanuska River drainage system and the eastward-flowing Nelchina River system to excellent views of this broad stream-crossed and lake-dotted valley and surrounding mountains from the top of Alascom (Alaska Communications) Dome. There are numerous informal campsites here.

MP 126.5: CHICKALOON-KNIK-NELCHINA WAYSIDE. This large paved wayside on the north side of the road has restrooms and information kiosks, and provides access to recreation trails for hiking, skiing, and ORVs.

MP 130: DRAINAGE DIVIDE AND HIGH POINT ON THE GLENN HIGHWAY. Near the high point of the Glenn Highway at Eureka Summit (3,322 feet), the drainage system changes from the westward-flowing Matanuska River drainage to the east-flowing Nelchina River drainage basin. Notice that the first stream channel crossing is of the eastward-flowing Little Nelchina River.

MP 160: ROAD TO LAKE LOUISE STATE RECREATION AREA. Drive this delightful, rolling road north 16 miles through an open-canopy boreal forest, past numerous fish-stocked lakes, tundra meadows, and marshes. Your destination is the lovely, island-dotted Lake Louise, where there are boat launches, campgrounds, and several lakeside lodges. Near the beginning of the road, look south for views of the massive Tazlina Glacier and Lake.

MP 170.5: ROAD ACCESS TO TOLSONA AND MOOSE LAKES. Take this road a few miles to enjoy boating, fishing, and hiking on these two state-stocked lakes.

Festivals and Fairs

Palmer Area

ALASKA STATE FAIR (FOURTH WEEK IN AUGUST AND FIRST WEEK IN SEPTEMBER): www.alaskastatefair.org. See 1,400-pound pumpkins and 100-pound cabbages.

PALMER COLONIAL DAYS (SECOND WEEK IN JUNE): www.palmer chamber.org/events.html.

Glennallen-Mendelta Area

MENDELTA CREEK MUSIC FESTIVAL (MEMORIAL DAY WEEKEND): bootsbisonranch@gmail.com or 907-727-2459.

COPPER BASIN 300 SLED DOG RACE (SECOND WEEK OF FEBRUARY): www.cb300.com.

Outfitters and Tour Operators

NOVA GUIDES, 800-746-5753 or 907-746-5753, www.novalaska.com. Offers glacier adventures and float trips on the Matanuska and tributary rivers.

USEFUL INFORMATION

MP 187: AHTNA NATIVE CORPORATION HEADQUARTERS IN GLENN-ALLEN, 907-822-3476, www.ahtna-inc.com. Contact the corporation for permits for traveling on Ahtna Land.

THE MILEPOST TRAVEL GUIDE: www.themilepost.com/highway-info/highways/glenn-highway-tok-cutoff

ALASKA.ORG ROAD GUIDE: www.alaska.org/guide/glenn-highway

GLENN HIGHWAY NATIONAL SCENIC HIGHWAY: www.glennhighway.org

LAKE LOUISE STATE RECREATION AREA: dnr.alaska.gov/parks/aspunits/matsu/lklouisesra.htm

12

THE OLD GLENN HIGHWAY COLLECTION (AK 1)

Glacial Streams, Valleys, and Lakes

FROM → TO: Anchorage to Palmer via the back and side roads

WHERE IT STARTS: Glenn Highway, 6 miles north of downtown Anchorage

WHERE IT ENDS: End of the Old Glenn Highway at the Knik River bridge in Palmer

ESTIMATED LENGTH: 60 miles on six different side roads, plus returns, all paved

ESTIMATED TIME: Three to six days, depending upon how much time you enjoy on each side trip

HIGHLIGHTS: Arctic Valley hikes, Eagle River Nature Center, Eklutna Lake, bridge and gravel bars of the Knik River

GETTING THERE: Drive 6 miles north of Anchorage on the new Glenn Highway to your first side road to Arctic Valley

This is a compilation of geographically related roads, including the **Old Glenn Highway,** which you access from the southern section of the new **Glenn Highway** (Drive #11) (AK 1). None of these roads are individually long enough to warrant their own entry, but each of these road segments has worthwhile treasures to offer that, taken together, create a nice little curated drive.

From the starting point 6 miles north of Anchorage, take a short 5-mile drive up the **Arctic Valley Road** to explore some beautiful alpine tundra, a whole slew of hiking and biking trails, access to the **Chugach State Park**, and, in the winter, a ski area. Return to and continue north along the New Glenn Highway to around MP 11, and travel 8 miles up **Hiland Road** (Highland Drive on some maps) along the South Fork of the Eagle River to find more hiking and biking trails. Again you return to and continue north on the New Glenn

LEFT: FISHING FUN ALONG THE EKLUTNA TRAIL RACE, NEXT TO THE KNIK RIVER

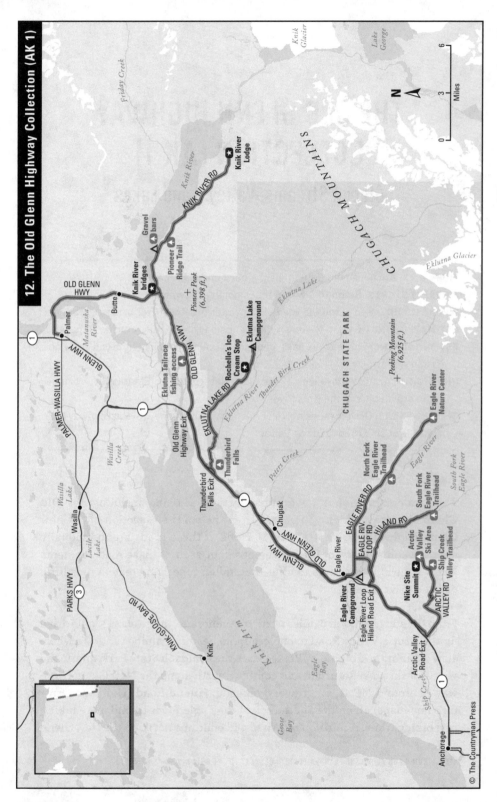

12. The Old Glenn Highway Collection (AK 1)

Highway to MP 13 to take the Eagle River Road exit, then drive 12 miles up the main stem of the Eagle River to the **Eagle River Nature Center** and its many outdoor offerings. Once again, return to the New Glenn Highway and drive farther north to around MP 26, where you detour up the Eklutna Lake Road to beautiful **Thunderbird Falls** and lovely **Eklutna Lake.** Then it's back, one more time, to the New Glenn Highway and on to MP 29, where you exit onto the longest remaining section of the Old Glenn Highway and the last two segments of this trip. Along this 8-mile-long segment, visit a popular fishing haven along the **Knik River**, explore and enjoy some buried cars, and then hang out on an old railroad bridge near the junction with the Knik River Road. From the railroad bridge you drive 11 miles on the Knik River Road, finding a trailhead to a classic local hike and enjoying multiple access points to the gravel bars of the Knik River.

There is also a shorter segment of the Old Glenn Highway that runs north of the town of Eagle River and parallels the New Glenn Highway. All these road segments exist within a 30-mile stretch of the beginning of the southern section of the New Glenn Highway, and all are within an hour of Anchorage. Together they offer a variety of stream channels of various sizes, lakes, waterfalls, hikes, and backcountry adventures that you can enjoy for multiple days. These road segments are particularly beautiful in autumn, when the golden colors of changing leaves painted against the dark green of boreal spruce forests are juxtaposed against the snow-topped peaks of the Chugach and Talkeetna Mountains.

IN THE AREA

Accommodations, Fuel, and Food

MP 8 (ON EKLUTNA LAKE ROAD): ROCHELLE'S ICE CREAM SHOP, 37501 Eklutna Lake Road, 907-688-6201. Ice cream and gold panning at MP 8 on the road to gorgeous Eklutna Lake. $.

MP 12: (ON KNIK RIVER ROAD) KNIK RIVER LODGE, 877-745-4575, www .knikriverlodge.com. Lodges, cabins, and restaurant at the very end of the Knik River Road. $–$$.

Camping

MP 8 (ON EAGLE RIVER ROAD): EAGLE RIVER CAMPGROUND, 907-694-7982, www.lifetimeadventures.net to make online reservations. Nearly 60 well-developed RV and tent campsites located on the North Fork of the

EKLUTNA LAKE OFFERS NUMEROUS ACTIVITIES INCLUDING BIKE AND KAYAK RENTALS

Eagle River five minutes from the town of Eagle but far enough for some peace and quiet. $.

MP 10 (ON EKLUTNA LAKE ROAD): EKLUTNA LAKE CAMPGROUND, 907-269-8400. Sixty well-developed campsites and a rental cabin surrounded by boreal forest near the shores of delightful Eklutna Lake. Includes bike, canoe, and kayak rentals, interpretive displays, access to hiking trails, and opportunities for winter sports. $.

Attractions and Recreation

MP 6 (GLENN HIGHWAY): ARCTIC VALLEY ROAD. Take the Arctic Valley Road exit off the Glenn Highway and drive east toward the mountains. The road turns to gravel and narrows and steepens at about mile 2. At the lower elevations you drive through a second-growth deciduous forest of aspen and birch trees. Slow way down for servicepeople from the nearby Joint Base Elmendorf–Richardson who frequent the road for training maneuvers. As you climb, enjoy views of the Anchorage Bowl to the south; the Northern Cook Inlet, its Knik Arm, and the Chigmat Mountains to the southwest; and the Arctic Valley to the east, which this road parallels. As you gain elevation, notice the appearance of spruce trees, cottonwoods, willows, and alders. When you approach the end of the road, at about mile 5, the spruce trees disappear as alpine tundra begins to dominate. Near the top of the road the Arctic Valley Road enters the Chugach State Park, where you find the Arctic Valley and Ship Creek trailheads. The road terminates in the Anchorage Ski Bowl, which in the winter offers ski lifts for alpine skiing and in the summer a plethora of roads for hiking and biking. Several parking areas provide access to multiple informal trails that crisscross the slopes.

GLACIER FED EKLUTNA LAKE, BETWEEN CHUGACH MOUNTAIN RIDGELINES

BEAUTIFUL HOMES NESTLE INTO WHITE SPRUCE FORESTS ALONG HILAND DRIVE

There is also the Nike Site Summit, which is on the National Register of Historic Places. You can gain the ridgeline by following the gravel road to the communication towers near the top of the main road. All summer and into the fall these hill slopes are covered with wildflowers, including lupine, fireweed, and dwarf fireweed, wild geraniums, monkshood, Indian paintbrush, and bluebells, and on the lower slopes tons of blueberries—bring your buckets! A gravel and dirt road leads north along the valley bottom from the ski up-and-over into the drainage basin of the Eagle River. Follow this road to trails that link with the Hunter Pass Trail and the South Fork trailhead over on Hiland Road. Keep your ears and eyes tuned for ground squirrels; you'll often hear their high-pitched squeaks before you see them. The Ship Creek Trailhead you passed on the way up is the western end of a trail that you can follow to the west for miles and connect with other trail systems in the Chugach State Park trail system.

MP 11.5 (GLENN HIGHWAY): HILAND ROAD. Exit east and take an almost immediate right turn onto paved Hiland Road. Drive 8 miles to West River Road and then to South Creek Road, through a rural residential area featuring nice homes nestled into the boreal forest. Enjoy the beautiful old birch trees, with many good views of the high Chugach peaks that frame the Eagle River Valley, on your way to the South Fork trailhead in Chugach State Park. This trailhead offers access to a variety of trails, including routes to Eagle and Symphony Lakes, the Hanging Valley Trail, as well as the Hunters

Pass Trail, which connects you to the Arctic Valley area (described above.) These trails begin near the tree line and take you across broad expanses of view-laden slopes.

MP 13.5 (GLENN HIGHWAY): EAGLE RIVER ROAD. Drive east to the Eagle River Loop Road and follow that around to the Eagle River Road, which begins in the town of the same name. Beginning around mile 8, you have wide views across the valley with grand scenes filled with the high Chugach peaks. At mile 8 is the Eagle River State Park, which offers picnicking, camping, and access to the fast-flowing river and the North Fork of the Eagle River Trail. At mile 12, the end of the road, you reach the Eagle River Nature Center, which offers natural history exhibits and access to a variety of trails, including the western end of the Crow Creek Pass Trail and a portion of the famous Iditarod National Historic Trail, whose eastern trailhead begins at the end of the Crow Creek Pass Road (see MP 88.5 Drive #14.)

MP 26.5 (GLENN HIGHWAY): EKLUTNA LAKE ROAD. Continuing north, take the Thunderbird Falls exit and follow the road to the parking area, where you'll find some information kiosks about the falls and the historical naming and use of this area by the Dena'ina Native tribes. Hike up the forested Thunderbird Creek Trail to beautiful Thunderbird Falls. Half a

ROCHELLE'S IS A MUST-STOP ON THE WAY TO EKLUTNA LAKE

EKLUTNA LAKE AND THE MONTANE VALLEY

mile north, turn right (southeast) onto Eklutna River Road and follow it 10 miles through a boreal forest to its end at gorgeous Eklutna Lake. While paved, this is a narrow highway with not much of a shoulder and only one narrow turnaround along the 10-mile-long trip to the lake. If you are pulling a trailer or a boat, you're committed to the road at least until you reach Rochelle's Ice Cream Parlor at mile 8, which is on the high point of the road and offers gold panning as well as ice cream. From the high point at Rochelle's, continue southeast down and toward Eklutna Lake, enjoying good views of the high Chugach Mountains in your front windshield. At mile 9 you enter the Eklutna Lake area, part of Chugach State Park, where there are 60 developed campsites; information kiosks about the glacial formation of the lake; canoe, kayak, and bike rentals; and access to an extensive system of varied hiking trails. Lakeside are birch and cottonwood trees, as well as large white spruce trees. Enjoy this lovely, quiet place for the day or the weekend. The only types of motorized craft allowed on this lake are electric-motored crafts, so it is very peaceful. Soak in the fabulous views of the lake and surrounding ridges and peaks. Wintertime offers terrific Nordic ski opportunities across the often flawless snow-covered lake surface. It's interesting to note that though this is a natural, glacially carved lake, it has been slightly augmented with the addition of a dam and spillway system that is used as a freshwater source and for hydroelectric power generation by the Eklutna Tailrace generation station, which you can visit on the next Old Glenn Highway segment along the Knik River.

MP 29 (GLENN HIGHWAY): Turn right (south) to access this longest remaining section of the Old Glenn Highway. This takes you along the southern bank of the Knik River, from which you can look to the north and see dramatic views of the high, jagged peaks of the Talkeetna Mountains as well as the braided stream channels of the glacially silted Knik River, whose source is the Knik Glacier about 20 miles upstream. There are multiple boat and fishing access points along this road. One of the most interesting and fun is the Eklutna Tailrace day-use fishing access area, located between MP 3 and MP 4, a favorite area for many local anglers who gather to enjoy fishing on the Knik River. Located just a couple hundred yards upstream from the parking area is the Eklutna Tailrace power generation station. The tailrace is the outfall of Eklutna Lake. The water exits from the tailrace and flows along a calm channel that passes by the parking lot, boat ramp, and fishing area. Walk the bridge over the power station tailrace runout onto a narrow island, which has been built up around old car bodies that are now buried deep in mud. These old cars are fun subjects for photographers, sketchers, and painters. From the Eklutna Tailrace area, the road continues north along the Knik River until MP 8.5, where you reach the Knik River bridges: the new one that you can drive over and a derelict one that you can walk over. Walk across the old bridge to enjoy some great views north up the channel of the Knik River and over to expansive views of the Talkeetna Mountains. This is also where the Old Glenn Highway intersects with the Knik River Road segment of our road collection.

MP 8.5 (OLD GLENN HIGHWAY): KNIK RIVER ROAD. After you've enjoyed your walk across the old Knik River bridge, turn right off the Old Glenn Highway and continue your drive east along the banks of the Knik River. You'll encounter numerous places to access the gravel bars that are above water during most of the year, except during spring runoff. I particularly enjoy dry camping out on the gravel bars in the fall, when the evenings are cool, the autumn colors warm, and the higher peaks show early-season snows. We refer to these early-season dustings of snow as "termination dust" that drives the *cheechakos* (visitors) out of Alaska and back to their warm winter homes. Another attraction along this road, near mile 4, is the

GROUP FISHING FUN ALONG THE SHORES OF THE KNIK RIVER

HIKE ACROSS THE OLD KNIK BRIDGE FOR GREAT VIEWS UP AND DOWN THE RIVER

trailhead for the Pioneer Ridge Trail, a steep, 4.5-mile-long climb to the top of Pioneer Peak, the tallest area peak and a favorite local landmark, in this section of the Chugach Mountains. Note: The upper half of this trail is for experienced mountain climbers only. Even if you don't hike this trail to the top, I encourage you to pack a lunch and some water and work your way up until you are at least above tree line. You'll be glad you did, because views of the Knik River Valley and the high peaks and ridgelines of the Talkeetna Mountains to the north are just breathtaking. Following your hiking adventure, continue east along the road, enjoying the scenery until MP 12, where you reach road's end at the Knik River Lodge. To return to the New Glenn Highway, retrace your journey along Knik River Road 12 miles to the intersection with the Old Glenn Highway and the twin bridges. From there you can continue to retrace your drive back along the Old Glenn Highway, or you can turn right (north) and cross over the new Knik River bridge, continuing along the Old Glenn Highway into the town of Palmer, where you can rejoin the New Glenn Highway.

Festivals and Fairs

ALASKA STATE FAIR (FOURTH WEEK IN AUGUST AND FIRST WEEK IN SEPTEMBER): www.alaskastatefair.org. See 1,400-pound pumpkins and 100-pound cabbages.

PALMER COLONIAL DAYS (SECOND WEEK IN JUNE): www.palmer chamber.org/events.html

Outfitters and Tour Operators

NOVA GUIDES: 800-746-5753 or 907-746-5753, www.novalaska.com. Offers glacier adventures and float trips on the Matanuska and tributary rivers.

ALASKA KAYAK ACADEMY: 907-746-6600, www.kayakcenterak.com. Offers kayak training and trips.

EAGLE RIVER NATURE CENTER (MP 12; THE END OF EAGLE RIVER ROAD): 907-694-2108, www.ernc.org. Fascinating nature center located at the end of Eagle River Road.

USEFUL INFORMATION

THE MILEPOST TRAVEL GUIDE: www.themilepost.com/highway-info/ highways/glenn-highway-tok-cutoff

ALASKA.ORG ROAD GUIDE—OLD GLENN: www.alaska.org/guide/old -glenn-highway-Scenic-Drive

ALASKA.ORG ROAD GUIDE—ARCTIC VALLEY: www.alaska.org/guide/ arctic-valley-road-scenic-drive

ALASKA.ORG ROAD GUIDE—EKLUTNA LAKE DRIVE: www.alaska.org/ guide/eklutna-lake-scenic-drive

13

THE HATCHER PASS ROAD
Through the Heart of the Talketna Mountains

FROM → TO: Palmer to Willow

WHERE IT STARTS: MP 51 on the Glenn Highway

WHERE IT ENDS: MP 72 on the Parks Highway

ESTIMATED LENGTH: 47 miles (first 17 miles is paved from Palmer, followed by 20 miles of gravel up and over the pass, and then 10 miles of paved road down and into town of Willow)

ESTIMATED TIME: One to two days

HIGHLIGHTS: Dry camping at pullouts; hiking, biking, and skiing the Archangel side road; historical mine site; summit area hiking; the Upper Willow Road

GETTING THERE: Drive 51 miles on the New Glenn Highway from its beginning in downtown Anchorage to the north side of the town of Palmer. Turn west on Palmer-Fishhook Road for Hatcher Pass. Note: This is also the starting point for Drive # 11. Alternatively, drive 72 miles north of Anchorage on the Glenn Highway and then the follow the Parks Highway to Willow-Fishhook Road to approach Hatcher Pass from the west. Driving to Hatcher Pass from the Palmer/east side is the fastest way up to the pass and offers the best views on the way in.

Hatcher Pass was named for Robert Hatcher, who discovered gold here in 1906. From MP 51 on the Glenn Highway, turn northwest and you are immediately driving through beautiful pastoral farm and ranch country as you head up into the Talkeetna Mountains. Within a few miles you enter a classic boreal forest dominated by spruce trees on the slopes with the addition of birches, aspens, and cottonwoods along the banks of the **Little Susitna River**, known locally as the "Little Su." Near the base of the pass road you

LEFT: THE BOULDER-FILLED STREAM CHANNEL OF THE LITTLE SU RIVER IN FALL

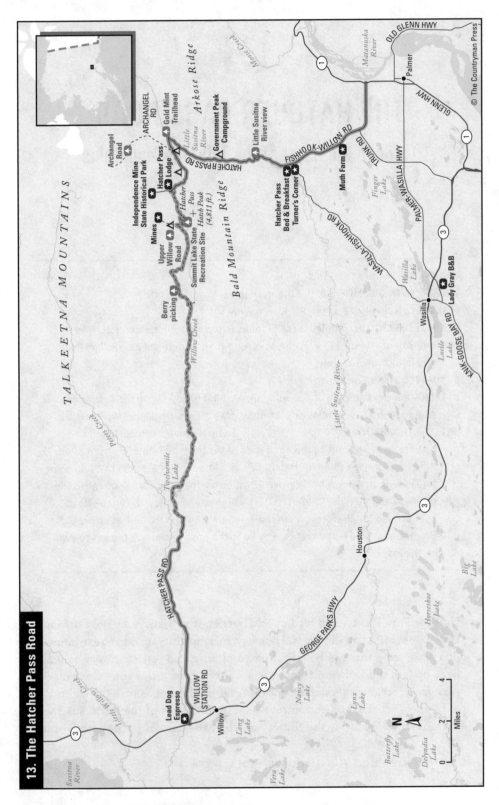

13. The Hatcher Pass Road

© The Countryman Press

THE HATCHER PASS HIGH COUNTRY OFFERS SWEEPING VISTAS

drive over the Little Su, where I encourage you to stop at the wayside and enjoy the stream channel and the information kiosks. From there, follow the boulder-strewn stream channel for several miles up to the Gold Mint wayside, which offers access to a beautiful, glacially carved valley via the **Gold Mint Trail**. From the Gold Mint wayside, the road begins to climb in earnest toward the **Independence Mine State Historical Park** located high up in the cirque bowl basin at the head of the valley. This section of the road cuts a long, diagonal path across the mountain front, offering numerous pull-outs with spectacular views of the surrounding Talkeetna Mountains, and out across the broad valleys of the Matanuska and Knik Rivers, over into the high peaks of the Chugach Mountains. From this section you also have access to the Archangel Road along which you can hike, ski, bike, or ORV/snowmobile back into the **Archangel basin**, where berry picking is prime. At about MP 17 you reach the end of the paved road at the Independence Mine site. Here you can enjoy all sorts of outdoor recreational fun, including hiking and skiing up and around the site's buildings; fabulous meadow and

TOP: THE HATCHER PASS TRAVERSE PROVIDES STUNNING VIEWS IN ALL DIRECTIONS
BOTTOM: LOOKING INTO THE HEART OF THE TALKEETNA RANGE FROM THE HATCHER PASS ROAD

ridge hiking throughout the spring, summer, and fall; spectacular Nordic skiing in the winter; and biking throughout much of the year.

From the Independence Mine site, continue up and over Hatcher Pass on a gravel road that is steeper and narrower than the paved road. (It's not recommended for long RVs and is closed in winter.) Take this upper road section to the top of the pass at the **Summit Lake State Recreation Site** for spectacular views on both sides of the alpine tundra–covered ridgelines and peaks of the rugged Talkeetna Mountains. After enjoying the pass area, continue your drive west down from the top of the pass. You'll reach **Upper Willow Road** near the bottom of the pass—feel free to take this drive up to an old and current mine site. The final 18 miles of the drive are westward along the Willow Creek valley, initially through prime brushy berry-picking tundra, followed by marshy tundra along Willow Creek, and then boreal forest. Finish with a treat at Lead Dog Espresso in the town of Willow on the Parks Highway.

IN THE AREA

Accommodations, Fuel, and Food

MP 6.5: TURNER'S CORNER, 907-745-6161. Offering gas, beer, wine, spirits, pizza, diesel, and a convenience store.

MP 9.5: HATCHER PASS BED & BREAKFAST, 9000 North Palmer-Fishhook Road, 907-745-6788, www.hatcherpassbb.com. Beautiful log cabins located on the west side of Hatcher Pass at the base of the Talkeetna Mountains. $$.

CABINS AT THE HATCHER PASS LODGE CABINS OFFER ACCESS TO THE HISTORICAL MINE SITE

MUTH FARM MAKES A CHARMING STOP

MP 17: INDEPENDENCE MINE HATCHER PASS LODGE, 907-745-1200, www.hatcherpasslodge.com. Rustic and homey cabins to rent and a restaurant near the end of the paved road on the east side of Hatcher Pass. We love to have hot chocolate, soup, and a sandwich at the lodge's restaurant after a day of hiking or skiing. Cabin 7 has the best views. Road, lodge, and cabins are open year-round. $–$$.

MP 39: LEAD DOG ESPRESSO, 100 S. Parks Highway, 907-465-5283, www .facebook.com/leaddogespresso. Very fun, small coffee, Danish, breakfast sandwich, and hot dog stand at the intersection of Willow-Fishhook and the Parks Highway. Look for the blue-sided building with the green cutouts of the sled dog teams. Check out the hot dog specials on Facebook. $.

MP 39 PLUS 10 MILES SOUTH OF PARKS HIGHWAY: LADY GRAY B&B, 907-373-1557 or 907-355-8454 (cell), www.ladygraybnb.com. Beautiful and spacious log home on 12 acres next to Cottonwood Creek. $$.

Camping

MP 11: GOVERNMENT PEAK CAMPGROUND. Small roadside camping area for tents and small RVs with access to the Little Susitna River.

MP 16: FISHHOOK PARKING AND CAMPING AREA. Partially developed camping with access to toilets. Large gravel parking lot for RV dry camping and nearby tent camping.

Attractions and Recreation

MP 3.7: MUTH FARM. Stop here to check out the beautiful pottery at one of the area's original homesteading farms.

MP 10: LITTLE SUSITNA RIVER VIEW AREA. Just after you cross over the bridge at the Little Susitna River, immediately pull off at the view area

THE HEADWATERS OF THE LITTLE SU RIVER CARVE THROUGH GOLD MINT VALLEY

and enjoy some beautiful scenes upstream of the Little Su bouncing over and around boulders of granitic and metamorphic rocks. Also, take some time to read the information kiosks on the geology and hiking areas of Hatcher Pass.

MP 12: GOLD MINT TRAILHEAD. Hike, bike, or horseback ride 9 miles along the upper reaches of the Little Su stream channel and through a classically U-shaped, glacially carved valley to the source of the meltwater from

DRIVE, HIKE, BIKE OR SKI THE ARCHANGEL ROAD INTO THE HEART OF THE TALKEETNA MOUNTAINS

the Mint Glacier. The trail passes through brushy and then marshy tundra, and alpine walking tundra at higher and drier locales as you slowly gain elevation while enjoying the proximity to the upper reaches and head-waters of the Little Su River channel. Be sure to watch for the resident beavers working hard on their latest construction projects.

MP 15: ARCHANGEL ROAD. Hike, bike, or ride your ORV into the glacially carved cirque bowl basin headwaters areas of Archangel and Glacier Creeks and the twin Read Lakes. In the late summer and fall this is a favorite berry-picking area, and in the winter it's used for Nordic skiing, fat-tire biking, and snowmobiling. From late spring through fall, be aware that the roadbed can be very badly rutted and have huge potholes, so proceed with caution. A turnout on the main road at the intersection of the Hatcher Pass Road and the Archangel Road is an excellent dry camping spot affording excellent morning and evening panoramic views.

MP 16: FISHHOOK PARKING, CAMPING, AND HIKING AREA. About a mile from the end of the road you'll pass this large gravel parking lot with restrooms and access to the Fishhook trailhead. This is a good base camp area for hiking to the ridgelines and beyond. The tundra near the parking area is squishy and brushy walking tundra, but upslope it becomes shorter, firmer, and easier to hike, even if the slopes become steeper. You can both dry and tent camp here.

MP 17: INDEPENDENCE MINE STATE HISTORIC PARK. At the end of the paved road on the east side of Hatcher Pass, this area offers parking and access to a plethora of adventure opportunities, including hiking, biking, and skiing to the historic Independence Mine site, which has a museum and information kiosks. This area is nearly as popular in the winter as it is in the summer due to the copious amounts of snow that fall each year at the higher elevations around Hatcher Pass. In the springtime Nordic skiers love to come up here for the satin-surfaced backcountry skiing, known as crust skiing.

MP 20: SUMMIT LAKE STATE RECREATION SITE. Located at the very top of Hatcher Pass (3,886 feet) is a small parking area offering access to several cross-the-alpine-tundra trails as well as no-trail hikes. (Note: The gravel road to the summit is closed in the winter.) Trails range in length and difficulty from short and easy (a flat 100 yards to a nice view of Summit Lake) to multiple-mile, more challenging cross-country treks. My favorite on-trail hike is along the April Bowl Trail, whose trailhead is directly across from the Summit parking area. This trail takes you through lovely walking tundra, past several alpine lakes, and up to a ridgeline that provides spectacular views of the mountains, lakes, and tundra meadows that characterize this Hatcher Pass high country. Off-trail, I often head over in the direction of Hatch Peak. Throughout early spring, summer, and into the fall this tundra high country offers up a varied community of wildflowers whose membership changes throughout the summer season. When hiking the high country, be sure to bring extra layers, including a hat, gloves, and rain jacket, because the weather at high elevations can change rapidly and dramatically.

MP 21: GRAVEL ROAD TO OLD/NEW MINE SITE. Just west of the west gate at the bottom of the Hatcher Pass Road is a rough, single-lane dirt road (labeling it a road is being generous), Upper Willow Road, that heads north into a steep-sided, glacially carved valley and cirque bowl basin. This old and current mining road follows Upper Willow Creek for about a mile. Whether you plan to stay for just the afternoon or you remain overnight, you can enjoy some wonderful cross-tundra hiking opportunities—dry, short-cropped tundra on the higher slopes or boggy marshy tundra along the stream channel, with every gradation in between. Camping overnight here is special, with the dark, star-filled sky framed by the high twin valley-forming ridges. Hike to the end of the road and find an on-again off-again mining operation that you can wander around, though be sure to leave things as you find them. As you walk up the road, look west and see a zigzag trail that seems to climb an impossibly steep slope. The trail was cut by a bulldozer starting at the top of the mountain. That's correct: from the top! At the very northern end and head of the valley, which just 10,000 years ago was an ice-filled cirque bowl of the glacier that occupied this valley, look carefully on the north wall and you'll find a subtle switchbacked hiking trail that will lead you all the way to the top of the ridgeline.

MP 24–25: BERRY PICKING. This is a favorite local berry picking area in the brushy tundra. Eat as much as you can and bucket the rest!

Festivals and Fairs

ALASKA STATE FAIR (FOURTH WEEK IN AUGUST AND FIRST WEEK IN SEPTEMBER): www.alaskastatefair.org. See 1,400-pound pumpkins and 100-pound cabbages.

PALMER COLONIAL DAYS (SECOND WEEK IN JUNE): www.palmer chamber.org/events.html

Outfitters and Tour Operators

HATCHER PASS SNOWMOBILING: 907-783-3600, www.alaskasnowmobile tours.com. Offering guided snowmobile trips in the Hatcher Pass area.

USEFUL INFORMATION

THE MILEPOST HATCHER PASS SLIDESHOW: www.themilepost.com/slideshows/43-hatcher-pass-slideshow

ALASKA.ORG ROAD GUIDE—HATCHER PASS: www.alaska.org/detail/hatcher-pass

14

THE SEWARD HIGHWAY NORTH (AK 1)

Turnagain Arm Tour of Tides and Glaciers

FROM → TO: Anchorage to the northern end of the Kenai Peninsula

WHERE IT STARTS: West end of Potter Marsh at the northwestern end of Turnagain Arm

WHERE IT ENDS: The north end of the Kenai Peninsula at MP 73

ESTIMATED LENGTH: 42 miles, all paved

ESTIMATED TIME: Two to four days

HIGHLIGHTS: Potter Marsh, the Bird Ridge Trail, the Alaska Wildlife Conservation Center, the Spencer Glacier Whistle Stop, Portage Valley Blue Ice Trail

GETTING THERE: From downtown Anchorage, drive south on the Seward Highway (AK 1) to Potter Marsh

MILEPOST NOTE: I use actual physical highway milepost marker references, beginning with milepost 0 in Seward, rather than the distance from the starting point at Potter Marsh.

The Turnagain Arm section of the Seward Highway offers 42 miles of coastlines, mountain views, glaciers, and their stream channels, along with a variety of adventures to enjoy between the city of Anchorage at the mouth of the Turnagain Arm of Cook Inlet and the beginning of the Kenai Peninsula near the southeast corner of the Turnagain Arm. The Seward Highway contains two very geographically distinct segments, both of which you can easily devote multiple days to exploring. This first section is a coastal drive around the Turnagain Arm of Cook Inlet, which is all about the tides, stream channels, and mountains of this massive, 35-mile-long, glacially carved fjord. This road offers many opportunities for outdoor recreation, including hiking trails, river rafting, paddleboard and kite and tidal bore surfing, skiing, and

LEFT: THE ALASKA RAILROAD HUGS THE COASTLINE OF THE TURNAGAIN ARM

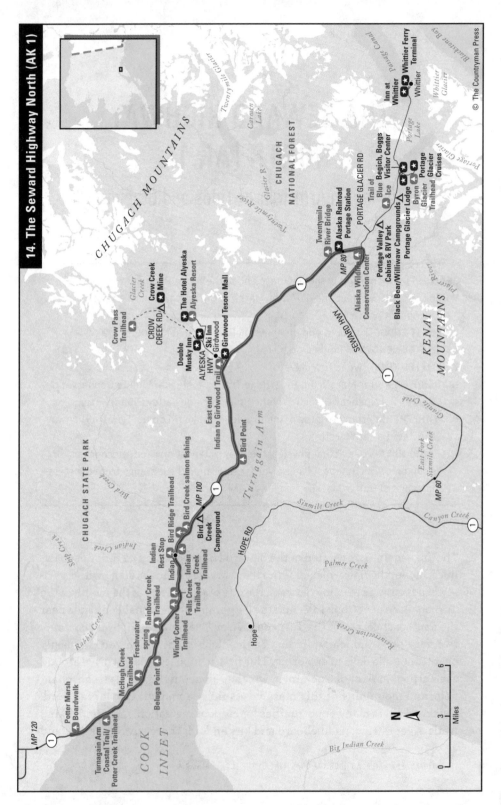

14. The Seward Highway North (AK 1)

MP 120

COOK INLET

Potter Marsh Boardwalk

Turnagain Arm Coastal Trail/ Potter Creek Trailhead

McHugh Creek Trailhead

Freshwater spring

Beluga Point

Rainbow Creek Trailhead

Windy Corner Trailhead

Falls Creek Trailhead

Indian Rest Stop

Indian

Indian Creek Trailhead

Bird Ridge Trailhead

Bird Creek salmon fishing

MP 100

Bird Creek Campground

Bird Point

CHUGACH STATE PARK

CHUGACH MOUNTAINS

Rabbit Creek

Ship Creek

Bird Creek

Indian Creek

Turnagain Arm

East end Indian to Girdwood Trail

ALYESKA HWY

Girdwood

Double Musky Inn

Ski Inn

Girdwood Tesoro Mall

CROW CREEK RD

Crow Creek Mine

The Hotel Alyeska

Alyeska Resort

Glacier Creek

Crow Pass Trailhead

Twentymile Glacier

Carmen Lake

Glacier River

Twentymile River

CHUGACH NATIONAL FOREST

Twentymile River Bridge

Alaska Railroad Portage Station

MP 80

Alaska Wildlife Conservation Center

PORTAGE GLACIER RD

Portage Valley Cabins & RV Park

Black Bear/Williwaw Campgrounds

Portage Glacier Lodge

Trail of Blue Begich, Boggs Ice Visitor Center

Byron Glacier Trailhead

Portage Glacier Cruises

Portage Lake

Passage Canal

Inn at Whittier

Whittier Ferry Terminal

Whittier

Whittier Glacier

Blackstone Bay

© The Countryman Press

SEWARD HWY

HOPE RD

Hope

Sixmile Creek

Palmer Creek

Resurrection Creek

Big Indian Creek

KENAI MOUNTAINS

Placer River

East Fork Sixmile Creek

Granite Creek

MP 60

Canyon Creek

N

0   3   6
Miles

THE POTTER MARSH WETLANDS ARE A HAVEN FOR SALMON AND WATERBIRDS

snowmobiling. In addition, I recommend three additional side roads, any of which you could easily explore for a day or more.

Travel Time Tip: If you're driving here in the summer, plan your day so that you are driving in either early morning or the evening. All these roads are two-lane with infrequent passing lanes. Driving between noon and 6 PM, you're almost certainly going to encounter substantial tourist traffic. Therefore, to reduce your frustration and increase your enjoyment, get going early, plan a midday off-road adventure, and then engage in more driving after 6 PM if you wish.

The **Turnagain Arm** fjord is so named because it is the eastern extension, or arm, of the north end of Cook Inlet, which itself is a northern extension of the Gulf of Alaska. The name Turnagain is derived from a voyage of Captain James Cook who, when they ventured into this arm of Cook Inlet, had to turn, and turn again, and turn again because of the narrow and shallow nature of the main channel up through the fjord. Begin your drive just south of Anchorage at the lovely, coastal, salmon spawning wetlands of **Potter Marsh**. From there, begin a 42-mile coastal highway journey that hugs the edges of Turnagain Arm and parallels the Alaska Railroad. Along the way you'll be treated to an amazing landscape of towering ice- and snow-clad peaks; huge, glacially carved valleys; stream channels choked with the fine silt of glacially ground sediment; and the spectacular sculptured channels of the mud flats that are recarved daily by tides up to 30 feet high. If you drive Turnagain Arm in the winter you'll be additionally wowed by amazing ice "sculptures" that are added to the glacial silt and water. At any time of year you'll notice the velocity of the tidal currents that flow in and out. And, if you happen to be driving during the change from low to high tide, you may see the bore tide wave that forms and moves up the channel when the tide switches. This wave is actually surfable, as YouTube videos will attest. In

TURNAGAIN ARM FJORD OFFERS DRAMATIC WINTER VIEWS

Fishing Options Abound Around Turnagain Arm

You can engage in combat stream fishing, where you are shoulder-to-shoulder with a couple hundred newfound fishing friends, along world-famous Bird Creek. You can also enjoy the fishing and camaraderie of others at the mouth of Twentymile Creek where it enters the eastern end of Turnagain Arm. Or, you can seek more solitary line tossing along the shores of the Portage River, which flows from the high peaks of the Chugach and Northern Kenai Mountains at the far eastern end of Turnagain Arm. Wind-powered boats are favorite crafts for navigating up the shallow, sediment-choked channels of Twentymile Creek for both fishing and sight-seeing adventures.

FAMILY FISHING AT THE MOUTH OF TWENTYMILE CREEK

addition to the massive tides, currents, and waves, Turnagain Arm is also famous for its strong and steady winds, which create perfect conditions for wind- and kitesurfers.

Sometimes those brisk winds become hurricane force, which requires the closure of the road. Until you approach the side road to Portage Valley at the head of Turnagain Arm, you drive next to soaring, steep slopes that drop down from the high peaks and ridges of the Chugach Mountains directly to the salty shores of Turnagain Arm. These create another winter attraction: massive and beautiful snow avalanche cones that routinely form at the base of the many steep ravines located next to the road and railway. Sometimes these snow avalanches cover the railroad tracks and the road, which forces their closure until they are removed.

There are several dozen turnouts along Turnagain Arm, each with a view seemingly more spectacular than the last. You may even be fortunate enough to see the beautiful white skin of the beluga whales that inhabit these waters. And, if you turn your eyes upslope, you're likely to see the white coats of Dall sheep that thrive on the craggy slopes. This entire area has a rich history of exploration and gold mining, much of which is well displayed and explained by the information kiosks that you can find at many of the turnouts along the way.

If you are a hiker, you'll find plenty of opportunities to pursue your passion on a variety of trails. Along the first 11 miles of this road you can enjoy the easy-to-hike Turnagain Arm Trail, which for the first 4 miles is very modestly sloped. Access this trail just south of Potter Marsh and hike through a beautiful spruce and aspen boreal forest while enjoying spectacular scenery. You'll also find many trailheads for more challenging hikes that climb the steep slopes to the surrounding ridgelines.

Another human-powered highlight opportunity is the 13.3-mile-long multiuse biking-walking-strolling trail that hugs the coastline between MP 103 at the town of Indian and MP 88.5 at Girdwood. Park a car at either end, or any one of multiple access points along its length, to walk or bike the entire length or any portion of the route. Pack a lunch and some drinks and plan to have a picnic at a point of your choosing along the way. If you don't want to tackle the steeper hiking trails, this gently undulating coastal trail will fit the bill perfectly. Water sports opportunities also abound. And, you can take The Alaska Railroad Whistlestop Train on a tour to view and access several glaciers and numerous more remote floating and hiking adventures.

IN THE AREA

Accommodations, Fuel, and Food

MP 88.5: GIRDWOOD TESORO MALL, 907-783-3486. Gas station, convenience store, ice cream shop, pizza parlor, and more. One of the busiest gas stations in Alaska and one of the few dependable fuel stops between Anchorage, Seward, and Soldotna. This is also the intersection of the side roads to Alyeska and Crow Creek Mine Roads. Open 24 hours.

MP 88.5 PLUS 2 MILES ON THE ALEYSKA HIGHWAY AND CROW CREEK PASS ROAD, DOUBLE MUSKY INN, 907-783-5520, www.doublemuskyinn.com. Historical eatery. $–$$.

MP 88.5 PLUS 4 MILES ON ALEYSKA HIGHWAY, ALEYSKA HOTEL, 800-880-3880 or 907-754-2275, www.alyeskaresort.com/hotel. Beautiful luxury hotel with all the amenities; hosts a lot of spring and summer festivals in a lovely alpine setting. $$$–$$$$.

MP 88.5 PLUS 3 MILES ON ALEYSKA HIGHWAY, SKI INN, 189 Hightower Road, Girdwood, 907-783-0002, www.akskiinn.com. Botique inn with nice rooms and affordable prices in downtown Girdwood. $–$$.

MP 77.3 PLUS 5 MILES UP PORTAGE VALLEY ROAD, PORTAGE GLACIER LODGE, 907-783-3117. Cafeteria, lodging, and tickets to Portage Glacier Boat Tour. $–$$.

MP 77.3 PLUS 12 MILES UP PORTAGE VALLEY ROAD AND THROUGH WHITTIER TUNNEL, THE INN AT WHITTIER, 907-472-3200, www.inn atwhittier.com. Full-service luxury waterfront lodging. $$.

Camping

MP 101: BIRD CREEK CAMPGROUND AND PUBLIC CABIN, www.dnr .alaska.gov/parks/aspunits/chugach/birdcreekcamp.htm. Chugach State Park campground with 28 campsites and two public use cabins close to fishing on Bird Creek. $.

MP 88.5 PLUS 4 MILES INTO THE CROW CREEK MINE ROADS: CROW CREEK MINE, 907-229-3105, www.crowcreekmine.com. Private camping and very fun gold-mining operation. $–$$.

MP 77.3: MULTIPLE CAMPGROUNDS ON PORTAGE GLACIER ROAD, 907-783-3242, www.forestcamping.com/dow/alaska/chuginfo.htm. Along this 5-mile-long road you will find three fully developed camping areas: Portage Valley Cabins and RV Park (private); and the Chugach National Forest campgrounds of Black Bear (MP 3.5) and the larger, more open Williwaw (MP 4.0). $.

Attractions and Recreation

MP markers: The milepost markers begin at MP 0 in Seward; therefore, this tour starts at MP 116.

MP 116: POTTER MARSH BOARDWALK. Enjoy a very pleasant stroll while spotting summer spawning salmon as well as a variety of aquatic and shorebirds, including white swans. Read the informational kiosks about the salmon and other wildlife that make this beautiful marshland their home.

MP 113: WESTERN END OF THE TURNAGAIN ARM COASTAL TRAIL AND POTTER CREEK TRAILHEAD. This is the beginning of the 14-mile-long Turnagain Arm Coastal Trail, and there is also access to the Potter Creek trailhead. It's 3 easy miles to the next trailhead at McCue Creek.

PORTAGE VALLEY IN WINTER IS A WONDERLAND OF CLEAR SKIES AND SNOWY PEAKS

The 1964 Earthquake

We feel earthquakes on a regular basis in Alaska, but in 1964 we got hit with a doozy, a magnitude-9.2 earthquake that dropped the eastern end of Turnagain Arm by 8 feet! You can still see remnants of this massive earthquake in the rows of dead spruce trees still standing in the marshes along the northern and eastern shores of Turnagain Arm. These ghost forests were once far enough above water level to live and thrive. The 1964 earthquake lowered their root systems so much that they are now soaked by the salty-brackish waters of the incoming tides or drowned by the fresh waters of the coastal marshes.

MP 110: MCHUGH CREEK TRAILHEAD. This trailhead is midway along the Turnagain Arm Coastal Trail and offers access to the 7-mile-long McHugh Creek Trail to McHugh and Rabbit Lakes. From here you can hike 3 miles back west to the beginning of the Turnagain Arm Coastal Trail, 4.2 miles east to the Rainbow trailhead, or 9.5 miles all the way to the end of the Coastal Trail at Windy. Note that the trail west toward Potter Creek is less challenging than the trail east, which has more ups and downs with an elevation gain of 800 feet. All the trails that head inland are much steeper upslope challenges.

MP 109: FRESHWATER SPRING. Here you find a freshwater spring coming directly out of the rock wall on the north side of the road. Park across the highway from the spring and carefully, and quickly, cross the highway, being very vigilant of the traffic. The spring water is delicious! Bring a milk jug or two to take some along with you!

MP 109: BELUGA POINT. This is a good viewpoint for searching for beluga whales. There's also a fun scramble across the rocks on the other side of the train tracks with wonderful views of Turnagain Arm.

MP 107: RAINBOW CREEK TRAILHEAD. This is three-quarters of the way along the coastal trail. Hike 4.2 easy miles back to the McHugh trailhead or 1.2 more challenging miles east to the Windy trailhead at the eastern end of the Turnagain Arm Coastal Trail.

MP 105: WINDY CORNER TRAILHEAD. This is the eastern end of the Turnagain Arm Coastal Trail and also a good viewing location for Dall sheep—look up!

CURRENTS CARRY ICE RAFTS ALONG TURNAGAIN ARM

MP 104: FALLS CREEK TRAILHEAD. The lower portion is a nice hike up the cool Falls Creek, with the upper section heading much more steeply for tree line above the stream channel.

MP 103: INDIAN REST STOP AND WEST END OF TURNAGAIN ARM BIKE/WALKING TRAIL. Park here to access the western end of the 13.5-mile-long Indian-to-Girdwood multiuse bike/walking trail. Park vehicles at each end for a terrific daylong hiking, biking, or strolling adventure.

MP 102: INDIAN CREEK TRAILHEAD. Have fun with gold panning and access to the Indian Creek Trail.

MP 100: BIRD RIDGE TRAILHEAD. This is a steep trail that proceeds directly up 3,400 feet (feel those thighs burn!) to the ridgeline of Bird Ridge for a spectacular Arctic tundra hike with amazing 360-degree views of the Chugach Mountains, Turnagain Arm, and the Northern Kenai Mountains.

MP 99.5: BIRD CREEK SALMON FISHING. This world-famous combat-fishing location (where you stand shoulder-to-shoulder with fellow fishing fanatics and battle for the bites) on Bird Creek is for those who really enjoy the company of others fishing a world-class salmon stream.

MP 94.6: BIRD POINT. A popular and well-developed rest area with tons of parking, this spot has a short paved walk out onto Bird Point, jutting out into Turnagain Arm. Enjoy some excellent views of the inlet and close access to rapidly flowing currents of incoming and outgoing tides.

MP 88.5: GIRDWOOD. Park here to access the eastern end of the 13.5-mile-long Indian-to-Girdwood multiuse bike/walking trail. Park vehicles at each end for a terrific daylong hiking, biking, or strolling adventure. This is also the location of Girdwood Mall for fuel and supplies.

MP 88.5: ALYESKA HIGHWAY. Drive north 3 miles to access the Crow Creek Road and then 4 miles to the town of Girdwood and the Alyeska Resort. The 7-mile-long Crow Creek Road provides access to a historic gold-mining location and several hiking trails, including the Iditarod National, Winner Creek, and Crow Creek Pass Trails. Note: The western end of the Crow Creek Pass trail is at the Eagle Nature Center located at the end of the Eagle River Road segment of Drive #12.

MP 79.2: TWENTYMILE RIVER BRIDGE, alaskabackcountryaccess.com. Access the Twentymile River for fishing from sandbanks at its mouth. Jet

HIKING TRAILS ABOUND ALONG THE NORTH SHORE OF TURNAGAIN ARM

boat rides are available for 50-mile trips upstream to ice-marginal Glacier Lake, formed in front of the glacier.

MP 78.3: ALASKA RAILROAD STATION FOR TRAINS TO SPENCER GLACIER, www.alaskarailroad.com. Take the Alaska Railroad Whistle Stop train to view numerous glaciers and access the Spencer Glacier recreation area, which offers multiple walking, hiking, floating, and paddling adventures.

MP 77.5: ALASKA WILDLIFE CONSERVATION CENTER, www.alaska wildlife.org. Stop by this unique wildlife rescue center at the eastern end of Turnagain Arm. See wild animals up close, including bears, moose, caribou, wolves, birds of prey, bison, and even on occasion musk ox. All are in the process of being rehabilitated from injuries. Ask about viewing feed times for the animals too.

MP 77.3: PORTAGE GLACIER ROAD TO PORTAGE VALLEY AND WHITTIER. Drive 5 miles along the beautiful, glacially carved Portage River Valley for spectacular views of the surrounding mountains; the Explorer and Byron Glaciers; and the beautiful, meandering, gravel-bottomed channel of the Portage River with its numerous side channels and contributory streams. Walk along the beautiful Blue Ice Trail, hike up to Byron Glacier,

THE PORTAGE GLACIER BOAT TAKES YOU TO THE FRONT OF THE GLACIER

or take a cruise across Portage Lake to the Portage Glacier. Visit the Begich, Boggs Visitor Center and camp at either of two Chugach National Forest campgrounds. Continue 1 mile though a tunnel to the Prince William Sound coastal town of Whittier, which offers an Alaska Marine Highway System ferry terminal and cruise ship dock, harbor-side accommodations and restaurants, and access to all manner of outdoor adventure activities, including glacier and wildlife tours as well as kayaking and hiking adventures into the spectacular College Fjord.

Festivals and Fairs

ALYESKA RESORT FESTIVALS: www.alyeskaresort.com. These festivals include:

FIDDLEHEAD MUSIC FESTIVAL (EARLY JUNE): Enjoy this very fun weekend celebration of the fiddlehead ferns and fiddle music in the Chugach Mountains. This is a family-oriented outdoors event with local arts and crafts, a beer and wine garden, and plenty of children's activities.

BLUEBERRY FESTIVAL (THIRD WEEK IN AUGUST): Join this outdoor celebration of blueberries during this family-oriented event featuring over two dozen arts and crafts booths in The Hotel Alyeska's Pond Courtyard. Also enjoy live music and all the blueberry concoctions you can eat.

MOUNTAIN BIKE FESTIVAL (FIRST WEEK IN SEPTEMBER): Even if you don't ride. this is a fun event to see, with three days of biking competitions, including whips, tricks, a wheelie competition, a downhill race, and the always popular Pond Crossing, where competitors attempt to cross a floating bridge without falling into the cold water.

ALYESKA CLIMBATHON (SECOND WEEK IN SEPTEMBER): How vertically challenged are you? Climb and test yourself or simply watch. Run or hike/walk 2.2 miles and 2,000 vertical feet up North Face Trail with friends and family while raising money to help end women's cancers.

OKTOBERFEST (THIRD AND FOURTH WEEKS IN SEPTEMBER): Come join all the German fun with beer, bratwurst, and live polka bands.

Outfitters and Tour Operators

Turnagain Arm

CHUGACH BACKCOUNTRY FISHING: 907-362-1224, www.chugachback countryfishing.com. Offers drift-in powerboat and hike-in fishing excursions on Northern Kenai rivers and lakes.

CHUGACH ADVENTURES: 907-783-1860, www.alaskanrafting.com. Spencer Glacier and other Chugach adventures.

ASCENDING PATH: 907-783-0505, www.ascendingpath.com/tours/spen cer-glacier-hike. Spencer Glacier and other tours.

ALASKA SNOWMOBILE TOURS AND RENTALS: 907-783-3600, www .alaskasnowmobiletours.com. Snowmobile tours and rentals near Portage Valley.

BLUE ICE JETBOATING: 907-783-3600, www.alaskabackcountryaccess .com/blue-ice-jetboat-ride. Jet boat rides up the Twentymile River.

Portage Valley

PORTAGE GLACIER CRUISES: 800-544-2206, www.portageglaciercruises .com. Cruise on Portage Lake.

Whittier

ALASKA SEA KAYAKERS: 877-472-2534 or 907-472-2534 in Alaska, www .alaskaseakayakers.com. Sea kayaking adventures around Whittier and in College Fjord. Single- and multiple-day trips, kayak rentals, and training.

EPIC CHARTERS: 907-242-4339, www.epicchartersalaska.com. Kayaking, water taxi, and glacier tours.

MAJOR MARINE TOURS: 907-274-7300, www.majormarine.com. Comfortable, state-of-the-art tour boats to see the glaciers and marine and bird life of Prince William Sound.

LAZY OTTER CHARTERS: 800-587-6887, www.lazyottercharters.com. Custom tours, kayaking trips, kayak rental, water taxi, and landing craft gear transport, plus a great cup of coffee at the Lazy Otter Café.

USEFUL INFORMATION

THE MILEPOST TRAVEL GUIDE: www.themilepost.com/highway-info/highways/seward-highway

ALASKA.ORG ROAD GUIDE—TURNAGAIN ARM: www.alaska.org/guide/turnagain-arm-drive

ALASKA.ORG ROAD GUIDE—PORTAGE AND WHITTIER: www.alaska.org/guide/portage-valley

SPENCER GLACIER WHISTLE STOP TRAIN: www.alaskarailroad.com/travel-planning/destinations/spencer-glacier-whistle-stop

ALASKA RAILROAD: www.alaskarailroad.com

KENAI PENINSULA HIKING INFORMATION: Visit www.taztallyphotography.com for a signed copy of *50 Hikes in Alaska's Kenai Peninsula.*

NATIONAL FOREST CAMPGROUNDS: www.forestcamping.com/dow/alaska/chuginfo.htm

CHUGACH NATIONAL FOREST HIKING AND CABINS: www.fs.usda.gov/chugach

PORTAGE BLUE ICE TRAIL: www.fs.fed.us/wildflowers/regions/alaska/TrailOfBlueIce/index.shtml

15

THE SEWARD HIGHWAY SOUTH (AK 1 AND AK 9)

Meandering the Northern Kenai Mountains

FROM → TO: Southeastern corner of the Turnagain Arm of Cook Inlet to Seward
WHERE IT STARTS: MP 73 on the Seward Highway
WHERE IT ENDS: The docks on Resurrection Bay in Seward at MP 0
ESTIMATED LENGTH: 73 miles, all paved
ESTIMATED TIME: One to two days
HIGHLIGHTS: Turnagain Pass, Tern Lake, Exit Glacier and Harding Ice Field side
road, Seward Sea Life Center, Caines Head State Recreation Area
GETTING THERE: From downtown Anchorage, drive south on the Seward Highway
(AK 1) to MP 73 (the end of Drive #16)

The Kenai Mountain section of the Seward Highway offers 73 miles of mountain adventures and explorations. This is a mountain drive that takes you up into the northern half of the mountains of the Kenai Peninsula, over Turnagain Pass, by numerous lakes and streams, and through gorgeous glacially carved terrains to the coastal town of Seward. In addition to the primary route, I'm recommending three side roads for you to explore, any one of which you could take a day or two to investigate and enjoy.

Travel Time Tip: If you travel the roads of the Kenai Peninsula in the summer, and particularly the section of this road between Turnagain Arm and Tern Lake, I recommend that you plan your day so that you are driving either in morning or evening to avoid traffic. Remember, during the summer it's light well beyond midnight in Alaska!

The **Kenai Peninsula** is known as Alaska's playground, and for good reason. The outdoor recreational opportunities here include hiking, biking, skiing,

LEFT: NORTHERN KENAI OFFERS WINTERTIME SKIING AND SNOWMOBILING

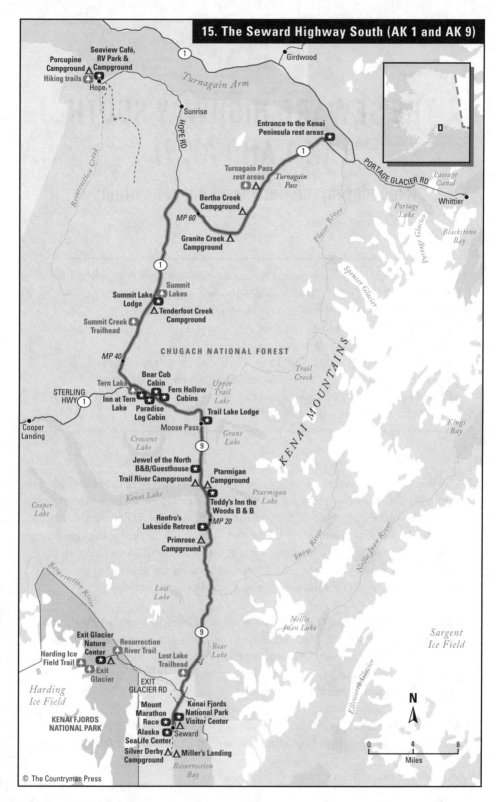

15. The Seward Highway South (AK 1 and AK 9)

Porcupine Campground
Hiking trails
Seaview Café, RV Park & Campground
Hope
Girdwood
Turnagain Arm
Sunrise
HOPE RD
Resurrection Creek
Entrance to the Kenai Peninsula rest areas
PORTAGE GLACIER RD
Passage Canal
Whittier
Portage Lake
Blackstone Bay
Portage Glacier
Turnagain Pass rest areas
Turnagain Pass
Bertha Creek Campground
MP 60
Placer River
Granite Creek Campground
Spencer Glacier
Summit Lakes
Summit Lake Lodge
Tenderfoot Creek Campground
Summit Creek Trailhead
MP 40
CHUGACH NATIONAL FOREST
Trail Creek
KENAI MOUNTAINS
Kings Bay
Bear Cub Cabin
Tern Lake
Fern Hollow Cabins
Upper Trail Lake
STERLING HWY
Inn at Tern Lake
Paradise Log Cabin
Trail Lake Lodge
Moose Pass
Grant Lake
Cooper Landing
Crescent Lake
Jewel of the North B&B/Guesthouse
Trail River Campground
Ptarmigan Campground
Kenai Lake
Teddy's Inn the Woods B & B
Ptarmigan Lake
Cooper Lake
Renfro's Lakeside Retreat
MP 20
Primrose Campground
Snow River
Nellie Juan River
Lost Lake
Nellie Juan Lake
Sargent Ice Field
Resurrection River
Exit Glacier Nature Center
Resurrection River Trail
Lost Lake Trailhead
Bear Lake
Harding Ice Field Trail
Exit Glacier
EXIT GLACIER RD
Ellsworth Glacier
Harding Ice Field
Mount Marathon Race
Kenai Fjords National Park Visitor Center
KENAI FJORDS NATIONAL PARK
Alaska SeaLife Center
Seward
Silver Derby Campground
Miller's Landing
Resurrection Bay

N

0   4   8
Miles

© The Countryman Press

snowmobiling, horseback riding, coastal walks, fishing, and more. At about MP 73 on your Seward Highway journey, you leave the coastal and fjord environments of Turnagain Arm and head directly up into the **Northern Kenai Mountains**. It is quite an abrupt transition; all of a sudden you are deep into steep-sided, forested canyons. Seven miles south of your entrance to the Kenai Peninsula, at about MP 69, you reach mountain-rimmed Turnagain Pass, which, at an elevation of 1,015 feet, is the second highest point on your Seward Highway drive. Turnagain Pass is busy and packed with outdoor adventure lovers all year long.

Moving south from Turnagain Pass you advance through towering mountains, crossing stream channels, lakes, and meadows as you continue your climb into and through the Northern Kenai Mountains. In winter this is a wonderland of snow, ice, and frozen waterfalls, and you'll be treated to a variety of shapes and sizes of snow avalanche cones that form at the bottom of the many steep-sided ravines. During spring, summer, and fall you can pause for a picnic or stop for the evening at any one of several **Chugach National Forest** or Alaska State Park campgrounds (my favorite is Granite Creek). You also have a variety of hiking trails to enjoy (my fave is Summit

EARLY AUTUMN HERE IS A STUNNING MIX OF FALL COLORS AND EARLY RIDGELINE SNOWS

Creek). Between MP 42 and MP 45 you reach the beautiful, glacially carved lower and upper **Summit Lakes** and the upper limits of the boreal forest, so all of the surrounding mountain slopes are tundra covered and wide-open. For hikers who are looking for cross-tundra hiking adventures, the **Summit Lake trailhead** is just a quarter mile south of the south end of Upper Summit Lake. From there, you begin a gradual downhill drive through lake-dotted boreal forest, past the trailhead to Devil's Pass, until you reach the very lovely **Tern Lake** at the junction with the Sterling Highway (Drive #16). If you didn't stop at Summit Lake, Tern Lake is an attractive alternative, with its marsh-lined shores nestled between multiple high peaks soaring thousands of feet above lake level.

Continuing on the Sterling Highway from Tern Lake, the state highway number changes from AK 1 to AK 9, with AK 1 continuing on the Sterling Highway (Drive #17). You pass Trail Lake on your way into the hamlet of **Moose Pass**, where you can find local accommodations and eateries as well as access to floatplane flights and several outfitters. From Moose Pass, continue downhill and parallel to the original route of the Iditarod National Historic Trail that runs just north of the highway. You are traveling mostly through boreal forest along the eastern end of aquamarine Kenai Lake, where you can access multiple camping areas and hiking trailheads. At MP 18 you cross the mouth of the braided channel of the Snow River where it empties into the eastern end of Kenai Lake. As you approach the road high point between Tern Lake and Seward, you will drive once again above tree line and your views will open up. Pull into the turnout at MP 12 to enjoy sweeping views of the **Upper Snow River Valley** as well as some kiosks about the Native history. At about MP 11 you cross the drainage divide between streams flowing eastward toward Resurrection Bay and westward-flowing streams that contribute to the Kenai Lake and River drainage basin. As you enter the outskirts of Seward you'll pass the trailhead to Lost Lake and then, at MP 3.5, the road to Exit Glacier. From there it's over the Resurrection River and into the coastal town of Seward, which is nestled in the Chugach

Mountains on the western end of the beautiful Resurrection Bay, where you will find all sorts of activities to enjoy.

IN THE AREA

Accommodations, Fuel, and Food

MP 56 PLUS 17 MILES TO HOPE: SEAVIEW CAFÉ AND RV PARK AND CAMPGROUND, 907-782-3300, www.seaviewcafealaska.com. Open noon–11 PM Wed.–Sun. $–$$.

MP 45: SUMMIT LAKE LODGE, 907-244-2031, www.summitlakelodge.com. Beautiful log lodge and cabins on the shores of lovely Summit Lake in the heart of the Northern Kenai Mountains. Check out their geothermal energy system! $$.

MP 35: INN AT TERN LAKE, 907-288-3667, www.innatternlake.com. Full-service, beautiful log- and wood-paneled inn. $$.

SUMMIT LAKE LODGE, IN THE HEART OF THE NORTHERN KENAI MOUNTAINS

MP 34: BEAR CUB CABIN (MOOSE PASS), 907-288-3667, www.moose passalaska.com/lodging/bearcubcabin. Historical, restored (originally built in the early 1900s), cozy, unique, and cute cabin. $–$$.

MP 34: PARADISE LOG CABIN (MOOSE PASS), 907-330-9085, paradise logcabin.business.site. Private, clean, custom-built, old-style log cabin. $–$$.

MP 28: TRAIL LAKE LODGE (MOOSE PASS), 907-288-3101, www.trail lakelodge.com. Full-service lodge with a restaurant. $.

MP 24: FERN HOLLOW CABINS (MOOSE PASS), 907-288-3678, www.fern hollowcabins.com. Beautiful shake-sided cabin, tucked in the woods, with the coolest cabin door ever! $–$$.

MP 24: JEWEL OF THE NORTH B&B/GUESTHOUSE (MOOSE PASS), 907-288-3166, www.bedbreakfasthome.com/jewelofthenorth. Modern, wood-paneled, streamside guest house. $–$$.

MP 22: TEDDY'S INN IN THE WOODS (MOOSE PASS), 907-288-3126, www.seward.net/teddys. Fun barn-style apartment that sleeps five near Kenai Lake. $–$$.

MP 18: RENFRO'S LAKESIDE RETREAT (MOOSE PASS), 907-288-5059, www.renfroslakesideretreat.com. Full-service cabins and RV sites at a lakeside resort. $–$$.

Camping

MP 56 PLUS 18 MILES TO END OF ROAD IN HOPE: PORCUPINE CAMP-GROUND. Thirty-four developed Chugach National Forest campground sites under old-growth boreal forest with great birch trees. Trailheads to Hope Point and Gull Rock hiking trails and near the north trailhead for the Resurrection Pass Trail. $.

MP 64: BERTHA CREEK CAMPGROUND. Twelve small, quiet, streamside, developed Chugach National Forest campground sites. $.

MP 63: GRANITE CREEK CAMPGROUND. Nineteen lovely campsites in an open canopy forest next to beautiful Granite Creek (my favorite developed Kenai campground). $.

MP 45.25: TENDERFOOT CREEK CAMPGROUND. Thirty-five-site developed National Forest campground on Upper Summit Lake, close to the Summit Creek trailhead. $.

MP 25: TRAIL RIVER CAMPGROUND. Large (63 sites) lakeside developed National Forest campground on eastern shore of Kenai Lake. $.

MP 22.7: PTARMIGAN CAMPGROUND. Small hike-in National Forest campground on shores of Ptarmigan Lake with 16 tent sites. $.

MP 17.7: PRIMROSE LANDING CAMPGROUND. Eight-site developed campground near northern trailhead for Primrose and Meridian Lakes Trails. $.

MP 11.6 (EXIT GLACIER ROAD): Exit Glacier Campground, 907-422-0500. Twelve walk-in tent sites near Exit Glacier. $.

MP 0: WATERFRONT PARK, 907-224-4055, www.cityofseward.us. City of Seward RV (with utilities) and dry tent camping next to waterfront near downtown. $.

MP 2.2 (BEACH DRIVE SOUTH OF SEWARD): SILVER DERBY CAMPGROUND, 13750 Lowell Point Road, Seward, 907-224-4711. Private RV and tent developed campground near Resurrection Bay. $.

MP 2.8 (BEACH DRIVE SOUTH OF SEWARD): MILLER'S LANDING, south end of Lowell Point Road, Seward, 907-331-3113 or 907-331-4040, www.millerslandingak.com. Private RV and tent developed campground next to Resurrection Bay with an array of servies and tours. $.

Attractions and Recreation

MP MARKERS: The MP markers begin at MP 0 in Seward; therefore, this tour starts at MP 73.

MP 73: ENTRANCE TO THE KENAI PENINSULA. There are several dry rest stops near here located on both side of the road.

MP 68.4: TURNAGAIN PASS. At the pass you are right about at tree line, so you have a variety of environments and activities from which to choose. Take hikes that begin in the boreal forest and climb above the tree line. You can enjoy fishing and bird and beaver watching down around the lowland marshy tundra. And, as you might imagine, you can take advantage of

TURNAGAIN ARM FROM THE HIGH SLOPES OF THE HOPE POINT RIDGE TRAIL

photographic opportunities galore. You can rest and just enjoy the incredible scenery, and dry camp overnight at one of two large Turnagain Pass rest areas with toilets, located on opposite sides of the road. The east side rest area provides access to hiking, skiing, and snowshoe trails, while the west side rest area tends to be frequented by four-wheelers in the summer and snowmachiners in the winter. Even in the middle of winter the stream at the base of the east-facing slopes on the west side of the valley still flows, creating fascinating ice, snow, and water sculptures. At just over 1,000 feet in elevation, the pass retains snow for a lot longer than the coastal areas, which allows for earlier and longer winter recreation seasons. During the summer months, the extensive grassy meadows that dominate here offer shoulder-high wildflowers for multiple months.

MP 56: THE HOPE ROAD. An 18-mile paved road leads to the historic mining community of Hope (population 200), located on the southwest shore of Turnagain Arm. It also provides access to the Gull Rock, Hope Point, and Resurrection Pass Trails, as well as the Chugach National Forest Porcupine Campground, all located near the end of the road close to Hope.

MP 45: UPPER SUMMIT LAKE, SUMMIT LAKE LODGE. At 1,266 feet in elevation, Upper Summit Lake is 200 feet higher than Turnagain Pass, making this the highest point on the Seward Highway, and in fact on any highway on the Kenai Peninsula. Pull off along Upper Summit Lake for a picnic and to enjoy the lake and the surrounding mountain slopes. Consider camping at the Tenderfoot Creek Campground, or stay overnight at the beautiful Summit Lake Lodge. And if you are interested, ask the lodge owner about his innovative renewable energy lake-water-based heat pump system.

MP 42.5: SUMMIT CREEK TRAILHEAD. This is one of my four favorite hikes on the Kenai Peninsula. Summit Creek Trail traverses three separate drainage basins and offers the highest starting elevation of any established Kenai trail. It is also the fastest way to the alpine tundra high country and, along with the Harding Ice Field Trail, reaches the highest elevation in the Kenai Peninsula inventory of maintained trails.

MP 36: TERN LAKE. This is a beautiful rest stop. Turn briefly north onto the Sterling Highway (Drive #16) at the second turnoff (you'll miss Tern Lake if you take the first turnoff) and drive 100 yards to the turnout rest area on the south side of the road. From spring through fall, look for the mating pair of beautiful white swans that make Tern Lake their summer home. In winter Tern Lake forms a terrific ice-skating surface before the snow falls and an easy-to-access Nordic ski and snowshoe surface once it is snow-covered.

BREATHTAKING HIGH-COUNTRY VIEWS FROM THE SUMMIT CREEK TRAIL

THE ALPINE TUNDRA SURROUNDING LOST LAKE IS GREAT FOR CAMPING AND HIKING

MP 28: MOOSE PASS. Stop off for lunch at the beautiful Trail Lake Lodge, stay overnight at any of several quaint and cute lodging options, or arrange for a flight-seeing tour or fishing trip.

MP 5: LOST LAKE TRAILHEAD. Turn south and follow signs for 0.7 miles to the trailhead for a wonderful hike through old-growth boreal forest to and across the gorgeous alpine tundra meadows and high peaks surrounding Lost Lake.

MP 3.5: EXIT GLACIER. Turn south onto Herman Lehrer Road (a.k.a. Exit Glacier Road) and drive 5 miles for access to multiple adventures, including the Kenai Fjords National Park Visitors Center, the Resurrection River, Exit Glacier, and Harding Ice Field Trails. Be sure to at least walk the half-paved trial that leads to the front of Exit Glacier.

MP 0: IN AND AROUND SEWARD. While in Seward, enjoy the Alaska Sea Life Center; a glacier and marine-mammal and bird tour; a hike up to Exit

EXIT GLACIER IS ACCESSIBLE AND STILL IMPRESSIVE, EVEN IN RETREAT

KAYAKING ON RESURRECTION BAY

Glacier and maybe even the Harding Ice Field; the Fourth of July Mount Marathon Race events; local art galleries and bistros; and hiking/kayaking along the Caines Head State Recreation Area from Miller's Landing.

Festivals and Fairs

SEWARD SILVER SALMON DERBY (ALL SUMMER): www.seward.com/ welcome-to-seward-alaska/seward-silver-salmon-derby-august

MOUNT MARATHON RACE AND STREET PARTY (JULY 4): www.mmr .seward.com

SEWARD MUSIC AND ART FESTIVAL (THIRD WEEK OF SEPTEMBER): www.sewardfestival.com

Outfitters and Tour Operators

MAJOR MARINE TOURS: 907-274-7300, www.majormarine.com. Top-notch marine tours out of Seward—glaciers, marine mammals, and bird habitats.

THE ANNUAL JULY 4TH MARATHON RACE ATTRACTS PARTICIPANTS FROM AROUND THE WORLD

KENAI FJORD TOURS: 877-777-4051, www.kenaifjords.com. They offer excellent tours of glacial fjords, marine mammals, and birds on large catamarans. An exclusive Fox Island tour too.

GONE AGAIN CHARTERS: 907-288-3655 or 907-362-1509 (cell), www.goneagain charters.com. Fishing charters in Seward and Prince William Sound.

ALASKAN COASTAL SAFARI: 907-362-4101, akcoastalsafari@hotmail.com. Fishing and wildlife tours and water taxi services.

ALASKA SEA LIFE CENTER: 301 Railway Avenue, Seward, 907-224-6300, www.alaskasealife.org. Marine aquarium, educational exhibits and programs, and a marine mammal rescue center.

USEFUL INFORMATION

THE MILEPOST TRAVEL GUIDE: www.themilepost.com/highway-info/highways/seward-highway

ALASKA.ORG ROAD GUIDE: www.alaska.org/guide/seward-highway

MOUNT MARATHON RACE: www.mmr.seward.com

NATIONAL FOREST CAMPGROUNDS: www.forestcamping.com/dow/alaska/chuginfo.htm

ALASKA STATE PARK CAMPING: dnr.alaska.gov/parks/units

Annual Fourth of July Mount Marathon Race and Community Party

Each July Fourth the community of Seward hosts the world-famous race up 3,022-foot Mount Marathon. Accompanying the race is a community party, for which streets are blocked off, that attracts mountain runners and observers from all over the world (Seward's population grows from about 2,500 to 40,000 during the event). The entire town gets involved in this multi-day party that is not to be missed if you are anywhere nearby.

ALASKA STATE PARK CAMPING ON THE KENAI: dnr.alaska.gov/parks/units/#kenai

KENAI NATIONAL WILDLIFE REFUGE: www.fws.gov/refuge/kenai. Download the information-packed PDF.

DISCOVERY GUIDE FOR THE ENTIRE KENAI PENINSULA: www.kenaipeninsula.org/discovery-guide

SEWARD CHAMBER OF COMMERCE: www.seward.com

ORDER A SEWARD TRIP PLANNER: www.seward.com/visit-seward/trip-planner

EXIT GLACIER RETREAT INFORMATION: www.nps.gov

MOOSE PASS LODGING: www.moosepassalaska.com/lodging

KENAI PENINSULA HIKING INFORMATION: To order a signed copy of *50 Hikes in Alaska's Kenai Peninsula*, visit www.taztallyphotography.com.

16

THE STERLING HIGHWAY NORTH (AK 1)

Land of Lakes and Streams

FROM → TO: Tern Lake to Swanson River Road

WHERE IT STARTS: Tern Lake at intersection of Seward Highway and Sterling Highway (MP 36 on Seward Highway; Drive #15)

WHERE IT ENDS: Swanson River Road, Soldotna

ESTIMATED LENGTH: 47 miles, all paved

ESTIMATED TIME: One to two days

HIGHLIGHTS: Tern Lake, floating and fishing the Kenai River, Rainbow Lake, Skilak Lake, Kelly Lake, Swanson and Swan Lakes canoe trail

GETTING THERE: Drive 80 miles east on Seward Highway (Drives #14 and #15, AK 1) to the second turnoff for Sterling Highway to Homer. If you take the first, very well-labeled turnoff for Homer, rather than the second turnoff at Tern Lake, you will be on the correct road but you will miss Tern Lake and the Tern Lake Rest Area.

MILEPOSTS NOTES: MP mileage numbers begin at Seward on AK 9 and continue along AK 1 starting at MP 36.

Your Sterling Highway drive begins at **Tern Lake**, a lovely alpine lake nestled between three mountain ridges, with resident swans and a pleasant rest and picnic area. For the first half of this drive you continue to enjoy the landscapes of the Northern Kenai Mountains. In addition, you'll be treated to views of numerous alpine lakes and stream channels. Eight miles south of Tern Lake you arrive at the shores of the mountain-rimmed, aquamarine-colored (due to its content of continuously suspended glacial rock flour) **Kenai Lake** and the beginning of the community of **Cooper Landing**. Cooper Landing, which spreads along 13 miles of the shores of

LEFT: THE NORTHERN STERLING HIGHWAY PASSES THROUGH THE HEART OF THE KENAI MOUNTAINS

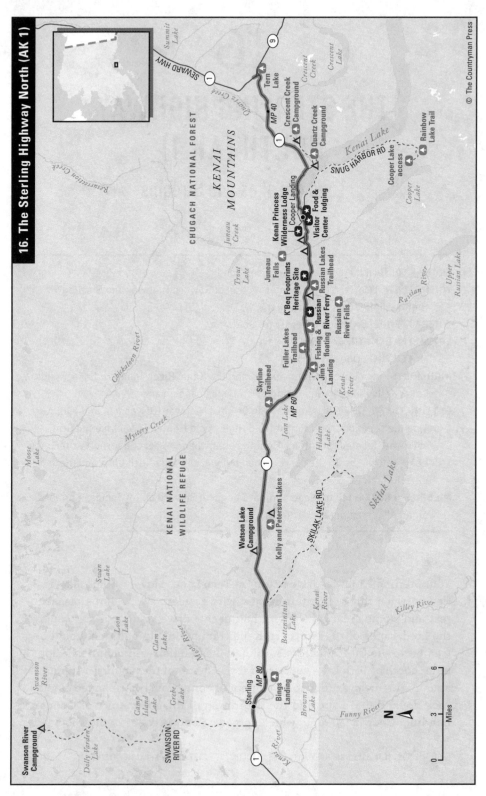

16. The Sterling Highway North (AK 1)

SEWARD HWY

Summit Lake

Quartz Creek

Tern Lake

MP 40

Crescent Creek Campground

Crescent Creek

Crescent Lake

Quartz Creek Campground

Kenai Lake

Rainbow Lake Trail

SNUG HARBOR RD

Cooper Lake access

Cooper Lake

CHUGACH NATIONAL FOREST

KENAI MOUNTAINS

Juneau Creek

Kenai Princess Wilderness Lodge

Cooper Landing

Visitor Food & Center lodging

Juneau Falls

Trout Lake

K'Beq Footprints Heritage Site

Russian Lakes Trailhead

Russian River

Upper Russian Lake

Russian River Falls

Russian Lake

Resurrection Creek

Fuller Lakes Trailhead

Fishing & Russian floating River Ferry

Jim's Landing

Skyline Trailhead

Jean Lake

MP 60

Kenai River

Hidden Lake

Skilak Lake

Chickaloon River

Mystery Creek

KENAI NATIONAL WILDLIFE REFUGE

Moose Lake

Swan Lake

Watson Lake Campground

Kelly and Peterson Lakes

SKILAK LAKE RD

Kenai River

Killey River

Leon Lake

Clam Lake

Moose River

Bottenintnin Lake

Loon Lake

Camp Island Lake

Grebe Lake

Dolly Varden Lake

Swanson River Campground

SWANSON RIVER RD

Swanson River

Sterling

MP 80

Bings Landing

Browns Lake

Funny River

Kenai River

N

0   3   6
Miles

© The Countryman Press

Kenai Lake, and its outflow, the Kenai River, offer lodging, restaurants, fuel, camping, hiking, as well as floating and boating adventures on and around the lake and river. Along the Kenai River road segment you will find a variety of outdoor adventure outfitters as well as numerous eateries. The entire Kenai Lake and River section of road is very narrow and twisty with no shoulder, so drive carefully and pull off to do your landscape viewing. At MP 48 you cross the bridge over the outlet of Kenai Lake, which is also the beginning of the world-famous salmon fishing stream and the aquamarine-colored Kenai River. Just south of the bridge crossing is the turnoff to **Snug Harbor Road** that you can drive along the east side of Kenai Lake.

The 10-mile-long section from the bridge over the Kenai Lake outlet to **Jim's Landing** is a water-oriented playground favored by many for floating and fishing. From time to time turn your binoculars up onto the mountain slopes to see if you can catch a glimpse of the mountain goats that frequent the high elevations. Along this section of road you also have access to the world-

RAFTING THE KENAI RIVER IS A FAVORITE PASTIME, FROM SPRING THROUGH FALL

LOWER RUSSIAN LAKE IS SECLUDED AND PEACEFUL

famous-for-fishing Russian River Ferry, which fishermen use to move back and forth across the Kenai River near its confluence with the **Russian River**. The rest stop and launching area are always a hub of activity throughout the spring, summer, and early fall.

In addition to the fabulous water sports opportunities, there are also trailheads for numerous wonderful hikes along this section of the Sterling Highway, including the Crescent Lake, Russian River, Resurrection Pass, Fuller Lakes, and Skyline hikes. All of these offer day hikes as well as longer multiday hiking opportunities. The Russian River Trail also boasts a wheelchair-accessible path to the Russian River Falls.

Floating Safety Note: Even though the Kenai River is mostly a Class I river, remember that these are all glacially fed waters that are very cold. Be sure to wear a life jacket anytime you are on the lake or river to help ensure your survival in the case of a boating mishap. All the major launch points provide free life jackets to borrow.

Bear Country Note: Alaska is bear country, and in areas like the Kenai River, where you have lots of fish and fishermen, bears and humans are likely to meet. Keep your eyes open for the curious and hungry bears, and if you see one approaching, move slowly away. And don't drag your fish with you!

Near MP 58 the road turns away from the Kenai River at its intersection with the east end of Skilak Lake Road. From Jim's Landing the river continues for several miles down into **Skilak Lake** while the main road leads away from the channel. The river here offers numerous wilderness paddling and hiking opportunities. From the intersection with Skilak Lake Road, you will continue for another 3 miles through the southern section of the **Northern Kenai Mountains**. You will have access to two more hikes: the Fuller Lakes trail, which takes you through boreal forest with gorgeous groves of big birches and lovely stands of mountain hemlock to twin alpine lakes at tree line, and the Skyline Trail, which leads you quickly up to the alpine tundra.

South of MP 62 you leave the Northern Kenai Mountains behind and enter the watery lakes country of the **Kenai National Wildlife Refuge**. From here to the Swanson Lake Road you travel through lowland forest featuring large groves of aspens and birches interspersed throughout the spruce. Just after MP 68 you arrive at a side road leading to Kelly and Peterson Lakes. (Look carefully for the sign, as it's easy to zoom right past it because there's no prior notification for it.) Your Northern Sterling Highway journey ends at MP 83.5 at the junction with the Swanson River Road, located in the small town of **Sterling**, which provides access to another section of the Kenai National Wildlife Refuge.

IN THE AREA

Accommodations, Fuel, and Food

MP 47.5: WILDMAN'S CONVENIENCE STORE AND VEHICLE SHUTTLE, 907-595-1456, www.wildmans.org. Stop here for coffee, beer, wine and spirits, ice cream, groceries, a bite to eat, and to arrange for vehicle shuttle for your Kenai River float/fishing trip.

MP 47.7: KENAI PRINCESS WILDERNESS LODGE, 17245 Frontier Circle, Cooper Landing, 907-595-1425, www.princesslodges.com/princess-alaska-lodges/kenai-lodge. Turn at Bean Creek Road on the north side of

WINTER ON THE KENAI PENINSULA

the bridge over the outlet of Kenai Lake, then drive 3 miles to this beautiful log cabin–style lodge located on a bluff above the Kenai River with great views of the Kenai River Valley and surrounding mountains. With full-service accommodations and a restaurant, this lodge is associated with Princess Tours, which offers train, ship, and bus tours and lodges all over Alaska. $$–$$$.

MP 47: ALASKA HEAVENLY LODGE, 866-595-2012, www.alaskaheavenly .com. Enjoy the rustic elegance of this beautiful log lodge for accommodations, meetings, and weddings. $$.

MP 48.2: COOPER LANDING GROCERY, 907-595-1341. Groceries, pizza, ice cream, and supplies.

MP 48.5: DRIFTERS LODGE, 907-595-5555, www.drifterslodge.com. Lodge, rafting, and fishing adventures. $–$$.

MP 48.5: THE HUTCH BED AND BREAKFAST (COOPER LANDING), 907-595-1270 or 907-598-1270 (cell), www.arctic.net/~hutch. Three-story rustic cedar lodge, welcoming owners, and nightly campfires. $–$$.

MP 48.5: GRIZZLY RIDGE CABINS AND RV SITES, 907-595-1260, www .grizzlyridgeak.com. Lodge and cabins plus RV sites. $–$$.

MP 49: SACKETT'S KENAI GRILL (COOPER LANDING), 907-595-1827. Known for its BBQ, pizza, and other comfort food. $.

MP 49.6: COOPER LANDING FISH CAMP, 907-595-3474, www.facebook .com/CooperLandingFishCampLLC. Cabins and guided fishing. $–$$.

MP 50.1: KENAI RIVERSIDE FISHING, 800-478-4100, www.kenairiverside fishing.com. Full-service lodge with a wide variety of guided fishing adventures on the Kenai River. $$.

MP 51.5: GWIN'S LODGE ROADHOUSE, 907-595-1266, www.gwinslodge .com. Good food, nice cabins, and a tackle shop at a long-standing and historic roadhouse, and they serve breakfast all day! One of our faves. Ask for the salmon chowder. $–$$.

MP 51.5: ALASKA HEAVENLY LODGE, 866-595-2012, www.alaskaheavenly .com. Classic log lodge–style accommodations on a large, beautiful riverside property with guided fishing. $–$$.

GWIN'S LODGE ROADHOUSE

MP 51: UPPER KENAI RIVER INN B&B, 907-595-3333, www.alaskabba .com/inns.php?id=121. Small, homey, bed & breakfast open all year. $–$$.

MP 51: RIVER HAVEN CABIN ON THE RIVER, 907-398-8834, www.river havencabin.com. Sweet cabins on the Kenai River. $–$$.

MP 51.5: ALPINE INN MOTEL, 907-595-1557, www.kenairivermotel.com. Fishing-oriented motel close to the Kenai River. $–$$.

MP 52: EAGLE LANDING RESORT, 907-595-1213 or 866-595-1213, www .eaglelandingresort.net. Cabins and guided adventures on the Kenai River. $–$$.

Camping

MP 45: QUARTZ CREEK CAMPGROUND (COOPER LANDING). Large (45 sites), very nice, highly developed campground on the shores of Kenai Lake with access to hiking and boating. $.

MP 45 PLUS 3 MILES UP CRESCENT CREEK ROAD: CRESCENT CREEK CAMPGROUND (COOPER LANDING). Partially developed, secluded campground snuggled in the boreal forest near the Crescent Lake trailhead. $.

MP 49.7: KENAI RIVERSIDE CAMPGROUND (COOPER LANDING). 888-536-2478, www.kenairv.com/kenai-riverside-campground/campground. Full-service RV camping with hookups. $.

MP 50.7: COOPER CREEK SOUTH AND NORTH CAMPGROUNDS (COOPER LANDING). Chugach National Forest developed campgrounds along the Kenai River.

MP 53: RUSSIAN RIVER CAMPGROUND. Large (80 sites) Chugach National Forest campground at the confluence of the Russian River with the Kenai River. Fishing paradise and trailhead for Russian Lakes Trail. $.

MP 68: KELLY AND PETERSON LAKES CAMPGROUND. Two partially developed campgrounds at Kelly and Peterson Lakes that are part of the

POPULAR ACTIVITIES ON THE KENAI RIVER

Kenai National Wildlife Refuge, with fire pit, toilets, and dirt boat ramp access to the lakes. Seven Lakes Trail northern trailhead too. $.

MP 82: WATSON LAKE STATE RECREATION SITE CAMPGROUND. Small (six sites) developed lakeside campground with a boat launch on a quiet lake. $.

Attractions and Recreation

MP 36–37: TERN LAKE AND TERN LAKE REST STOP. Regardless of which way I'm heading—Anchorage, Seward, Homer, or just for some outdoor adventure in between—I always stop here to enjoy Tern Lake. There's a turnout along the lake just after you turn onto the Sterling Highway, or, if you'd like a little bit longer and quieter respite, drive half a mile to the Tern Lake rest stop, where you will find picnic tables, pit toilets, a salmon-viewing platform near the lake outlet, and a couple of short hikes. In particular, walk back across the bridge over the stream channel and take the short hike up onto the overlook knoll for some wonderful views across the lake and the surrounding mountainous countryside.

MP 45: QUARTZ CREEK AND CRESCENT CREEK. There are camping, boating, and hiking opportunities galore here.

MP 47.7: ACCESS TO JUNEAU FALLS SECTION OF THE RESURRECTION TRAIL. Turn west on Bean Creek Road to the trailhead that leads to the Juno Falls section of the Resurrection Trail. This is also the access road for the Kenai Princess Wilderness Lodge.

MP 48: KENAI RIVER OUTLET BRIDGE AND COOPER LANDING STATE RECREATION SITE. Slow down as you drive over the bridge for terrific views east across Lake Kenai and west down the Kenai River. A quarter mile past the south end of the bridge you can access the Cooper Landing State Recreation Site, which has a boat launch ramp (human powered only) for the river. There is frequently fun and fascinating activity happening around the boat launch.

MP 48: SNUG HARBOR ROAD. Drive this 13-mile-long, mostly gravel road for north-facing views across Kenai Lake into the Northern Kenai Mountains; a sweet little hike along a marshy tundra trail to Rainbow Lake; access to the northern trailhead of the wild and woolly Resurrection River Trail; and the secluded lakeshore of little-visited Cooper Lake to camp near the end of the road.

MP 48.7: COOPER LANDING VISITOR'S CENTER. This visitor's center includes a museum with fascinating mining-era artifacts.

MP 52.6: K'BEQ FOOTPRINTS HERITAGE SITE. This is an Alaskan Native Heritage Site of the Kenaitze Indian Tribe's Dena'ina ancestors, offering interpretive displays.

MP 53: RUSSIAN LAKES TRAILHEAD ACCESS. Enjoy a short hike up to the Russian River Falls (wheelchair accessible) or a longer one through the high country.

MP 53.5: RESURRECTION PASS TRAILHEAD ACCESS. This 39-mile-long wilderness track leads up to and through the tundra-covered high country of the Northern Kenai Mountains.

MP 48–58.5: FISHING AND FLOATING THE KENAI RIVER. The Kenai River is world famous for its king salmon fishing, so during the summer months you have no shortage of fishing friends here. The Kenai River also offers fun Class I and II floating opportunities, as well as access to hiking.

SKILAK LAKE AND THE CENTRAL KENAI MOUNTAINS

MP 55: RUSSIAN RIVER FERRY. If you are a fisherman, this is one of those must-stop, world-famous salmon-fishing locations. In addtion to a large parking and launch area, there's a ferry across the Kenai River for shuttling fishermen around to their favorite line-tossing locations.

MP 58: JIM'S LANDING AND SKILAK LAKE ROAD. Turn south onto the eastern end of the Skilak Lake Road and take an immediate left to Jim's Landing, which is the end of the 10-mile float trip down the Kenai River from the outlet of Kenai Lake. There is parking, toilets, and a Kenai River boat ramp. Enjoy plenty of activity from folks taking out of the river after their fishing and floating trips.

MP 58: SKILAK LAKE ROAD. This 18-mile-long favorite of mine, which can be accessed from either MP 75 or MP 58 on the Sterling Highway, is

EARLY MORNING, KELLY LAKE

a generously wide two-lane gravel road. It traverses a forested landscape containing over a dozen gem-like lowland lakes, including the massive and beautiful Skilak Lake, seven hiking trails, and five well developed campsites with boat ramps, all within the Kenai National Wildlife Refuge. You can easily devote several days to exploring the lakes and trails of the beautiful Skilak Lake country. And if you are a trout fisherman or fisherwoman, huge brown and rainbow trout in the large and glorious Skilak Lake are awaiting your line tosses. Skilak Lake is also one of my favorite winter Nordic ski haunts, and I often have the whole lake to myself.

MP 58: FULLER LAKES TRAILHEAD. Hike to several high-country, alpine tundra–surrounded lakes, passing through boreal forest with groves of big, beautiful birch trees and mountain hemlocks. From trail's end you can also access a scenic high elevation alpine ridgeline traverse over to the Skyline trail.

MP 61: SKYLINE TRAILHEAD. Hike up above the tree line for gorgeous views of the surrounding Skilak Lake country. You can join the Fuller Lakes Trail via a high alpine ridge traverse.

MP 68.8: KELLY AND PETERSON LAKES. Part of the Kenai National Wildlife Refuge, these two lowland lakes provide great picnic sites as well as boating and fishing opportunities. Kelly Lake offers delightful early morning or late afternoon strolls along the Seven Lakes Trail for which it is the northern trailhead; the trail's other end is on the Skilak Lake Road (see MP 58). Kelly Lake is also home to a family of very industrious beavers. You can hike to a cabin, located a half mile along the shoreline.

MP 75: WESTERN END OF THE SKILAK LAKE ROAD. See MP 58.

MP 80: BINGS LANDING STATE PARK. This road provides access to a powerboat launch site for the western portion of the Kenai River.

MP 83.5: SWANSON RIVER ROAD. This wide, two-lane, well-maintained, mostly gravel road leads 9.1 miles north across the marshy, lake-dotted lowlands of the Kenai River Flats, through boreal forest toward Cook Inlet, and into the northern section of the Kenai National Wildlife Refuge. The road terminates at the Swanson River Campground at a put-in on the Swanson River Canoe Trail. Highlights include fishing, canoeing, birding, and camping at over 20 campsites.

Festivals and Fairs

KENAI RIVER FESTIVAL (SECOND WEEK IN JUNE): Celebration of the Kenai River, kenaiwatershed.org/community-outreach/kenai-river-festival

SOLDOTNA PROGRESS DAYS (THIRD WEEK IN JULY): Chain saw carving competition, parade, Dutch oven competition, www.visitsoldotna.com/events/progress-days

Outfitters and Tour Operators

MP 47.5: WILDMAN'S CONVENIENCE STORE AND VEHICLE SHUTTLE, 907-595-1456, www.wildmans.org. Stop here for coffee, beer, wine and spirits, ice cream, groceries, a bite to eat, and to arrange for vehicle shuttle for your Kenai River float/fishing trip.

MP 48.5: ALASKA TROUTFITTERS, 907-595-1212, www.aktroutfitters .com. Guided fishing specializing in Dolly Varden trout, with an Orvis pro shop.

MP 48.5: KENAI RIVER FLOAT-N-FISH, 907-595-3505, www.kenaifloat-n -fish.com. Small mom-and-pop fishing trips.

MP 49.5: ALASKA RIVERS COMPANY, 888-595-1226, www.alaskarivers company.com. Cabins, fishing, rafting, paddleboarding, and glacier tours.

MP 50.1: KENAI RIVERSIDE FISHING, 800-478-4100, www.kenairiver sidefishing.com. Wide variety of guided fishing adventures on the Kenai River.

MP 51: ALASKA RIVER ADVENTURE, 907-595-2000, www.alaskariver adventures.com. Lodging and guided rafting and fishing tours and hikes.

MP 51: KENAI CACHE OUTFITTERS, 907-268-4849, kenaicache.com. Complete tackle shop, fish processing and freezing, plus fishing trips.

MP 52: ALASKA RIVERS COMPANY, 888-595-1226, www.alaskarivers company.com. Guided fishing, boating, and rafting trips. Kenai River cabin rentals too.

MP 75: DOT'S KENAI RIVER FISH CAMP, 907-262-5650. Secluded fish camp on the banks of the Kenai River.

USEFUL INFORMATION

THE MILEPOST TRAVEL GUIDE: www.themilepost.com/highway-info/highways/sterling-highway

ALASKA.ORG ROAD GUIDE: www.alaska.org/guide/sterling-highway

KENAI NATIONAL WILDLIFE REFUGE: www.fws.gov/refuge/kenai. Download the information-packed PDF.

DISCOVERY GUIDE FOR THE ENTIRE KENAI PENINSULA: www.kenai peninsula.org/discovery-guide

17

THE STERLING HIGHWAY
SOUTH (AK 1)

A Playground of Beaches, Lakes, and Streams

FROM → TO: Soldotna to Homer

WHERE IT STARTS: At the Soldotna Visitor Center just north of the Kenai River bridge in Soldotna

WHERE IT ENDS: End of the Homer Spit

ESTIMATED LENGTH: 80 miles, all paved

ESTIMATED TIME: One to two days

HIGHLIGHTS: Cook Inlet view at MP 142.5, Anchor Point Beach, "The View" from the Skyline Drive side road, Homer Spit, Homer's art galleries, Kachemak Bay State Park hiking, kayaking, and taxi tour

GETTING THERE: Drive 80 miles east from Potter Marsh in Anchorage on Seward Highway (Drive #14, AK 1) to the second turnoff for Sterling Highway to Homer. If you take the first, very well labeled turnoff for Homer, rather than the second turnoff at Tern Lake, you will be on the correct road but you miss Tern Lake and the Tern Lake Rest Area. Then drive 95.6 miles on the Northern Sterling Highway (Drive #16) to the Soldotna Visitor Center just north of the Kenai River bridge at MP 95.

Begin your southern Sterling Highway drive near the **Kenai River bridge**, where you have your last view of the lovely, aquamarine-colored (due to its suspended glacial sediment), king salmon fishing haven of the Kenai River. The Kenai River may be the most famous fishing stream in the world, and with good reason. Pulling 50- to 70-pound king salmon out is not uncommon, with a record for this stream being a 97-pound monster caught in 2003. As you head south from the Kenai River you will encounter a number of other appealing streams, including the **Kasilof River**, which drains giant

LEFT: A GLORIOUS VIEW OF 10,000+ FOOT HIGH MOUNT ILIAMNA VOLCANO FROM ANCHOR POINT BEACH

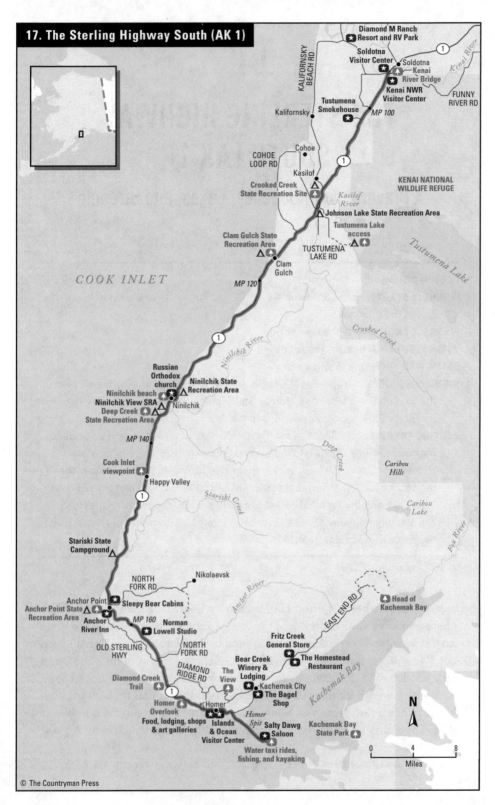

17. The Sterling Highway South (AK 1)

Diamond M Ranch
Resort and RV Park

Soldotna
Visitor Center

Soldotna

KALIFORNSKY BEACH RD

Kenai River Bridge

Kenai NWR Visitor Center

FUNNY RIVER RD

Tustumena Smokehouse

Kalifornsky

MP 100

Kenai River

COHOE LOOP RD

Cohoe

Kasilof

Crooked Creek State Recreation Site

Kasilof River

KENAI NATIONAL WILDLIFE REFUGE

Johnson Lake State Recreation Area

Tustumena Lake access

Clam Gulch State Recreation Area

TUSTUMENA LAKE RD

Tustumena Lake

COOK INLET

Clam Gulch

MP 120

Ninilchik River

Crooked Creek

Russian Orthodox church

Ninilchik State Recreation Area

Ninilchik beach

Ninilchik View SRA

Deep Creek State Recreation Area

Ninilchik

Deep Creek

Caribou Hills

MP 140

Cook Inlet viewpoint

Happy Valley

Stariski Creek

Caribou Lake

Fox River

Stariski State Campground

Nikolaevsk

North Fork Rd

Anchor River

Head of Kachemak Bay

EAST END RD

Anchor Point

Sleepy Bear Cabins

Anchor Point State Recreation Area

MP 160

Anchor River Inn

Norman Lowell Studio

Fritz Creek General Store

The Homestead Restaurant

OLD STERLING HWY

NORTH FORK RD

DIAMOND RIDGE RD

Bear Creek Winery & Lodging

Diamond Creek Trail

The View

Homer

Kachemak City

The Bagel Shop

Kachemak Bay

Homer Overlook

Food, lodging, shops & art galleries

Islands & Ocean Visitor Center

Homer Spit

Salty Dawg Saloon

Kachemak Bay State Park

Water taxi rides, fishing, and kayaking

N

0   4   8
Miles

© The Countryman Press

CAMPING ON THE HOMER SPIT

Lake Tustumena, as well as **Crooked Creek**, **Deep Creek**, and the **Anchor River**, all of which offer excellent opportunities for floating and fishing.

The first 20 or so miles you roll through an open-canopy boreal forest interspersed with large sections of marshy tundra that surround numerous lakes and interconnecting stream channels. The higher and drier slopes are dominated by white spruce, aspen, and birch, while black spruces, willows, and grasses dominate the lower and wetter marshy and muskeg areas. I call these "3M" areas, which stands for "marshes, meadows, and moose." Thousands of moose live in the southern half of the Kenai Peninsula, and they are wonderful to see and have as neighbors. Unfortunately, between 100 and 200 of them are killed in vehicle collisions each year, so please drive with vigilance, and particularly at night, don't outdrive your headlights.

Beginning at **Clam Gulch** (MP 78), your drive is dominated by views west across Cook Inlet over to the Chigmit Mountains, including three spectacular intermittently active and easily visible volcanoes that are, from north to south, **Mounts Spurr**, **Redoubt**, and **Iliamna**, all of which rise from sea level to over 10,000 feet. Two additional, more southerly located volcanoes, **Mounts Augustine** and **Douglas**, are visible on clear days as you approach the southern end of the Kenai Peninsula. Between Clam Gulch and Anchor Point you have nearly continuous views across Cook Inlet with numerous pullout viewing points, including my favorite at MP 142.5. In addition to crossing four major stream channels, you have access to a number of lakes, including the large, spectacular and wild Tustumena Lake and its more well

KAYAKING THE FJORDS OF KACHEMAK BAY

developed neighbor, Johnson Lake. One of the features of this road that sets it apart from so many others in Alaska is its proximity to multiple **state beach recreation areas**.

Most of Alaska's connected road system tends to offer up mostly rocky shorelines, but here, in the southern Kenai Peninsula, you can enjoy beaches that rival those found anywhere else in the world. Kenai beaches extend for dozens of miles, are often backed by high bluffs up to 1,000 feet high, and are meshed with beautiful coastal stream channels. These beaches experience big waves and enormous tidal ranges of up to 30 feet and provide some wonderful tide-pooling opportunities at low tide. Southern Kenai beaches are strewn with cobble- to boulder-sized specimens of a wide range of igneous, metamorphic, and sedimentary rocks, known as glacial erratics, that have been dragged down from and across the Kenai and Alaska Peninsula mountains by glaciers that covered the entire Cook Inlet region just a few thousand years ago. When these glaciers retreated, they dumped all these rocks here for us rock jocks to pick through and enjoy. Examples of some of these great beaches include **Clam Gulch, Ninilchik, Stariski, Anchor Point,** and **Diamond Gulch State Recreation Areas,** as well as along the southern shores of the world famous Homer Spit. You can walk these wonderful beaches for miles in either direction. One of my favorite long beach walks is the 15-mile stretch from Anchor Point to Homer. The highway and viewpoints south of Clam Gulch are largely across grasslands that grow to the edge of high bluffs which soar hundreds of feet above the beaches. They provide spectacular views across the 50-mile-wide Cook Inlet, up and down the beaches, and across to the mountainous, volcano-topped Alaska Peninsula. When the skies are clear, views are breathtaking. The access roads to the state recreation areas lead you from the bluffs down to beach level. Along the west side of the peninsula, there are numerous fishing charter companies in the towns of Clam Gulch, Ninilchik, and Anchor Point that will take you fishing on Cook Inlet or any number of the fish-rich coastal streams.

From **Anchor Point** to the end of the road at Homer, the highway turns east and dips back inland through alternating environments of open-canopy boreal forests, meadows, and marshy tundra (moose heaven) before weaving back to the coastline again at **Homer**. Stop at the overlook on the outskirts of Homer, where you are some 1,000 feet above the shoreline and water. Here you are treated to jaw-dropping views of Homer Spit; Kachemak Bay; the glacial, fjord-laced Southern Kenai Mountains, which are topped by glaciers flowing from the Harding Ice Field; the Herring Islands; and all three of the southern Cook Inlet volcanoes—Iliamna, Augustine, and Douglas—more than 70 miles away on the western and southern horizons. This one view has been the initiating force behind many of us moving to Homer. Drive onward down to sea level and out onto the end of **Homer Spit**, jutting 4½ miles out into amazing **Kachemak Bay**. While here you can enjoy a range of explorations and activities, including Homer Harbor and its delightful harbor walk; numerous restaurants, art galleries, and clothing shops; fishing and

FISHING AND BEACH WALKING ARE HIGHLIGHTS OF VISITING THE HOMER SPIT

TUTKA BAY FJORD FROM GRACE RIDGE IN KACHEMAK BAY STATE PARK

other outdoor adventures with outfitters offering everything from fishing to bear viewing; and water taxi services to kayaking and hiking adventures all around Kachemak Bay State Park and Wilderness Area. Enjoy access to the Kachemak Bay Water Trail, which follows the shores of Kachemak Bay for 125 miles along gorgeous beaches, beautiful bays, and spectacular fjords, all with wonderfully remote camping locations. And, there are 18+ hiking trails across the bay in Kachemak Bay State Park.

If you're in the Homer area during the first week of May, be sure to attend the Kachemak Bay Shorebird Festival, the second largest shorebird festival in the United States, which annually attracts thousands of visitors and world-renowned keynote speakers. There are dozens of activities and myriad birding-oriented viewing stations and programs for beginners and experts alike.

KENAI PENINSULA INFORMATION GUIDES

FOR THE ENTIRE KENAI PENINSULA: www.kenaipeninsula.org/dis covery-guide

KENAI NATIONAL WILDLIFE REFUGE "REFUGE REFLECTIONS" VISITORS GUIDE: www.fws.gov/refuge/kenai

IN THE AREA

Accommodations, Fuel, and Food

Soldotna

MP 93: ST. ELIAS BREWING COMPANY, 434 Sharkathmi Avenue, Soldotna, 907-260-7837, www.steliasbrewingco.com. A brewpub serving pizza and other American comfort food in a fun atmosphere. $.

MP 94: THE MOOSE IS LOOSE RESTAURANT, 44278 Sterling Highway, Soldotna, 907-260-3036. They feature Alaskan home-cooked meals and have a great bakery. $.

MP 95.6: DIAMOND M RANCH RESORT AND RV PARK, 48500 Diamond M Ranch Road, Kenai, 907-283-9424, www.diamondmranch.com. $–$$.

Kasilof

MP 101.4: TUSTAMENA SMOKEHOUSE, turn west and drive 1 mile on Tote Road, 907-262-0421, tustumenasmokehouse.com. Smoked Alaskan salmon, crab legs, reindeer sausage, and more. $.

Anchor Point

MP 156 PLUS 0.8 MILE UP NORTH FORK ROAD: SLEEPY BEAR CABINS, 34053 North Fork Road, Anchor Point, 866-235-5630, www.sleepy bearalaska.com. Cute, clean, quiet, well equiped cabins near Anchor River. Open year-round. $–$$.

MP 157: ANCHOR RIVER INN, 34358 Old Sterling Highway, Anchor Point, 907-235-8531, www.anchorriverinn.com. Accommodations and restaurant near mouth of famous trout stream. $–$$.

Homer

HOMER BED & BREAKFAST ASSOCIATION, www.homerbedbreakfast .com. Email them to enquire about bed & breakfast inns. $–$$.

DRIFTWOOD INN AND HOMER SEASIDE LODGES, 135 W. Bunnell Avenue, Homer, 229-469-9019, www.thedriftwoodinn.com. Nice, affordable lodging close to beach and town. $–$$.

OCEAN SHORES MOTEL, 3500 Crittenden Drive, Homer, 609-681-2985, www.oceanshoresalaska.com. Great view and close to downtown with beach access. $–$$.

HOMER INN & SPA, 895 Ocean Drive Loop, Homer, 907-891-8920, www .homerinnandspa.com. Lovely oceanfront inn with day spa. $$.

BEAR CREEK WINERY AND LODGING, 60203 Bear Creek Drive, Homer, 907-235-8484, www.bearcreekwinery.com. They have wonderful wines made on-site and beautiful rooms. $$.

AJ'S OLDTOWN STEAKHOUSE AND TAVERN, 120 West Bunnell Avenue, Homer, 907-235-9949, www.facebook.com/AJsOldTownSteakhouse. Excellent steak and seafood with great atmosphere plus entertainment. $.

TWO SISTERS BAKERY, 233 East Bunnell, Homer, 907-235-3380, www .twosistersbakery.net. The bakery is a favorite hangout for many locals, with famous sticky buns. $.

CAPTAIN PATTIE'S FISH HOUSE, 4241 Homer Spit Road, Homer, 907-235-5135, www.captainpatties.com. Excellent fish fare. $.

FINN'S PIZZA, Cannery Road Boardwalk, Homer Spit Road, Homer, 907-235-2878, finnspizza.co. Excellent homemade pizza. $.

CAFÉ CUPS, 162 West Pioneer Avenue, Homer, 907-235-8330, www.cafe cupshomer.com. Fine dining in a cute building. $$.

COSMIC KITCHEN, 510 East Pioneer Avenue, Homer, 907-235-9355, www .cosmickitchenalaska.com. Affordable, good American, Mexican, and vegan food in a central location. $.

THE BAGEL SHOP, 3745 East End Road, Homer, 907-299-2099, www.the bagelshopalaska.com. Fabulous breakfast and lunch bagels. $.

ALICE'S CHAMPAGNE PALACE, 195 East Pioneer Avenue, Homer, 907-226-2793, www.alices.club. Good food and spirits in a great atmosphere with frequent entertainment. $.

FRITZ CREEK GENERAL STORE, 55770 East End Road, Homer, 907-235-6753. Excellent homemade foods in a historic building, with a post office to boot! $.

THE HOMESTEAD RESTAURANT, 55829 East End Road, Homer, 907-235-8723, www.homesteadrestaurant.net. Upscale dining in a more formal atmosphere. $$.

Camping

MP 109 PLUS 2 MILES: JOHNSON LAKE STATE RECREATION AREA. Beautiful, fully developed lakeside camping with boat launch. $.

MP 109 PLUS 3 MILES: CROOKED CREEK STATE RECREATION SITE. Fishing heaven with fully developed streamside camping, grocery store, and supplies. $.

MP 117.5: CLAM GULCH STATE RECREATION AREA. Beachside camping with access to razor clam digging at low tides. $.

MP 135.7: NINILCHIK STATE RECREATION AREA. Camping in a beautiful, mature boreal forest with lovely, large birch trees. $.

MP 135: NINILCHIK BEACH CAMPGROUND. Camping on the beach in historic Ninilchik. $.

MP 135: NINILCHIK VIEW STATE RECREATION AREA. Bluff-top camping with great views across Cook Inlet. $.

MP 137.3: DEEP CREEK CAMPGROUND. RV and tent camping on the beach at the mouth of Deep Creek. Excellent halibut and king salmon fishing. $.

MP 151: STARISKI STATE CAMPGROUND. Small, quiet bluff-top camping with panoramic views of Cook Inlet. Tent camping and small RVs. $.

MP 157: ANCHOR POINT BEACH STATE RECREATION AREA. Five campgrounds are available in the state recreation area: Halibut, Cohoe, Silver King, Slide Hole, and Steelhead. Halibut is my favorite because it's right on the beach. Fabulous beach walking, fishing, tractor boat launch facilities, and of course fishing, both on Cook Inlet and the Anchor River. $.

Attractions and Recreation

MP 95.5: SOLDOTNA CHAMBER OF COMMERCE AND VISITOR CENTER. Stop here, just north of the Kenai River bridge, for information on the whole Kenai Peninsula.

MP 98: KENAI NATIONAL WILDLIFE REFUGE VISITOR CENTER. Provides current information on the sprawling Kenai National Wildlife Refuge, including road conditions, wildlife sightings, and good berry-picking locations.

MP 110: TUSTUMENA AND JOHNSON LAKES. Access is via Johnson Lake Road. Johnson Lake is close to the highway and offers developed camping and a motorboat-accessible boat ramp. Tustumena Lake is more remote, much larger, and very wild, with more primitive camping at the end of the road where the outlet of Tustumena Lake forms the headwaters of the Kasilof River. It's worth the ride down here just to see the lake and the forest, and if you're looking for wilderness lakeshore kayaking adventures, there are few locations that are better.

MP 111: CROOKED CREEK STATE RECREATION AREA. For excellent fishing that many locals frequent, drive west (toward Cook Inlet) on Cohoe Road and turn right into the Crooked State Recreation Area, where there's a campground, grocery store, and even a marina to meet all your fishing needs. There is great streamside wading here, and you're bound to make friends with both local and visiting fishermen.

MP 117.5: CLAM GULCH STATE RECREATION AREA. Drive west to Clam Gulch Beach, where locals dig for large razor clams. This is also a terrific walking beach with great views of the towering volcanoes rising on the western side of Cook Inlet. The large boulders sitting prominently on the beach are glacial erratics that were dragged across Cook Inlet by monster glaciers during the Pleistocene Epoch, and then left on this side when the glaciers retreated.

MP 134.6: RUSSIAN ORTHODOX CHURCH. Russian-Alaska history buffs enjoy visiting this well-maintained Russian Orthodox chapel, on a bluff-top above Ninilchik Beach. Photographers can get a good shot of the chapel with the volcanoes in the background.

MP 135: NINILCHIK VILLAGE AND BEACH. Take a short drive along the lower portions of the Ninilchik River to its mouth at Cook Inlet, where you

THE RUSSIAN ORTHODOX CHURCH AT NINILCHIK, ABOVE COOK INLET

can walk the beaches, camp at the beachside RV park, and view the small commercial boat harbor and the Russian-built coastal fishing community of Ninilchik (population 883).

MP 137. 3: DEEP CREEK STATE RECREATION SITE BEACH. This area offers a variety of attractions, including another wonderful walking beach, a stream- and beachside campground, and a tractor boat launch service that fishing vessels can use to launch and retrieve their boats into and from Cook Inlet during the summer months. And the launching and retrievals are fun to watch!

MP 142.5: BEST COOK INLET, BEACH, AND VOLCANO VIEWPOINT. There are a dozen established pullouts and viewpoints between Clam Gulch and Anchor Point. If you only can the stop at one, this should be it. From here you have great views of both Mount Iliamna and Mount Readout, and on clear days even Mount Spurr to the northwest and Mount Augustine to the Southwest. There is plenty of safe parking well away from the road on a large, paved pull-off rest area. Take a short walk across the field on a well-worn path for some spectacular high-bluff views of the volcanoes across Cook Inlet, as well as awesome vistas up and down the beach. Caution: Be careful at the edge of the cliff because it is overhung. Note: This is private land that the owners allow people to transit to enjoy the spectacular views, so please stay on the unofficial path, don't litter, and please pick up any trash that you find.

MP 156.6: ANCHOR POINT STATE RECREATION AREA BEACH. One of my favorite beaches is located at the end of the most westerly point on the North American highway system. This area offers a nice beachside campground; access to the mouth of the Anchor River (famous for its trout as well as its salmon); a fascinating tractor boat launch and retrieval service for fishing boats that want to launch out into Cook Inlet; and access to miles of

BOULDER-STREWN DIAMOND BEACH OFFERS WORLD-CLASS BEACH WALKING AND VIEWS

spectacular beaches, habitat for many shorebirds, and a natural rock hound heaven. I enjoy walking the mile or so north to the mouth of the Anchor River. I particularly enjoy this trek in the winter, when I typically have the beach to myself and can enjoy the natural sculptures of Anchor River–contributed ice rafts that are strewn all over this gorgeous beach.

MP 160.9: NORMAN LOWELL STUDIO, www.normanlowellgallery.net. Between Anchor Point and Homer, turn north on Norman Lowell Road and drive a third of a mile to the Norman Lowell Studio to view the massive landscape paintings for which he is famous.

MP 164.5: NORTH FORK ROAD/OLD STERLING HIGHWAY LOOP. This approximately 30-mile-long loop drive is a delightful twisting and turning, rising and falling drive. It traverses the Southern Kenai Peninsula uplands, continues down to Anchor Point, and then returns via the Old Sterling Highway to MP 165 a mile east of the original turnoff.

MP 167: DIAMOND RIDGE ROAD AND DIAMOND CREEK TRAIL ACCESS. Turn left to access Diamond Ridge Road and drive 8 miles up and over to "The View." You can see nearly the entire gorgeous fjord-indented coastline of Kachemak Bay; the rugged ridgeline of the Southern Kenai Mountains topped by the Harding Ice Field feeding four visible glaciers; the Herring Islands; and of course the iconic Homer Spit. Or, turn right off the Sterling Highway and drive south about a mile. Take the half-mile-long trail that descends 600 feet to amazing Diamond Beach, which is on the very southern tip of the Kenai Peninsula offering spectacular views east across Kachemak Bay to the Southern Kenai Mountians, and south and west across Kamishak Bay and Cook Inlet to the volcanoes of the Aleutian Peninsula and the Chigmit Mountains.

MP 169.6: HOMER OVERLOOK. Over a thousand feet above the surrounding waters of Southern Kachemak Bay and Cook Inlet, this is the view that has captured so many hearts. You can see the entire southern half of Kachemak Bay, including Homer Spit, dramatic views of the high ridgeline of the Harding Ice Field–topped Southern Kenai Mountains and the glaciers that flow from this ice field, in addition to three volcanoes the rim the southern end of Cook Inlet.

MP 173: DOWNTOWN HOMER AND EAST END ROAD. Turn left on Pioneer Avenue to enjoy art galleries, restaurants, and many local shops. Drive approximately 30 miles along Pioneer Avenue and then East End Road to the head of Kachemak Bay, stopping at historic Fritz Creek Store for homemade food, with more amazing views along the way.

CAMPING AT KACHEMAK BAY

MP 173.1: HOMER CHAMBER OF COMMERCE. The office is packed with information on the area.

MP 173.2: ISLANDS AND OCEAN VISITOR CENTER. Plan to devote some time here to learn about the 3.4-million-acre Alaska Maritime National Wildlife Refuge, including the spectacular Aleutian volcanic island chain, home to hundreds of species and millions of birds.

MP 175–179: HOMER SPIT AND BEACHES. Enjoy Homer (the largest harbor in Alaska), with its nice harbor walk, beaches, and the Homer Spit hiking and biking trail. Visit the famous Salty Dawg Saloon, art galleries, shops, and restaurants out near the end of the spit. You can also catch a fishing charter, rent some kayaks, take a taxi ride around or across glorious Kachemak Bay, or go kayaking in the fjords or around the Herring Islands, which are part of the fabulous 125-mile-long Kachemak Bay Water Trail.

Festivals and Fairs

KACHEMAK BAY SHOREBIRD FESTIVAL (FIRST WEEK IN MAY): One of the largest shorebird festivals in the U.S., with speakers, tours, and view stations galore. www.homeralaska.org

SALMON FEST (FIRST WEEK OF AUGUST): A weekend celebration of music, fish, and fun. www.salmonfestalaska.org

WINTER KING TOURNAMENT (THIRD WEEK IN MARCH): King salmon fishing on Kachemak Bay. www.homeralaska.org

FIREWEED IS RESPLENDENT ALL OVER THE KENAI PENINSULA IN LATE SUMMER

THE NUMEROUS COMMERCIAL AND PRIVATE BOATS OF HOMER HARBOR

HOMER JACKPOT HALIBUT DERBY (ANNUAL ALL SUMMER): www
.homeralaska.org

Outfitters and Tour Operators

MAKO'S WATER TAXI: 907-235-9055, www.makoswatertaxi.com. Water
taxi rides and tours, and kayak rentals around Kachemak Bay.

ASHORE WATER TAXI: 907-235-2341, www.homerwatertaxi.com. Water
taxi and freight transportation around Kachemak Bay.

TRUE NORTH KAYAK ADVENTURES: 907-235-0708, www.truenorth
kayak.com. Kayaking, paddleboarding, and hiking adventures around
Kachemak Bay.

ST. AUGUSTINE KAYAKING TOURS: 907-299-1894, www.homerkayaking
.com. Kayaking adventures on Kachemak Bay.

Fishing and Wildlife Viewing Charters

HOMER OCEAN CHARTERS: 800-426-6212, www.homerocean.com. Offers a wide range of fishing charters.

BAY EXCURSIONS: 907-235-7525, www.xyz.net/~bay. Bird viewing and whale watching around Kachemak Bay.

RAINBOW TOURS: 907-235-7272, www.rainbowtours.net. Whale-watching and fishing tours.

USEFUL INFORMATION

THE MILEPOST TRAVEL GUIDE: www.themilepost.com/highway-info/highways/sterling-highway

ALASKA.ORG ROAD GUIDE: www.alaska.org/guide/sterling-highway

KENAI NATIONAL WILDLIFE REFUGE: www.fws.gov/refuge/kenai. Download the information-packed PDF.

DISCOVERY GUIDE FOR THE ENTIRE KENAI PENINSULA: www.kenaipeninsula.org/discovery-guide

SOLDOTNA CHAMBER OF COMMERCE AND VISITOR CENTER: visit soldotna.com/visitors

HOMER CHAMBER OF COMMERCE AND VISITOR CENTER: www.homeralaska.org

KACHEMAK BAY WATER TRAIL: www.kachemakbaywatertrail.org

ISLANDS AND OCEAN VISITOR CENTER: www.fws.gov/refuge/Alaska_Maritime/about.html

18

THE REZANOF-PASAGSHAK DRIVE TO FOSSIL BEACH

A Kodiak Island Adventure of Beaches, Bays, and Coves

FROM → TO: Kodiak to Fossil Beach

WHERE IT STARTS: Beginning of Rezanof Drive West

WHERE IT ENDS: Fossil Beach

ESTIMATED LENGTH: 46 miles (about 40 miles paved, 6 miles gravel)

ESTIMATED TIME: One to two days

HIGHLIGHTS: Kalsin Bay Beach, Surfers and Fossil Beaches, Fort Abercrombie State Historic Park, Termination Point Trail

GETTING THERE: Take the Alaska Marine Highway ferry or fly to Kodiak. From the Ferry dock, drive northwest a quarter mile down Center Avenue into the middle of Kodiak to the four-way intersection of East Rezanof Drive, Lower Mill Bay Road, Center Avenue, and Rezanof Drive West. Then, turn left/southwest on Rezenof Drive West.

Kodiak is a mountainous, wild island on the western edge of the Gulf of Alaska. There are few roads on the island, in fact, less than 5 percent of it is reachable by roads. Kodiak's connected road system is restricted to a small section of the island's northeastern peninsula. While the roads are not numerous, those that do exist on Kodiak lead to some pretty great places. There are four primary drive-to destinations on Kodiak Island: Fossil Beach, Cape Chiniak, Anton Larsen Bay, and Monashka Bay. Here I am treating the drive to Fossil Beach as the primary drive and describing the others as side roads.

The first 30 miles to **Fossil Beach** is a coastal drive along West Rezanof Road, which closely hugs the rugged northeastern coastline of Kodiak

LEFT: DRIFTWOOD-STREWN BEACH ON THE SHORES OF MONASHKA BAY

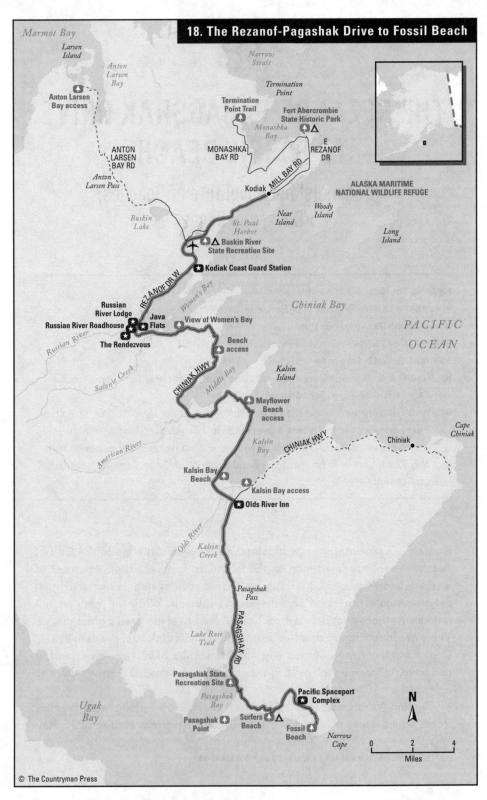

Marmot Bay

Larsen
Island

Anton
Larsen
Bay

Anton Larsen
Bay access

ANTON
LARSEN
BAY RD

Anton
Larsen
Pass

Narrow
Strait

Termination
Point

Termination
Point Trail

Monashka
Bay

MONASHKA
BAY RD

Fort Abercrombie
State Historic Park

E
REZANOF
DR

MILL BAY RD

Kodiak

ALASKA MARITIME
NATIONAL WILDLIFE REFUGE

Buskin
Lake

St. Paul
Harbor

Near
Island

Woody
Island

Long
Island

Buskin River
State Recreation Site

Kodiak Coast Guard Station

Chiniak Bay

PACIFIC
OCEAN

Russian
River Lodge

Russian River Roadhouse

Java
Flats

View of Women's Bay

Women's Bay

The Rendezvous

REZANOF DR W

Russian River

Salonie Creek

Beach
access

Middle Bay

Kalsin
Island

CHINIAK HWY

American River

Mayflower
Beach
access

Kalsin
Bay

CHINIAK HWY

Chiniak

Cape
Chiniak

Kalsin Bay
Beach

Kalsin Bay access

Olds River Inn

Olds River

Kalsin
Creek

Pasagshak
Pass

Lake Rose
Tead

PASAGSHAK RD

Pasagshak State
Recreation Site

Pasagshak
Bay

Ugak
Bay

Pasagshak
Point

Surfers
Beach

Pacific Spaceport
Complex

Fossil
Beach

Narrow
Cape

N

0   2   4
Miles

© The Countryman Press

THE ALASKA MARINE HIGHWAY SYSTEM PROVIDES YEAR-ROUND ACCESS TO DOZENS OF COMMUNITIES

Island. Begin on the western edge of Chiniak Bay, where at MP 6 you reach the largest US Coast Guard station in the Pacific. Continuing south, you drive around three large, glacially carved bays separated by two elongated headlands. From north to south the three bays are **Women's Bay**, **Middle Bay**, and **Kalsin Bay**, each having its own noteworthy features. The road over the two narrow, rocky headlands twists, dives, and climbs through coastal oak forest interspersed with stands of alders and spruce. The heads of all three bays offer excellent birding opportunities along the tidewater marshes, in particular during the spring and fall migrations. As you drive across the wetlands, you also cross over four major coastal stream channels, including the Russian River (Women's Bay), the American River (Middle Bay), and the Olds and Kalsin Rivers (Kalsin Bay), all offering good fishing streamside, picnicking, and camping, as well as floating if you want to make your way upstream. Of the three bays, Kalsin offers a particularly spectacular beach that is well worth a wander.

Glance at the map and you'll notice that all three bays and headlands have a strong southwest-to-northeast orientation, which is the result of the southwest-to-northeast movement, and resulting scouring, of the glaciers that formed in and flowed from the mountains of Kodiak during the recent (geologically speaking) Pleistocene glaciation.

At MP 30 you reach a T in the road in front of the Olds River Inn. Turn right/west on Pasagshak Road to continue your drive to Fossil Beach (a left-

THE DRAMATIC SWEEP OF PASAGSHAK BAY

hand turn will take you on the Cape Chiniak side road drive). Follow the Pasagshak Road along the floodplain of the Kalsin River, up and over **Pasagshak Pass**, then down along Lake Rose Tead and the 3-mile segment of the lower Pasagshak River that flows into Pasagshak Bay. Around MP 38 you can enjoy picnicking and fishing at the Pasagshak State Recreation Area. Via the small side road of Furin Way, you can reach and walk along the long and beautifully crescent-shaped beach fronting **Pasagshak Bay**. Please be conscious of private property and remain on obvious public rights-of-way. From Pasagshak Bay the road becomes gravel as you drive up and over the Pasagshak Point ridgeline.

From here, drive down and across grassy slopes past another lovely crescent-shaped beach, known locally as Surfer's Beach, where you can stop and picnic, camp, or just walk. From Surfer's Beach drive up and over a rolling ridgeline and past the Alaska Aerospace Launch Complex and then on to Fossil Beach bay. Fossil Beach is so named because of the abundance of fossils you find outcropping on the headlands of **Narrow Cape**, located just across the beach from the end of the dirt road that terminates on a bluff just above the beach. If you are a beach person, you might want to enjoy a full two days meandering around Surfer's and Fossil beaches. At lower tides you can walk around the headland between the two beaches. Hike up onto the bluff tops for spectacular views east and south out across the Gulf of Alaska and Northern Pacific Ocean.

IN THE AREA

Accommodations, Food, and Fuel

MP 30: OLDS RIVER INN, 3223 Pasagshak Road, Kodiak, 907-486-6040, www.oldsriverinn.com. Accommodations, restaurant, bar, convenience store, and cabins located at the T turnoff to Fossil Beach and Chiniak. $–$$.

MP 12 (BELLS FLATS): THE RENDEZVOUS, 734 Willow Circle, Kodiak, 907-487-2233, www.facebook.com/rendezvous.kodiak. Good food and drinks on the Chiniak Highway. $.

MP 12 (BELLS FLATS): RUSSIAN RIVER ROADHOUSE, 907-942-18630 or 907-487-9700, www.russianriverroadhouse.com. Good food and cabin rentals.

MP 12 (BELLS FLATS): RUSSIAN RIVER LODGE, 907-487-4460 or 907-942-7809 (cell), www.kodiakrussianriverlodge.com. Full-service lodge also offers help with a wide range of outfitting services, particularly for fishing. $–$$.

MP 12 (BELLS FLATS): JAVA FLATS, 907-487-2622, www.javaflats.com. Coffee and tea and bakery on the road to Fossil Beach or Chiniak. $.

MP 42 BEYOND THE T ON CHINIAK HIGHWAY, Roads End Restaurant, 907-486-0438. Restaurant at the end of the road in Chiniak. Look them up on Facebook. $.

Camping

MP 1 (MONASHKA BAY SIDE TRIP): FORT ABERCROMBIE STATE HISTORIC PARK. Lovely coastal forest, lake, and beach camping and hiking.

MP 4.5: BUSKIN RIVER STATE RECREATION SITE. Well-developed coastal campground famous for its fishing.

Attractions and Recreation

MP 0: MONASHKA BAY DRIVE. From the four-way intersection in Kodiak, drive 7.5 miles north on Lower Mill Bay Road through the town of Kodiak to the intersection with East Rezanof Drive; turn left. This is a 15-mile-long coastal drive with several very unexpected and delightful treats. The first

HIKING THE COASTAL CLIFF TO
TERMINATION POINT

treat is Fort Abercrombie State Historic Park, which features unexpectedly beautiful coastal forest, meadow, and beachside hiking trails, a wonderful cobble and driftwood-strewn barrier beach, lovely barrier-beach-protected Gertrude Lake, and fascinating WWII gun emplacements and information kiosks as well. The second, equally unexpected, treat is the spectacular coastal Termination Point hiking trail that begins at the end of the road. This hike leads you alternately up and along the sheer cliffside edge of gorgeous Monoshka Bay though a wonderful old growth spruce forest poised above roiling waves crashing against giant boulders 100 to 200 feet below, and then down to and along cobble, kelp, and driftwood log–strewn beaches and back up again into the cliffside forest and out onto elevated grass covered headlands with breathtaking views.

MP 4.5: BUSKIN RIVER STATE RECREATION SITE. This is good, well-developed, near-to-town picnicking, camping, fishing, and wildlife-viewing coastal park. It is next to the airport, but flight traffic into and out of Kodiak is light.

MP 4.5: ANTON LARSEN BAY FJORD. Drive this 11-mile-long, mostly gravel road up and over the mountainous spine of Kodiak Island to easy, open-field hiking across oak tree–dotted meadows at Anton Larsen Pass to the beautifully deep and narrow, forest rimmed Anton Larsen Bay fjord. There you'll find a mini floating marina put-in for boats and kayaks and a road's-end trailhead.

MP 6: KODIAK COAST GUARD STATION. This is a completely self-contained community that is famous for its air and sea rescue capabilities and heroics, and houses a submarine base as well. The Coast Guard station offers tours at 1 PM on the first and third Wednesdays from May through September. However, you must submit a tour request form 45 days before the requested tour date. Tour request forms are available from the Coast Guard's website.

MP 13: VIEW TURNOUT. Stop here for some great views across Women's Bay.

MP 16: BEACH ACCESS. Park in a small turnout on the north side of the road to take a short path down to a sweet beach.

MP 24: MAYFLOWER BEACH ACCESS. Park and walk to the shore and waters of delightful Kalsin Bay. This area can be flooded at high tide.

MP 28.5: ACCESS TO KALSIN BAY BEACH. Drive down to and walk the broad, often windswept beaches of Kalsin Bay. You can access this beach from either end of the head of Kalsin Bay and walk down to the outflows of the American and Olds Rivers. If you access the beach from the southeast end (along the first mile of the Chiniak Highway), you'll be treated to some spectacular views of the surrounding mountain ridgelines. Be aware that there is private property leading up to the beaches, so remain on the public access roads until you reach the beach.

MP 30: CHINIAK HIGHWAY. Turn left at the T in front of the Olds River Inn to begin your drive toward Chiniak along the southern edge of Kalsin Bay. Within the first mile, turn left on a sand road to the beach on the southern end of Kalsin Bay, where you can enjoy some delightful views of the central mountainous spine of Kodiak Island. Continue on for nearly continuous views of the coastline and a variety of erosional features, including arches, pillars, and sea stacks. You'll also see rocky bays and inlets and beaches, including isthmus beaches that commonly protect backwater ponds that are occasionally breached at the highest tides. There are numerous beach access points as well as boat-launching locations on your way to Chiniak.

MONASHKA BAY HAS FASCINATING TIDAL PATTERNS

REFLECTIONS AT ABERCROMBIE STATE PARK

Traveling past Chinak is iffy and requires permission from Leisnoi Native Corporation, reachable at 907-222-6900.

MP 38.7: PASAGSHAK STATE RECREATION SITE. Enjoy picnicking, camping, and world-class fishing for Dolly Varden, sockeye, pink, chum, and silver salmon on this 3-mile-long Pasagshak River section that drains Lake Rose Tead into Pasagshak Bay. You can also enjoy walks on Pasagshak Bay beach.

MP 40: PASAGSHAK POINT. For some off-road adventure (high ground clearance four-wheel-drive vehicles required), drive slowly along a 2.8-mile, very rough dirt track to the base of Pasagshak Point. Then hike/climb 500 feet vertically to the top for spectacular views of the ocean and Pasagshak Bay to the north and Surfers and Fossil Beaches to the south.

MP 42: SURFERS BEACH. A fabulous beach framed by high headlands. Perfect for picnicking, surfing, walking, and dry camping.

MP 44.5: PACIFIC SPACEPORT COMPLEX. If you've ever heard about those missile tests over the Pacific, this is one of the missile launch facilities from which those tests are flown. This is a privately owned (Alaska Aerospace) launch facility which provides launch services to the U.S. government and other commercial space customers.

MP 46.5: FOSSIL BEACH. Camp near the end of the road at Fossil Beach. Walk south to the first rock outcrop at the base of Narrow Cape to find and enjoy 10 million-year-old fossil mollusks. Also, hike up onto and across the Narrow Cape plateau flower-strewn-in-summer grasslands to enjoy expansive views of the ocean and have fun noodling around old World War II gun emplacements.

DRAMATIC SHORELINES ALONG MONASHKA BAY

Festivals and Fairs

KODIAK CRAB FESTIVAL (MEMORIAL DAY WEEKEND): Annual celebration of the crab-fishing industry and lifestyle and all that they contribute to Kodiak. Lots of food, fun, and entertainment. www.kodiakchamber.org

Outfitters and Tour Operators

SEA HAWK AIR: 506 Trident Way, Kodiak, 907-486-8282, www.seahawkair .com. Seaplane service offering kayaking, cabins, fishing, hunting, and wildlife viewing.

ALASKA WILDERNESS ADVENTURES: 907-487-2397, www.kodiakswild side.com. Kayaking, whale watching, paddle with puffins, wildlife viewing and photography, mountain climbing, and winter adventures.

SPIRIT OF ALASKA WILDERNESS ADVENTURES: 866-910-2327, www .spiritofalaska.com. Guided trips for sea kayaking, wildlife viewing and photography, and fishing. Customized trips too.

GRASSY HEADLANDS SURROUNDED BY CRASHING WAVES AROUND KODIAK

SURFERS BEACH, KODIAK

LARSEN BAY LODGE: 800-748-2238 or 907-847-2238, www.larsenbaylodge .com. Fly into the mouth of Larsen Bay for a high-end, full-service resort offering fishing, hunting, and bear and other wildlife viewing in a stunning, secluded location.

KODIAK WILDERNESS ADVENTURES: 907-454-2418, www.kodiakwilder ness.com. Beautiful lodge on Port Lions Island offering fishing and hunting adventures around Kodiak.

USEFUL INFORMATION

ALASKA.ORG ROAD GUIDE—CHINIAK HIGHWAY: www.alaska.org/ guide/chiniak-highway-guide

ALASKA.ORG ROAD GUIDE—PASAGSHAK BAY: www.alaska.org/guide/ pasagshak-bay-road

ALASKA.ORG ROAD GUIDE—MONASHKA BAY: www.alaska.org/guide/ monashka-bay-road-guide

ALASKA.ORG ROAD GUIDE—ANTON LARSEN BAY: www.alaska.org/ guide/anton-larsen-bay-road

DISCOVER KODIAK: www.kodiak.org

19

THE NOME TO TELLER ROAD
Across the Tundra to Port Clarence Bay

FROM → TO: Nome to Teller

WHERE IT STARTS: At west end of Nome on Bering Street where the road crosses the Nome River

WHERE IT ENDS: Native village of Teller

ESTIMATED LENGTH: 71 miles (about 4 miles is paved and the remainder is mostly high-quality, well-maintained gravel); this road is not open in winter

ESTIMATED TIME: One day

HIGHLIGHTS: Glacier Creek Road (all of it!), dwarf tundra ridge hiking, Sinuk River bridge and salmon information kiosk, high point on the Road, Bluestone River, Port Clarence Bay, and Teller View

GETTING THERE: Drive west on Front Street and turn right/north on Bering Street near the western end of town; drive about ½ mile to MP 0 on the Nome-Teller Highway where Bering Street crosses the Nome River

---

Nome is not known for its roads, but it should be. Many people travel to Nome for the end of the Iditarod Trail Sled Dog Race, the gold mining, and the rough-and-tumble entertainment of Nome itself. Most visitors don't realize that there are three roads out of Nome (or three and a half, if you count Glacier Creek Road, and you should) that take you to some really amazing landscapes, spectacular scenery, and fascinating locations.

The road between **Nome** and the Native community of **Teller,** 71 miles to the west, negotiates large swaths of marshy and tussock tundra at low elevations near the coast, and massive slopes of brushy and close-cropped dwarf alpine tundra where the road rolls across broad, higher, and drier

LEFT: THE LOVELY COLORS AND DETAILED TEXTURES OF THE ALPINE TUNDRA

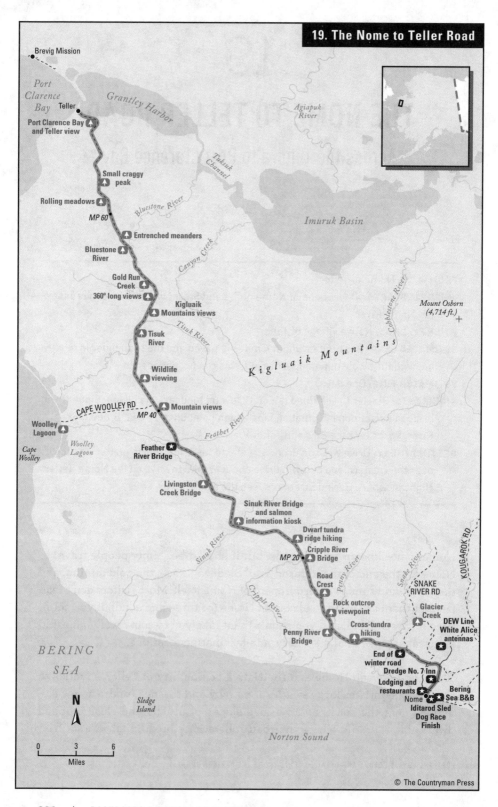

Brevig Mission

Port Clarence Bay

Teller

Port Clarence Bay and Teller view

Grantley Harbor

Agiapuk River

Tuksuk Channel

Imuruk Basin

Small craggy peak

Rolling meadows

MP 60

Bluestone River

Entrenched meanders

Bluestone River

Canyon Creek

Gold Run Creek

360° long views

Kigluaik Mountains views

Tisuk River

Tisuk River

Wildlife viewing

Mount Osborn (4,714 ft.)

Cobblestone River

CAPE WOOLLEY RD

Mountain views

MP 40

Feather River

Woolley Lagoon

Woolley Lagoon

Cape Woolley

Feather River Bridge

Kigluaik Mountains

Livingston Creek Bridge

Sinuk River Bridge and salmon information kiosk

Sinuk River

Dwarf tundra ridge hiking

Cripple River Bridge

MP 20

Road Crest

Penny River

Cripple River

Rock outcrop viewpoint

Snake River

SNAKE RIVER RD

Glacier Creek

KOUGAROK RD

Penny River Bridge

Cross-tundra hiking

DEW Line White Alice antennas

End of winter road

Dredge No. 7 Inn

BERING SEA

Lodging and restaurants

Nome

Bering Sea B&B

Iditarod Sled Dog Race Finish

Sledge Island

N

Norton Sound

0   3   6
Miles

© The Countryman Press

THE TOWN OF NOME RETAINS MUCH OF ITS BOOMTOWN SPIRIT

south-facing mountain slopes. At the beginning of the road you are immediately driving through lowland marshy tundra as you pass by the historic
Dredge No. 7 Inn, named after one of the massive dredges used to mine the
gold-bearing gravels on which Nome is built. Several of these old dredges
are scattered around Nome and along the three roads where they still sit in
the ponds where they were working when they were shut down. The Teller
Road leads initially north and then immediately swings west as you quickly
leave Nome behind and head out across a broad plain of marshy tundra.
Begin looking for signs of wildlife, including moose, musk ox, red fox, and
a variety of aquatic and shorebirds. The lowland tundra through which you
are driving at the beginning of the road offers good wildlife-viewing opportunities, particularly for moose and aquatic birds. If you are interested in
seeing musk ox and fox, you'll find that these creatures prefer the higher
and drier slopes. Having binoculars is a great help because both the moose
and the musk ox sport textures, tones, and colors that allow them to blend
in well with their surroundings. Scan slowly across the landscape, looking
for slight movements.

Between Nome and Teller you drive over the eight major stream channels
of the Nome, Snake, Penny, Cripple, Sinuk, Feather, Tisuk, and Blue Rivers
and across their beautiful valleys, as well as over six massive, tundra-covered
mountain slopes. You also cross the **Kigluaik Mountains** and then head down
onto the coastal plain to the waters of beautiful **Port Clarence Bay**. For the
first two-thirds of the route you are treated to southern-facing slopes and
foothills with long views across broad landscapes. On the last third of the
road you drive through the southern foothills of the Kigluaik Mountains
while passing through some of the historic mining locations that developed
along this road. You also cross the beautiful Bluestone River and its incised
valley, with its bold entrenched meanders, and then ultimately follow rolling
meadows down into the Native community of Teller on the shores of Port
Clarence Bay. As you descend the open slopes toward the town of Teller, at

the last ridge above the town, pull off, stop, and pan your eyes and binoculars west to enjoy the lovely view of the arc-shaped spits of sandy land that define Port Clarence bay. Then train your binoculars farther west along the coast, where on clear days you can see along the barrier island and spit coastline to the Native village of Brevig Mission, which is only accessible by boat, and most commonly launches from the Teller Spit, and floatplane.

Teller (population 300) is a Native Alaskan community, with 85 percent Inupiat peoples, most of whom are living a traditional subsistence lifestyle, including berry picking, fishing, and hunting. As in many of Alaska's remote native villages, you will find small houses nestled next to one another, with

Native Lands Access, and Hunting and Fishing Resources

Much of the land beyond the 50-foot right-of-way on both sides of the roads out of Nome is owned by four Alaska Native Corporations: Sitnasuak, Bering Straits, Council, and King Island Native Corporations. While I encourage you to strike off across the tundra-covered hillsides and ridgelines, do check in with the Native tribes to obtain their permission to do so. The tribes are often happy to share access to and views from their beautiful lands; they just ask that you request permission and then do no harm. In addition, keep in mind that many members of the Native communities depend upon subsistence hunting, fishing, and berry picking to feed their families, which is a matter of survival and not sport. If you are interested in hunting or fishing on Native lands, you should specifically inquire about that. And, if you do hunt and fish, do so for food rather than for trophy so that the animal resources remain viable. The Teller Road is surrounded largely by Sitnasuak Native Corporation lands; the side road to Woolley Lagoon on the Nome-Teller Highway is King Island land; the Kougarok Road runs through largely Bering Straits Native Corporation lands; and the road to Council runs largely through Council Native Corporation lands. Following is contact information for the various Native Corporations:

Sitnasuak Native Corporation: 214 Front Street, Second Floor, Nome, AK 99762; 877-443-2632 or 907-387-1200; www.snc.org

Bering Straits Native Corporation: 110 Front Street, Suite 300, Nome, AK 99762; 800-478-5079 or 907-443-5252; www.beringstraits.com/contact

Council Native Corporation: 606 Fifth Avenue, Nome, AK 99762; 907-443-6513; tc.cou@kawerak.org

Solomon Native Corporation: P.O. Box 243, Nome, AK 99762; 907-443-7526; tc.sol@kawerak.org

King Island Native Corporation: 907-443-5494; www.kingislandnative.com

MUSK OX ARE A FREQUENT SIGHT ALONG NOME'S ROADSIDES

satellite dishes to provide internet, cable television, and connection with the outside world; driveways lined with trucks, four wheelers, and snowmachines; open-skiff boats filled with nets and anchored alongside the river; pieces of wood standing tall and tied together where fish are dried in the summer months; a native corporation-operated community store; a washateria (laundromat); a school; a church; and a native council building. Park your car and walk around the town and along the shore and spit. Strike up conversations with the locals and learn about the history of this area, including that it was once a gold rush and whaling port boomtown of 5,000 people. Also, ask about authentic, locally hand-crafted native items, including whale and walrus bone art, that may be available for purchase from local artists. Be sure to ask permission before taking photographs of community members or walking around private property or through the cemetery.

IN THE AREA

Accommodations, Fuel, and Food

MP 1: DREDGE NO. 7 INN, 1700 Taylor Highway, 907-304-1270, www.dredge 7inn.com. Comfortable, state-of-the-art ecolodging with historic turn-of-the-century ambience, operated by an authentic multigenerational Alaskan mining family. They also offer rental vehicles. $$–$$$.

DOWNTOWN NOME: AURORA INN, 302 Front Street, Nome, 907-443-3838, www.aurorainnome.com. A modern hotel with standard rooms, suites, and kitchenettes. Rental vehicles near the east end of town. $$–$$$.

DOWNTOWN NOME: NUGGET INN, 315 Front Street, Nome, 877-443-2323, www.nomenuggetinnhotel.com. Famous old-style hotel on Main Street at the west end of town. $–$$.

DOWNTOWN NOME: POLARIS HOTEL, 200 Bering Street, Nome, 907-443-2000, www.visitnomealaska.com/polaris-hotel. Hotel, restaurant, and bar in the middle of town. $–$$.

NOMES SWEET HOMES B&B, 406 West Fourth Avenue, Nome, 907-387-0478, www.visitnomealaska.com/nome-sweet-homes. Comfortable, nice, quiet B&B close to downtown Nome with full breakfast. $–$$.

BERING SEA B&B, 1103 East Fifth Avenue, Nome, 907-443-2936, www .beringseabb.com. $–$$.

SWEET DREAMS B&B, 406 W. Fourth Ave, Nome, 907-443-2919, www.visit nomealaska.com/sweet-dreams. Nice B&B close to downtown, $–$$.

SOLOMON B&B, 34 miles east on Nome-Council Highway, 907-443-2403, www.solomonbnb.com. Historic B&B at east end of Safety Sound. $–$$.

THE KUGLIAK MOUNTAINS VIEWED FROM THE TELLER ROAD

Vehicle Rentals

DREDGE NO. 7 INN: 1700 Teller Highway, 907-304-1270, www.dredge7inn .com. Four-wheel-drive vehicle rentals.

STAMPEDE CAR RENTALS: Aurora Inn, 302 Front Street, 907-443-3838.

Camping

There really are not any established campgrounds between Nome and Teller. However, there are numerous places to dry camp along the main and side roads. Remember that most of these roads are Sitnasuak Native Corporation lands, so contact them to obtain permission.

Attractions and Recreation

MP 2: DEW LINE/WHITE ALICE ANTENNAS. Look north to the top of Anvil Mountain to see the Distant Early Warning (DEW) Line (a.k.a. White Alice) antennas that the United States used as part of the nation's nuclear early warning system during the Cold War.

MP 5.6: GLACIER CREEK TURNOFF. Drive 8 miles up this mostly ORV (after 2 miles) road that follows the meandering, gravel-bottomed Glacier Creek to a wonderful ridgeline overlook that also provides immediate access to some terrific dwarf tundra hiking.

MP 6: EXTENT OF WINTER ROAD. During the winter, deep snows and highways create huge snowdrifts that close the Nome to Teller Road from here west for the duration of the winter months.

MP 9–10: CROSS-TUNDRA HIKING. If you don't intend to drive the entire road, this is a good spot to enjoy some cross-tundra hiking. Explore the walking tundra ridgelines to local hilltops at both MP 9 and MP 10.

MP 12.5: PENNY RIVER BRIDGE. Park on the far side of the bridge and walk back across for beautiful views of the stream. You may see spawning salmon. Scan the local slopes for herds of musk ox that frequent this area.

MP 13–13.5: ROCK OUTCROP VIEWPOINT. Scramble up the rock outcrop for some beautiful views of the surrounding Penny River Valley. This is a good location for viewing musk ox, reindeer, and moose, so bring your binoculars and camera gear. Also, turn your eyes skyward for raptors that like to hunt from these rock outcrops. Looking south, you'll see a beaver dam, pond, and lodge. There are also lots of fascinating microenvironments to explore in and among the rocks.

MP 15: ROAD CREST. This is a terrific place to stop for some excellent hiking across dwarf tundra through short-cropped grasses and sedges. This location also provides a good view of the well-known rock outcrop known as House Rock or Cabin House, plus dramatic views of the east face of the deeply incised Kigluaik Mountains. You will enjoy wide-open landscape views across the broad, tundra-covered slopes and lake-dotted lowlands. Being able to hike freely across these lands is a huge benefit of checking in with the Sitnasuak Native Corporation prior to heading out. It's well worth the small amount of time and effort required to obtain their permission.

MP 19: CRIPPLE RIVER BRIDGE. The bridge is a terrific place for a rest while enjoying great views up and down the clearwater, rocky bottom channel of the Cripple River. Take the dirt access road just east of the Cripple River bridge for some good gravel bar hiking, except during spring runoff, when the channel will be full.

MP 21: DWARF TUNDRA RIDGE HIKING. Pull off and up to the right into a gravel parking area for access to excellent hiking across the dwarf tundra.

MP 26: SINUK RIVER BRIDGE AND SALMON INFORMATION KIOSK.
Stop on the west side of the ridge to view the largest and longest of the stream channels you cross on this road, the headwaters of which are at a glacial lake far up in the Kigluaik Mountains. Also take time to read the interesting salmon information kiosk. This is another prime location for salmon viewing and it offers good musk ox sighting opportunity as well.

MP 31: LIVINGSTON CREEK BRIDGE. Look for rare views of stream channel cuts into exposed layers of icy permafrost.

MP 36: FEATHER RIVER BRIDGE. Drive down the east side of the stream channel to an old road-construction camp and landing strip where musk oxen were once flown in. Four-wheel drive only.

MP 37–38: HIGH POINT ON THE ROAD. Stop for sweeping views across massive, tundra-covered mountain front slopes and the high peaks and ridges of the southern end of the Kigluaik Mountains.

MP 40: WOOLLEY LAGOON. Drive 7.5 miles down this side road through marshy tundra with freshwater lakes to a small coastal community at the mouth of the river. Along the roadside where the soil has been undercut, look for sections of exposed permafrost. You'll notice both full-sized houses and some small fishing shacks owned by members of the King Island Native community. The small fishing shacks are used throughout the summer months as family fishing retreats. Keep your eyes open for sand-

SANDHILL CRANES GRACE THE COASTAL SLOUGHS OF WOOLEY LAGOON

hill cranes that love to hang out and feed along the edges of the tidewater stream channels.

MP 42–44: WILDLIFE VIEWING. Turn off into two gravel pits and stand on top of your rig for some good wildlife viewing, including herds of reindeer that frequent these slopes. This is a good, safe, and quiet place to set up spotting scopes.

MP 47: TISUK RIVER. Look for lingering ice sheets in the stream channel, remnants of yearly ice dams that commonly form here. You pass over Eldorado Creek just before you reach the Tisuk River bridge. At low water levels you can take a short hike down the Eldorado Creek bed to its confluence with the Tisuk River less than a quarter mile downstream.

MP 48–50: KIGLUAIK MOUNTAINS VIEWS. Look north along this section of road for some of the best and most dramatic views into the high peaks and ridgelines of the Southern Kigluaik Mountains. If you drive this road in the fall you'll enjoy the wonderful contrast between the golden yellows of the cottonwoods, aspens, birch, and willows juxtaposed against the bright white of the snowcapped Kigluaik peaks.

MP 51: 360-DEGREE LONG VIEWS. Hike up the tundra-covered ridgeline just south of and parallel to the road for 360-degree long views south to the coast and north into the high peaks and ridges of the Kigluaik mountains. You'll also enjoy sweeping views of the surrounding tundra-covered countryside.

MP 52: GOLD RUN CREEK CROSSING. This stream is a good place to look for both salmon and arctic grayling. As you drive downstream following Gold Run Creek, you're driving through one of the most currently active gold-mining areas along the Teller Road. Look for the old derelict gold dredge sitting in the channel of Gold Run Creek, which is visible starting at about MP 53.5.

MP 57: BLUESTONE RIVER. This provides a good picnic spot on the east bank of the north-flowing Blue River, which gets its name from the blue schist minerals that carpet the bottom of the stream channel.

MP 59: ENTRENCHED MEANDERS. As you climb west out of the steep-walled canyon of the Bluestone River, pull off on the riverside and scramble up on top of your camper for some spectacular views of the entrenched meanders of the Bluestone River. These meanders formed when the earlier Bluestone River channel was meandering across lowland flats closer to sea level. They remained in place and carved the current channel as this area was uplifted, allowing the formation of this beautiful, sinuous deep-walled canyon.

MP 60–71: ROLLING MEADOWS. Follow the stair-step topography gradually downslope to sea level, across rolling, flower-packed meadows as you finish your drive toward the Native village of Teller and the coast.

MP 64: SMALL CRAGGY PEAK. Scramble up this small, craggy peak that pops up above the surrounding low-slope plain just south of the road for a terrific 360-degree view of the landscape.

ENTRENCHED MEANDERS OF THE BLUE RIVER FROM THE TELLER ROAD

MP 72: PORT CLARENCE BAY AND TELLER VIEW. Stop on the last stair-step down toward Teller for a fabulous view of Teller resting on the circular shores of the protected waters of beautiful Port Clarence Bay.

MP 71: NATIVE VILLAGE OF TELLER. Feel free to walk around the Native village of Teller and stop at the Native village store to say hello and make a few friends. While you're in town you might have the opportunity to purchase some hand-carved ivory art pieces, many of which are quite skillfully crafted and available for very reasonable prices. You can also park at the west end of town and walk out to the end of the spit for some good views across Port Clarence Bay. If you would like to chat with one of the local Natives, stop by the local store or the city office and ask for Daniel Komok, who is the town's unofficial ambassador. He is very friendly and would be delighted to tell you all about Teller.

Festivals and Fairs

IDITAROD SLED DOG RACE FINISH (EARLY MARCH): Race starts the first Saturday in March in Willow and ends about 10 days later in Nome. www.iditarod.com.

MIDNIGHT SUN FESTIVAL (JUNE 21): Longest-day-of-the-year party, including the Polar Bear Swim sponsored by the Nome Rotary Club. www.alaska.org/detail/midnight-sun-festival.

SALMONBERRY JAM FOLK FEST (LATE JULY–EARLY AUGUST): Three days of music and dancing, as well as dance workshops featuring local and guest musicians.

BLUEBERRY AND MUSIC FESTIVAL (LATE AUGUST–EARLY SEPTEM-BER): One-day festival with music and plenty of blueberry recipes.

Outfitters and Tour Operators

INTO THE WILD ALASKA ADVENTURE RENTALS, 907-841-0736, www
.akadventurerentals.com. Offers outdoor rentals for biking and float trips.
Also, some tour leading around Nome.

ALASKA GOLD & RESORT, Glacier Creek Road, 760-500-1329 or 760-855-
2855, www.akaugold.com. A resort for gold mining with historic relics, gold
panning, and gold prospecting consulting.

USEFUL INFORMATION

NOME INFORMATION: www.visitnomealaska.com

"ALASKA'S NOME AREA WILDLIFE VIEWING GUIDE": A helpful guide
published by the Alaska Department of Fish and Game's Division of Wildlife Conservation, dfg.dwc.hc-info@alaska.gov

"NOME ROADSIDE FISHING GUIDE": Contact the Alaska Department of
Fish and Game's Nome Office, 907-443-2271

NOME HOTELS AND B&B LISTINGS: www.visitnomealaska.com/places
-to-stay

NOME EATERIES LISTING: www.visitnomealaska.com/restaurants-and
-shopping

20

THE NOME TO KOUGAROK RIVER ROAD

Into the Kigluaik Mountains and Beyond

FROM → TO: East end of Nome to the Kougarok River bridge

WHERE IT STARTS: 2 miles east of downtown Nome on the Nome-Council Road

WHERE IT ENDS: Bridge over the Kougarok River

ESTIMATED LENGTH: 85 miles, all gravel

ESTIMATED TIME: One to three days

HIGHLIGHTS: Cape Horn viewpoint, Lake Solomon, Grand Central views, hiking the Crater Creek Area, floating the Pilgrim and Kuzitrin Rivers

GETTING THERE: Starting on Front Street in downtown Nome, drive east 1 mile past the dredge exhibit on the Nome-Council Road and turn left/north on Beam Road (a.k.a. the Kougarok/Taylor/Beam/Kuzitrin Road)

ROAD NAME NOTE: As indicated above, this road has various names. The official name of the entire road is the Nome-Taylor Highway. The name on the sign where you turn north from the Nome-Council Road is Beam Road. Many locals refer to this as the Kougarok Road because its final destination is a bridge that crosses the Kougarok River. (The road stops 25 miles south of the remote mining community of Taylor.) Some folks do refer to this as the Taylor Road. Welcome to road naming in Alaska! I will refer to it as the Kougarok Road.

The **Kougarok Road** takes you through a variety of terrains and environments. For the first third of the road you follow the stream channel and valley of the Nome River, with its multiple braided channels, meanders, oxbow lakes, backwater sloughs, and beaver ponds. As you head north toward its headwaters in the **Kigluaik Mountains**, you drive alternately through lowland, marshy tundra along the stream channels, and brushy tundra that inhabits the higher and drier slopes away from the wetlands. Look for musk ox, moose, beaver, hares, and a variety of birds. As you drive along the river you'll see

LEFT: THE NOME-KOUGAROK ROAD LEADS INTO THE GLORIOUS KOUGAROK MOUNTAINS

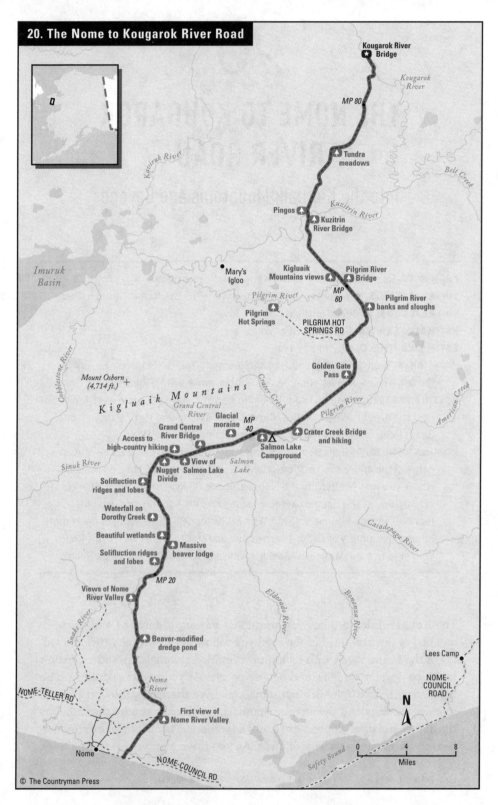

20. The Nome to Kougarok River Road

Kougarok River Bridge ★

Kougarok River

MP 80

Tundra meadows

Belt Creek

Kuziruk River

Pingos

Kuzitrin River

Kuzitrin River Bridge

Imuruk Basin

Mary's Igloo

Kigluaik Mountains views

Pilgrim River Bridge

MP 60

Pilgrim River banks and sloughs

Pilgrim River

Pilgrim Hot Springs

PILGRIM HOT SPRINGS RD

Golden Gate Pass

Mount Osborn (4,714 ft.) +

Crater Creek

American Creek

Kigluaik Mountains

Grand Central River

Glacial moraine

MP 40

Pilgrim River

Crater Creek Bridge and hiking

Grand Central River Bridge

Access to high-country hiking

Cobblestone River

Salmon Lake Campground

Sinuk River

Nugget Divide

View of Salmon Lake

Salmon Lake

Solifluction ridges and lobes

Casadepaga River

Waterfall on Dorothy Creek

Beautiful wetlands

Massive beaver lodge

Solifluction ridges and lobes

MP 20

Eldorado River

Bonanza River

Views of Nome River Valley

Beaver-modified dredge pond

Lees Camp •

NOME-COUNCIL ROAD

Snake River

Nome River

NOME-TELLER RD

N

First view of Nome River Valley

Nome

NOME-COUNCIL RD

Safety Sound

0   4   8
Miles

© The Countryman Press

lots of dredge spoils and dredge spoils ponds, evidence of both historic and current gold-mining operations. The local beavers are not only industrious but also highly adaptable. You'll find many places where beavers have redecorated dredge spoil ponds and made them their own. Another interesting feature is the parallel ridges of rumpled-looking soil that you find on many hillsides. These are known as solifluction ridges or lobes, depending upon their geometry. They indicate areas where, during the summer months, saturated near-surface soil is slowly melt-moving downhill on top of an underlying layer of solid frozen permafrost. Once you reach the base of the mountains, the road turns northeast as you cross over your first pass into the beautiful **Salmon Lake Valley**. Here you will drive parallel along the front of the Kigluaik Mountains between their high ridgelines and Salmon Lake. Along this section of the road you have many opportunities to stop and enjoy some cross-country hiking adventures, both up beautiful braided stream channels and across the rugged and beautiful Sawtooth Range portion of the Kigluaik Mountains. You can encounter terrain and topography here that is as dramatic as any in Alaska. Recent glacier activities have carved deep valleys and produced some spectacular horns and cirque bowl basins. The glacially carved, lake-dotted, U-shaped valleys that are currently being modified by stream channel processes are simply gorgeous. After driving along the shores of Salmon Lake, follow the road as it parallels the **Pilgrim River** from its headwaters on the northeast end of Salmon Lake, where you turn north and cross

A CLASSIC U-SHAPED VALLEY NEAR GRAND CENTRAL

over your second pass as the road moves out of the Kigluaik Mountains. A few miles north of the pass you reach the side road to **Pilgrim Hot Springs**. For the last third of your trip along the Kougarok Road you drive across dry tundra–covered uplands and along the marshy floodplains of the Pilgrim and Kuzitrin Rivers, crossing the channels of both as you go. The road comes to an abrupt end at a bridge that crosses the Kougarok River, a major tributary of the Kuzitrin River. Your Kougarok Road adventure allows you to enjoy the stream channel and surrounding environments of three major rivers, gawk at the beautiful montane environments of Salmon Lake, and hike the rugged mountain terrains of the Kigluaik Mountains. If you'd like to take a soak in some hot springs, you have an opportunity to do just that by taking the side road to Pilgrim Hot Springs, where you can sample the waters and explore the renewable energy projects that are being developed there.

IN THE AREA

Camping

MP 40: SALMON LAKE CAMPGROUND. This is a BLM-run campground on the shores of beautiful Salmon Lake, offering a sandy beach, picnic tables, BBQ pits, trash bins, and a restaurant. There's no running water, but you can fill up on fresh springwater at MP 36. In recent years, massive runs of sockeye salmon have returned to spawn in Salmon Lake after decades of low productivity due to earlier overfishing. The recovery of the salmon runs in Salmon Lake is a good case study for how we can undo previous harms, benefiting both the fish and ourselves, when we put our heads together and work cooperatively with good information. The east end of the lake provides access to a floating put-in at the head of the Pilgrim River. $.

Attractions and Recreation

MP 5: FIRST VIEW OF THE NOME RIVER VALLEY. Stop for a good view of the Nome River's multiple braided channels and floodplain.

MP 13: BEAVER-MODIFIED DREDGE POND. Take the gravel road on the east side of the Nome River Bridge to see an excellent example of a dredge pond that has been modified by beavers. Look for their lodge along the eastern edge. Walk back across the bridge to look for salmon and Dolly Varden trout in the Nome River.

MP 16–18: GREAT VIEW SECTION. Stop along this section of high road, known as Cape Horn, for expansive views of the Nome River and its flood-

plain. Look for the multiple braided stream channels as well as abandoned meanders and oxbow lakes, both evidence of where previous channels of the Nome River once flowed. This is also a good location to haul out your binoculars and look for moose in the marshy lowlands and musk ox on the higher and drier slopes.

MP 21–22: SOLIFLUCTION RIDGES AND LOBES. Look on hill slopes on both sides of the road for rumpled-rug-looking ridges and lobes that form where water-saturated summer soils are slumping downhill on top of the still-frozen permafrost layers beneath.

MP 22: MASSIVE BEAVER LODGE. Pull off into a flat gravel area on the east/right side of the road to check out what is likely to be the largest beaver lodge you'll ever see. Please do not disturb the beaver lodge, acquire your firewood elsewhere.

MP 24: BEAUTIFUL WETLANDS. Slow down along this section of road that allows you intimate views into a streamside wetland. This is also great moose habitat.

MP 26: WATERFALL ON DOROTHY CREEK. Although there is no trail, at very low water you can make your way across the channel of the Nome River. (Prepare to be wet and use hiking poles downstream for safety.) Most hikers approach the creek from the tundra slope above to reach a lovely waterfall about 1 mile up Dorothy Creek.

MP 29: MORE SOLIFLUCTION. Excellent examples of solifluction ridges and lobes.

MP 31–32: DRAINAGE DIVIDE PASS. Known as the Nugget Divide, this is your first of two passes on this road. Here you move from the Nome River drainage basin into the Salmon Lake and Pilgrim River drainage.

MP 33: SALMON LAKE VALLEY VIEW. See stunning views of Salmon Lake and valley.

THE SALMON LAKE SHORELINE IN EARLY SPRING

MP 31–35: ACCESS TO HIGH-COUNTRY HIKING. You'll find multiple accesses to cross-country dwarf tundra hikes here. Walk first across the low slopes, which in turn lead to the high ridgelines that will take you back into the heart of the Sawtooth Range of the Kigluaik Mountains. If you follow the ridgelines north far enough, you will earn jaw-dropping views of the cirque bowl basin that fronts Mount Osborn. If you do hike back up onto the ridgelines, take a good look at the exposed rock outcrops and you are likely to find some excellent specimens of garnet schists and gneisses containing very visible almandine garnets up to a centimeter in diameter.

MP 35.3: GRAND CENTRAL RIVER BRIDGE. Here you have awesome views up the Grand Central River valley into the high peaks of the Sawtooth Range of the Kigluaik Mountains, including Mount Osborn, which at 4,714 feet is the tallest peak on the Seward Peninsula. Notice how this broad valley is beautifully U-shaped, clear evidence of its glacially carved origin. Spawning salmon are often visible from the bridge in August.

MP 36: FRESHWATER SPRING. Stop here to fill up your water bottles with this fresh, spring-fed water that is piped to the side of the road through a white plastic pipe.

MP 38: GLACIAL MORAINE. Look west into the valley before you. At the mouth of the valley, where it leaves the mountain front, you'll notice a low ridgeline oriented perpendicular across the front of the valley. This is a recessional moraine of sand and gravel that was left behind when a glacier, which had recently carved and occupied this valley, paused here and deposited the moraine before continuing its retreat west up the valley. The stream channel has since cut through this moraine.

MP 40: SALMON LAKE OUTFLOW. Take the Salmon Lake Campground road to the outflow of Salmon Lake that becomes the Pilgrim River. You can put in here for a float down the Pilgrim River and take-out where the road crosses the river at MP 60.

MP 43: CRATER CREEK BRIDGE AND HIKING. Stop here to view the beautiful braided gravel and cobble-bottomed stream channel of Crater Creek as it flows down from the high peaks of the Kigluaik Mountains. Park along the section of road north of the bridge and don your backpack for some wonderful hiking across dwarf tundra. You can enjoy a day hike or a multiday backpack up the Crater Creek drainage. You'll find examples of marshy, brushy, and dwarf tundra. Stick to the higher, drier ridgelines for easy walking across the dwarf tundra. You can also make your way down to and hike up the braided stream channel of Crater Creek.

MP 51: GOLDEN GATE PASS. Enjoy wide-open slopes of dwarf tundra as you approach and then pass over Golden Gate Pass. This section offers terrific views of the Pilgrim and Kuzitrin Rivers' drainages. Look for migrating caribou here in spring and fall.

THE KOUGAROK MOUNTAINS VIEWED FROM THE NORTHERN TUNDRA PLAINS

THE OLD CHURCH AT PILGRIM HOT SPRINGS

MP 53.6: ROAD TO PILGRIM HOT SPRINGS. Follow this 7-mile-long dirt road, which may be impassable in wet weather, through a variety of forest, meadow, and wetland habitats, with some dramatic views to the west of the north face of the Kigluaik Mountains along the way, to reach a good soak in some hot spring tubs. Also take time to appreciate the fascinating hot spring microclimate and habitat, that provides migrating birds snow and ice free areas in the early spring.

MP 57–58: PILGRIM RIVER BANKS AND SLOUGHS. This riverside section provides great waterfowl viewing in a complex riparian environment of back channels, gravel channels, sloughs, and lakes, with cottonwood trees and willow thickets offering habitats for a variety of species. Pull off to the side, haul your camp chair to the top of your camper, then hang out and watch the show!

MP 60: PILGRIM RIVER BRIDGE. Walk out to the middle of the bridge and look west for some excellent views of the north face of the Kigluaik Mountains. This is also a good exit point for float trips on the Pilgrim River for those who put in at the outflow of Salmon Lake at MP 40.

MP 61: KIGLUAIK MOUNTAINS VIEWS. Enjoy panoramic views of the north face of the Kigluaik Mountains across the Pilgrim River and floodplain.

MP 68: KUZITRIN RIVER BRIDGE. This is a nice viewpoint for looking up and down the Kuzitrin River, and it's also good viewing territory for curlews and wimbrels. The bridge is also where you take out if you put in for a float trip down the Kougarok River.

MP 68.5: PINGOS. As you drive across the marshy tundra–covered, lake-studded lowlands north of the Kuzitrin River, look south across the flat surface for small bumps in the topography. These small local rises are pingos, which are formed when small pockets of the underlying permafrost push toward the surface, causing these small, tundra-topped bubbles.

MP 68–86: TUNDRA MEADOWS. For the final 18 miles of your Kougarok Road adventure, you travel across wide-open tundra-covered meadows. In the spring and fall these broad meadows are highways for migrating caribou, as well as a good habitat for bears, moose, musk ox, and wolves. My birding friends also swoon about the opportunities to see bristle-thighed curlews in their nesting habitat.

MP 86: END OF THE ROAD AT THE KOUGAROK RIVER BRIDGE. It's an odd sight to see this road cross this substantial bridge across the Kougarok River and then just terminate in a small, flat, muddy area. If you look past the end of the road you'll see a small ATV trail that continues north. If you were so inclined, you could follow this mud path north for another 25 miles to the private mining community at Taylor. You can put in a raft here and float down to the river's confluence with the Kuzitrin River, and then float the Kuzitrin down to the take out at the Kuzitrin River bridge at MP 68.

Float Trips Notes: Both float trips on the Pilgrim and Kougarok/Kuzitrin Rivers are easy floats that can be executed in a single day. However, it's important on both floats that you do not miss the take-outs at the bridges at MP 60 and MP 68. If you miss the take-outs you'll end up many miles to the west in the large flat waters, channels, and lakes of the Imuruk Basin. Some people do, by design, float from the MP 60 Pilgrim River bridge downstream to the Pilgrim Hot Springs; however, you want to thoroughly research this before trying it and make sure there is someone at the Pilgrim Hot Springs end of the float to retrieve you. Contact the folks at Into The Wild Alaska Adventure Rentals, www.facebook.com/AKadventurerentals.

For places to stay, eat, and fuel; vehicle rentals; Nome festivals and fairs; outfitters and tour operators; and useful information, see the Nome to Teller Road (Drive #19).

SNOW REMAINS INTO THE SUMMER ON NORTH FACING SLOPES

21

THE NOME TO COUNCIL ROAD
A Shore, Sound, and Mountain Adventure

FROM → TO: Nome to Council

WHERE IT STARTS: 1 mile east of downtown Nome on the Nome to Council Road at the Swanberg Dredge exhibit

WHERE IT ENDS: On the south bank of the Niukluk River across the river from the Native town of Council

ESTIMATED LENGTH: 72 miles, all paved

ESTIMATED TIME: One to two days

HIGHLIGHTS: Safety Sound and particularly sandhill cranes gathering over Safety Sound in the autumn, the garnet beach just west of Cape Nome, walking deserted beach east of Bonanza, hiking the alpine tundra ridges around Skookum Pass

GETTING THERE: Drive 1 mile east of downtown Nome on Front Street to N Street for your first stop

If you can, choose early autumn to visit **Nome**. Late August on Safety Sound offers one of nature's great spectacles: the gathering of thousands upon thousands of sandhill cranes who each summer gather on uncounted lakes and meadows all over the giant Seward Peninsula. Each fall huge numbers of these cranes gather over Safety Sound to prepare for their annual migration south. It is truly thrilling to lie back on the hood of your car and watch and listen as thousands of cranes gather, their beautiful, asymmetrical V formations passing overhead at various elevations as they begin their multi-thousand-mile journeys to their winter homes. I promise you it's a sight you will always remember.

LEFT: DRAMATIC SUNSET VIEWS ACROSS THE BERING SEA

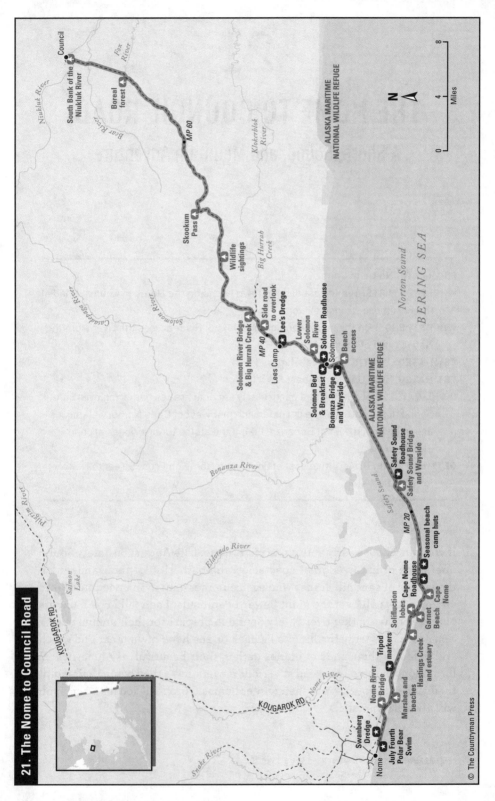

21. The Nome to Council Road

Council

South Bank of the Niukluk River

Niukluk River

Fox River

Boreal forest

Bear River

MP 60

Klokerblok River

ALASKA MARITIME NATIONAL WILDLIFE REFUGE

Skookum Pass

Wildlife sightings

Casadepaga River

Big Hurrah Creek

Solomon River

N

0   4   8 Miles

Solomon River Bridge & Big Hurrah Creek

MP 40

Side road to overlook

Lee's Dredge

Lower Solomon River

Solomon Roadhouse

Lees Camp

Solomon

Beach access

BERING SEA

Norton Sound

Solomon Bed & Breakfast

Bonanza Bridge and Wayside

Bonanza River

ALASKA MARITIME NATIONAL WILDLIFE REFUGE

Safety Sound Roadhouse

Safety Sound Bridge and Wayside

Safety Sound

KOUGAROK RD.

Salmon Lake

Pilgrim River

Eldorado River

MP 20

Seasonal beach camp huts

Cape Nome Roadhouse

Solifluction lobes

Garnet Beach

Cape Nome

Tripod markers

Hastings Creek

Nome River Bridge

Marshes and beaches

Nome River

KOUGAROK RD.

Swanberg Dredge

July Fourth Polar Bear Swim

Nome

Snake River

© The Countryman Press

THE WATERFOWL RICH WATERS OF BEAUTIFUL SAFETY SOUND

Safety Sound, along with its adjoining parallel beach, is the second of five major sections along the Nome to Council Road. The first 14-mile-long section from Nome to **Cape Nome** is a coastal segment of road that runs between, and sometimes through, marshy tundra on the north side of the road and along sections of broad, sandy beaches on the south side. The second section, from Cape Nome to **Solomon**, also spans a long section of beach, but on the north side of the road are the grass-bordered marshes of Safety Sound, replete with waterfowl and opportunities for spectacular kayaking, canoeing, wildlife viewing, and of course photography. The third section of the road follows upstream along the Solomon River through boreal forests and streamside wetlands to its ridgeline headwaters in the coastal ranges. This **Solomon River** section of the road provides some fascinating up-close looks at historical mining operations, including a dredge, and some excellent views of the river and floodplain environments along with fascinating side channels and backwaters. The fourth section takes you up and over **Skookum Pass** in the Coast Range and along alpine meadows and dwarf alpine tundra–covered slopes and ridgelines that offer excellent hiking opportunities and 360-degree panoramic views. While driving the Solomon River and Skookum Pass segments, drive slowly, stop frequently, and scan the stream channel wetlands for moose and the higher and drier slopes for musk ox, fox, and caribou. The fifth and final section takes you down from the high, tundra-covered ridgelines around Skookum Pass, through the stream channels of the Fox and Bear Rivers, and ultimately across marshy tundra lowland and floodplains to the south bank of the **Niukluk River** opposite the town of **Council**. You could easily spend a day in each of these environments.

IN THE AREA

Accommodations, Fuel, and Food

MP 26: SAFETY SOUND ROADHOUSE, 907-434-2982, www.facebook
.com/safetyroadhouse. Good selection of locally made brews and a wide
variety of comfort foods. $

SOLOMON BED AND BREAKFAST, 34 miles east on Nome-Council Highway, 907-443-2403, www.solomonbnb.com. Historic B&B at east end of
Safety Sound. $–$$

**See the Nome to Teller Road (Drive #19), for more accommodations and
eatery information.**

Attractions and Recreation

**MP 0.5: MINING-ERA ARTIFACTS AND ANNUAL JULY FOURTH POLAR
BEAR SWIM LOCATION.** On the east end of Front Street, across from the
beach and just past N Street, you'll find a collection of mining era artifacts
that are quite fun to noodle around and photograph. The beach side is the
location of the annual July Fourth Polar Bear Swim, in which I have partic-
ipated once and with which I have chosen not to torture myself again. This
section of beach is easy to access from downtown Nome and a great walk
anytime.

MP 1: SWANBERG DREDGE. This roadside dredge is in good shape and
has a wheelchair-accessible boardwalk. Stop here and peruse some excellent informational displays on the dredge, the history of dredges around
Nome, and the recent geologic history of local beach levels and dunes and
their impact on the location of gold deposits. This stop is well worth a visit,
although you might be eager to hit the road and visit this dredge later.

MP 2–34: TRIPOD MARKERS. These are winter navigational markers used to mark the location of the roadbed when the road along Safety
Sound and other beaches is covered with ice and snow. These are used by
the Iditarod dogsled racers to mark their race path along their final stretch
into Nome.

MP 2–34: SEASONAL BEACH CAMP HUTS. Along nearly all the beaches
around Nome you'll see series of small cabins perched just above high tide.

THE SWANBERG DREDGE NEAR NOME IS AN ICONIC FEATURE

These are summer fishing huts used by Native families. Some are very simple and others are more elaborate. Please respect this private property.

MP 3.5: NOME RIVER BRIDGE. This is a prime birding location near the mouth of the Nome River. Here the river is a tidal estuary stream channel and marsh, so you have the chance to see both fresh and saltwater species intermixing. Set up spotting scopes on either end of the bridge or on top of your rig. This is the mouth of the same Nome River that you follow north up into the Kigluaik Mountains along the Kougarok Road described in Drive #20.

MP 3.5–12: MARSHES AND BEACHES. Drive along and through coastal marshes that are naturally separated from the ocean by a dune environment. These ancient barriers were created during the rising and falling of sea levels, now largely stabilized by brushy tundra and marshy grasses. They also form natural beach benches and habitat as well. Parts of the Nome-Council Road are built on some of these higher and drier ancient dune benches.

SUMMER FISH CAMPS ALONG SAFETY SOUND

MP 9.4: HASTING CREEK AND ESTUARY. This is a beautiful marsh estuary with tons of driftwood supporting a variety of habitats for both fresh and saltwater birds as well as aquatic mammals such as beavers and otters.

MP 10–12: SOLIFLUCTION LOBES. Look on the side slopes, particularly during late afternoons with low sun angles, and you'll see rumples of water-soaked soil that are slowly moving downhill on top of underlying permafrost.

MP 11: GARNET BEACH ACCESS. Near Golden Gate Creek you can access the section of beach that is just north of Cape Nome. Drive down to the beach, then walk along it and notice the red color of the sand. Pick up a handful and take a close look. You'll see that the sand includes translucent red grains of garnet sand. These are almandine (iron-rich) garnets that have weathered out of the metamorphic gneisses which in turn compose portions of the rock that forms the Cape Nome headlands. If you are an admirer and collector of beach sands, this is one sample you will want to add to your collection. The beach access road takes you by numerous private beach huts, so please respect their private property and continue down to the beach.

MP 12: CAPE NOME. There is lots of construction going on here, but if you are a rock hound this is well worth a stop. Among the rock types you'll find here are granites that have intruded into limestones, forming contact metamorphic deposits featuring large feldspar, allanite, and epidote crystals, as well as gneisses containing significant garnets, which resist both mechanical and chemical weathering and populate the beaches to the west, giving them their red appearance. Birders also appreciate this stop due to the variety of birds that nest on the steep cliffs.

MP 14: CAPE NOME ROADHOUSE. This is one of three remaining road-houses, part of a series of roadhouses that served the significant mining population in the early 20th century. At one point it was a state orphanage, and it is now privately owned.

MP 14–34: SAFETY SOUND. The highway bifurcates a wonderful shore and sound environment featuring dunes and beaches on the ocean side, and the marshes, coastal grasslands, meadows, and open water on the Safety Sound side. Look for Canada geese and sandhill cranes among the diverse community of aquatic and shorebirds that call Safety Sound home for at least part of each year. Numerous access roads take you to the beach, but please respect the private property surrounding the fishing camp huts. (Tip: Read the detailed and fascinating description of the ecology of Safety Sound in the "Alaska's Nome Area Wildlife Viewing Guide" referenced in the combined Nome Useful Information section.)

MP 22: SAFETY SOUND BRIDGE AND WAYSIDE. Cross over the bridge and pull into the wayside on its east side to enjoy the boardwalk and information panels, as well as some beautiful views of Safety Sound. This is an excellent put-in spot for kayaks and canoes. It's also a perfect place to haul out your cooler and beach chair, grab your binoculars, set up your spotting scope, and settle in for some seriously good viewing. From this location you can see two fascinating pieces of recent geologic history. First, the elongated islands located in the middle of the sound and oriented parallel to the coast are old beach dune lines formed by periods of changing sea levels. Second, take a look at a cross section of the soil profile along the edge of the outlet water channel where the current has cut into the soil, and you'll find layers of peat that were formed in an ancient coastal marsh well

THE SAFETY ROADHOUSE OFFERS REFRESHMENTS FOR SUMMERTIME VISITORS

shoreward of a previous beach line that existed further south of the current beach. These ancient salt marsh muds, now covered with sand, offer further evidence of the migration of the beach/strand lines and their related marsh deposits over thousands of years.

MP 22.5: SAFETY SOUND ROADHOUSE. This roadhouse serves food and drink in the summer.

MP 32–33: BONANZA BRIDGE AND WAYSIDE AND BEACH ACESS. There is much to see here. "The Last Train to Nowhere" exhibit provides details about the Council City and Solomon River Railroad, whose construction began during the heyday of the Gold Rush but eventually and quite literally, stopped in its own tracks. The locomotives, tracks, and various railroad paraphernalia are slowly but surely rusting away and melding into the surrounding marsh environment. It's a fun place to look around and read about the railroad. If you are a macro photographer, you'll love all the textures. But don't just look at the ancient railroad pieces. This end of Safety Sound, where the waters of Bonanza Creek and the Solomon River mix with the local tides, is packed with swans, geese, and a variety of other breeding birds. This is also a great launch location for canoes and kayaks. And, just before you turn off the beach highway to cross over the bridge, you will find a beach access through the dunes where you can enjoy walking farther east along a roadless, little-visited section of the coast.

MP 34: TOWN OF SOLOMON AND SOLOMON ROADHOUSE. This is a historic Native fishing village and site of a Gold Rush boomtown. The current roadhouse is run by the Solomon Native tribe, which offers rooms for rent and meals.

MP 34–40: LOWER SOLOMON RIVER. As you drive north away from the coastal beaches, marshes, and estuaries, you move up onto higher, drier tundra-covered slopes that parallel the lower sections of the Solomon River. These lower segments offer some beautiful natural channels and streamside environments. As you proceed upstream you'll see the channel has been increasingly disturbed by historic mining dredges, as evidenced by extensive rows of dredge spoils and the creation of dredge ponds. However, if you look closely, you can also see that the river's natural processes of erosion and deposition, as well as the establishment of riparian vegetation, are slowly but surely reclaiming the river and its surrounding environments. Meanwhile, the ever-industrious and creative beavers are performing their own version of rural renewal projects by adopting and modifying many of the dredge ponds for their own purposes.

MP 39.5: LEE'S DREDGE. This last of the 13 once active dredges on the Solomon River is an easy-to-access gem, so don your rubber boots and wade in. Photographers love all the angles and surfaces, particularly in low-angle sunlight. Birders are attracted to all the nesting sites in the dredge remains.

MP 40.5: SIDE ROAD. This easy-to-miss dirt side road takes you to an overlook on the Solomon River along a section of narrow, steep, rock-walled canyon with good views up and down the river. This is a nice lunch spot and a

RUSTING REMNANTS OF THE GOLD TRAIN TO NOWHERE

good place to view raptors zooming around the Solomon River Valley. The semicircular side road takes you back to the main road at MP 41.

MP 42: SOLOMON RIVER BRIDGE AND BIG HURRAH CREEK. The highway crosses the Solomon River near its confluence with Big Hurrah Creek. This was a huge boomtown area during the Gold Rush, complete with a train system that ran down to the coast. Currently this is a beautiful river confluence that is well worth a walk back across the bridge to enjoy the view.

MP 42–53: FREQUENT WILDLIFE SIGHTINGS. As you continue north upstream along the Solomon River from Hurrah Creek and then over and up the East Fork of the Solomon River, keep your eyes open for megafauna such as musk ox, grizzly bear, caribou, and moose. Every time I drive this road I see one or more of these big beasts! The moose tend to prefer the lower, wetter elevations where they can munch on water-loving plants, while the grizzly bear, caribou, and musk ox are partial to the higher and drier slopes. Take advantage of the numerous pull-off areas to stop and scan for them while enjoying the gorgeous valley and high country. During the fall the subtle colors of autumn add a lovely painterly effect. Huge snowdrifts form here during the winter from the consistent north winds and can be found along the north sides of the road well into summer. Also, as you make your way toward Skookum Pass, sweep your eyes across the slopes, where you can see some very good examples of solifluction lobes formed by water-saturated topsoil that is sliding downhill over top of the underlying permafrost.

MP 53: SKOOKUM PASS. As you proceed upslope along the East Fork of the Solomon River, the environments become drier and the tundra shorter as you approach Skookum Pass and the drainage divides between the Solomon, Skookum, and Fox Rivers. Even if you are not a hiking enthusiast, I

encourage you to park your vehicle and wander off across the easy-hiking tundra. Start walking across the dwarf tundra–covered side slopes toward a nearby ridgeline and onto one of the nearby peaks for some spectacular landscape viewing. Take your time and enjoy your journey. Along the way, don't forget to look down and appreciate some of the beautiful micro landscapes of the tundra. The patterns, textures, and colors of dwarf tundra lichens are some of nature's most fascinating works of abstract art.

MP 53–72: SKOOKUM PASS TO FOX RIVER AND COUNCIL. As you continue your drive, the highway gradually drops down from the pass into and along the drainage basin of the Fox River. The river is inhabited by numerous beavers, as evidenced by their many lodges, dams, and ponds. You'll notice that the spruce-dominated boreal forest is much more present on the north side of the pass and ridgeline than what you drove through on the way up to the pass. By going over the pass you moved from a moister and more consistent coastal environment to a drier and more variable continental environment that exhibits more temperature extremes for which spruce and willow–dominated boreal forests are well adapted. At the higher elevations along this road you can enjoy sweeping views of the lower slopes, as well as some long-distance views into Norton Sound. As you lose elevation you will notice that the size and distribution density of the spruce trees increases. On your way to Council you cross over the stream channels of the Fox and Bear Rivers, which are surrounded by stands of tall white spruce. Between the streams are larger areas of wetland—marshy tundra containing some smaller-statured, widely spaced black spruce that are adapted to moister conditions and permafrost. These are interspersed with groves of larger, white spruce–dominated boreal forest that favor the more well-drained environments closer to stream channels. As you approach the town of Council, take a good look at the dense boreal forest that carpets the mountain slopes behind and uphill from the town. In the fall those dense, dark green, spruce-covered hillsides will be splashed with the yellows and golds of aspens and willows.

MP 72: SOUTH BANK OF THE NIUKLUK RIVER. Your journey ends on the south shore of the substantial channel of the Niukluk River. The Native village of Council is on the opposite shore, and there is no bridge. The river is fordable at lower levels, and you'll need a sturdy, heavy-duty four-wheel-drive vehicle with lots of ground clearance to get there. However, don't attempt to cross the river on your own! Wait for one of the residents of Council to arrive with one of their vehicles and discuss the crossing with them. If they are confident that your vehicle will make it across, then follow them. They will know where the fordable pathway exists. Better yet, if you're interested in visiting Council, arrange for a ride over and back. Hang out for a while and perhaps make a few new friends who might show you around.

For places to stay, eat, and fuel; camping; vehicle rentals; Nome festivals and fairs; outfitters and tour operators; and useful information, see the Nome to Teller Road (Drive #19).

Index

Note: Page references in **bold** indicate photographs.